E-Government for Good Governance in Developing Countries

E-Government for Good Governance in Developing Countries

Empirical Evidence from the eFez Project

Driss Kettani and Bernard Moulin

ANTHEM PRESS
LONDON · NEW YORK · DELHI

International Development Research Centre
Ottawa • Cairo • Montevideo • Nairobi • New Delhi

Anthem Press
An imprint of Wimbledon Publishing Company
www.anthempress.com

This edition first published in UK and USA 2014
by ANTHEM PRESS
75–76 Blackfriars Road, London SE1 8HA, UK
or PO Box 9779, London SW19 7ZG, UK
and
244 Madison Ave #116, New York, NY 10016, USA

A copublication with
International Development Research Centre
PO Box 8500
Ottawa, ON K1G 3H9
Canada
www.idrc.ca / info@idrc.ca
ISBN 978-1-55250-561-8 (IDRC ebook)

© International Development Research Centre 2014

British Library Cataloguing-in-Publication Data
A catalogue record for this book is available from the British Library.

Library of Congress Cataloging-in-Publication Data
Kettani, Driss.
E-government for good governance in developing countries : empirical evidence from the
eFez project / Driss Kettani and Bernard Moulin.
pages cm
Includes bibliographical references and index.
ISBN 978-0-85728-125-8 (hardback : alk. paper)
1. Internet in public administration–Developing countries. I. Moulin, Bernard, 1954– II.
Title.
JF1525.A8K477 2014
352.3'802854678–dc23
2014007505

ISBN-13: 978 0 85728 125 8 (Hbk)
ISBN-10: 0 85728 125 9 (Hbk)

Cover photo: Plus69 / Shutterstock.com

This title is also available as an ebook.

CONTENTS

Acknowledgments   ix

Foreword   xi

Chapter 1: Global Context
   I.   Introduction   1
   II.   The eFez Prolog (Narrated by Dr Kettani)   5
   III.   The eFez Project   11
   IV.   eFez Project Global Outputs/Outcomes   13
   V.   Why This Book?   21
   VI.   Targeted Population   22
   VII. Book Structure   23

Chapter 2: The Two Facets of ICT for Development
   I.   Introduction   25
   II.   A Journey through the Evolution of ICT   25
   III.   The Rise of Information and Communication Technology
        for Development   28
   IV.   The Ubiquitous and Pervasive Nature of ICT   33
   V.   The Transformative Capabilities of ICT   35
   VI.   ICT Is Not an Option: It Is Either an Opportunity or a Threat!   36
   VII. Leapfrogging as a Mechanism for Developing Countries to
        Capitalize on Past Experiences and Lessons Learned   40
   VIII. Conclusion   42

Chapter 3: E-Government and E-Governance
  I.   Introduction   43
  II.   E-Government versus E-Governance   44
  III. E-Government and E-Governance as a
        Means for Good Governance   47
  IV.   E-Government Application Areas   48
  V.   E-Governance Application Areas   52
  VI.   E-Government and E-Governance Benefits   54
  VII. Risk Factors   57
  VIII. E-Government and E-Governance Maturity   60
  IX.   Conclusion   67

Chapter 4: Evaluation of Outcomes/Impacts on Good Governance
  I.   Introduction   69
  II.   E-Government Evaluation Approaches   71
  III. Defining and Measuring Good Governance   74
  IV.   The eFez Method for Assessing Good Governance   83
  V.   Conclusion   94

Chapter 5: Adopting a Transformative Approach in E-Government
           Systems Development
  I.   Introduction   97
  II.   Fundamental Questions Asked when Starting
        ICT4D/E-Government Projects   99
  III. Important Management Issues for ICT4D/
        E-Government Projects   107
  IV.   ICT4D/E-Government Projects Are Transformation
        Processes   113
  V.   A Biological View of the Transformation Process   117
  VI.   Toward a Principled Approach to Manage the Transformation 119
  VII. Managing a Transformation Pilot Project   121
  VIII. Conclusion   134

Chapter 6: A Generic Roadmap for ICT4D/E-Government Projects
  I.   Introduction   137
  II.   A Generic Roadmap   139
  III. A Common Template for the Five Phases
        of the Generic Roadmap   145
  IV.   The TPP Phase   148
  V.   The LSDDA Phase   157
  VI.   The GSDDA Phase   166

VII.   Transition to Autonomy (TTA) Phase   173
VIII. Conclusion   180

Chapter 7: The eFez Project Roadmap
    I.   Introduction   181
    II.   The eFez Approach   182
    III. The TPP Phase of the eFez Project   190
    IV.   The LSDDA Phase of the eFez Project   202
    V.   The GSDDA Phase of the eFez Project   206
    VI.   The TTA Phase of the eFez Project   214
    VII. Conclusion   222

Chapter 8: Technology Enablers for E-Government Systems
    I.   Introduction   223
    II.   Key Issues in the Design and Implementation
          of E-Government Systems   223
    III. Global Orientations   228
    IV.   E-Government Design and Architecture   231
    V.   Security, Authentication and Access Control   236
    VI.   Hardware Platforms and Cloud Computing
          for Back-end Systems   241
    VII. Software Platforms for E-Government Systems   245
    VIII. Networking and Interconnection   247
    IX.   Conclusion   250

Chapter 9: Conclusion
    I.   Testimony of the Late Senator Titna Alaoui   252
    II.   Final Recommendations   255

Appendix: A Synthetic View of Critical Issues for a Successful ICT4D/
E-Government Project   259

References   273

Index   281

ACKNOWLEDGMENTS

This book could not have been released without the support of IDRC, in terms of help with finances and knowledge. Through these few words, we would like to acknowledge and express our gratitude to this wonderful organization and to its entire staff. In particular, we would like to recognize the immense work done by Dr Adel El Zaïm and Laurent Elder throughout the eFez Project. They were always supportive, available and keen to propose solutions and alternatives when problems arose. We would also like to thank Matthew Smith, who was patient and perseverant and never hesitated to do what needed to be done in order to facilitate the production of this book.

The authors would like to thank their respective institutions, Al Akhawayn University in Ifrane and Laval University in Quebec City. In particular, we would like to mention the contributions and support of Dr Amine Bensaid, President Rachid Benmokhtar and President Driss Ouaouicha.

Writing a book is extremely challenging and time-consuming. If it were not for the dedication and support of the eFez Project team members, and a number of other research partners, we could not have succeeded in this task. We would like to thank and recognize the significant contributions of Asmae El Mahdi and Houda Chakiri, who gathered the raw data (literature surveys, papers, technical reports, benchmarks, etc.) and made it available to us in order to build the foundations of this book. Asmae and Houda have been key actors in our research team and significantly contributed to the success of the eFez Project. We would like to thank Dr Michael Gurstein for his contribution to the impact assessment framework we present in this book. A big thank-you goes to Dr Tajje-Eddine Rachidi who accepted an offer to co-author Chapter 7 with us and enriched it with his valuable knowledge and expertise in the fields of security and networks.

We would like to commend the excellent cooperation and contributions of the decision makers and staff of the Fez/Agdal Municipality. We would particularly like to thank the late Mohamed Alaoui Idrissi Titna for his faith in the eFez Project and continuous support. As he passed away shortly before the production of this book, we decided to dedicate the conclusion to him.

We also thank Abdelhadi Hilali, Mostafa Alami, Rabia Mekkaoui and Bouchra Sefrioui. Without their dedication, the eFez Project would not have been a success and we certainly would not have been motivated to write this book to share this wonderful experience.

Writing and producing this book took us more than three years of hard and continuous work, with a lot of ups and downs, difficult situations to manage and despair when, sometimes, we thought we would not be able to meet this challenge! In these difficult moments (and in many others), the support of our respective families was instrumental and essential. Driss would like to thank his wife Nawal for her indefectible support during all these years, and his kids Lyna and Neil who are the best gifts Life/God gave him. Bernard would like to thank his family warmly for their continuous support and understanding, both during the eFez Project and the writing of this book.

FOREWORD

In a world that is becoming increasingly virtual – in which what we write disappears into a series of digital codes – it is reassuring to find that individuals continue to publish the kinds of books – like this one – which we can feel and touch.

It is a pleasure when the book in one's hand is the result of the productive collaboration of three renowned institutions: from Canada, Laval University and the International Development Research Centre (IDRC); and, from Morocco, Al Akhawayn University in Ifrane.

It is an even greater pleasure when the main author of this book is the product of two systems of education – Canadian and Moroccan – and has been able to draw the best from both cultures.

As the Canadian ambassador to Morocco, prefacing this book is an excellent opportunity to celebrate the depth and breadth of the relations between our two countries, and to demonstrate the excellence that our cooperation can produce.

Through the use of information and communication technologies (ICT), this book addresses the fundamental question of how services are delivered by a government to its citizens – and, more profoundly, the obligation of a government to respond to the needs and expectations of its people.

More broadly, it looks at the questions of good local governance, the role of citizen participation and the lynchpin of real democracy.

Morocco has been engaged since its independence in an ambitious effort to decentralize and modernize its state structures. The road is a long and winding one but, under the guidance of His Majesty Mohammed VI, much distance has already been covered and now significant regionalization is part of the new constitution.

Because of its size and diversity, Canada has necessarily undertaken significant decentralization and can offer lessons learned to other countries, including Morocco, from its own experience. We have supported Morocco's efforts through the project "Gouvernance Locale Maroc" (GLM), which is often praised by the regional governments who participated for its practical, hands-on approach.

In a context where economic pressures and the turbulence of the Arab Spring have led to greater calls for social engagement, Morocco is pursuing a path toward a better future, in particular thanks to the tremendous potential and talent of its youth.

Canada is very proud to contribute to the growth of this country through its most important resource: its citizens.

Sandra McCardell
Canadian Ambassador to Morocco

Chapter 1

GLOBAL CONTEXT

I. Introduction

Information and communication technologies (ICT) have tremendous potential to enhance the lives of people in general and, particularly, those in developing countries. Use of ICT can boost business, support education and healthcare systems and also enhance all levels of government in their development processes worldwide. Currently, it is difficult to imagine our lives without computers. They exist in cars, phones, aircrafts, banks, schools, etc. Technology-mediated applications are increasingly popular and have become part of our daily lives. Examples of such applications include, but are not limited to:

- Appliances (coffee makers, microwave ovens, toasters, etc. – for instance, a toaster uses an internal program to determine when the bread will pop up);
- In-car automated surveillance, which is used to monitor driving behaviors and to promote driving and traffic safety;
- Text messaging to arrange meetings and appointments;
- Car equipment such as mobile/smart phones, GPS localization/driving services, laptops/notebooks to carry out daytime work and portable printers to prepare handouts;[1]
- PDAs or fitness watches (equipped with fitness software) to monitor one's workout program and track fitness targets (heart rate, weight loss, etc.);
- The internet, which can be used to communicate with friends and family members, or even for mass communication to engage in forms of activism; and[2]
- Distance learning programs to pursue an academic degree to further advance career opportunities.

One defining feature of our time, in developed countries (DC), is the omnipresence of technology and the related prevalence of internet access.

---

1   http://www.cnet.com/1990-11212_1-6398697-1.html?tag=flash (accessed June 2009).
2   http://www.certmag.com/read.php?start=8121&in=3840 (accessed June 2009).

The increase of technology-mediated activities is an uncontested trend. Such activities are found in almost every domain conceivable, and usage is continuously increasing at home, in the workplace and in the leisure domain.

Several factors contributed to this growth, which has transformed the computer into an essential tool – not only to do business but also to support and boost the social or personal activities of individuals. These factors include the appearance of the internet, the integration of informatics devices and telecom infrastructures, the miniaturization of devices and the considerable decrease of acquisition costs. Gradually, in developed countries, society's perception of computers has progressively shifted from considering them as purely technical devices to "all-in-one" support tools for almost all human activities. The term "ICT" has appeared in order to accompany this shift and is defined as the set of facilities/features (inherent in the combination of computing machinery, the internet and the telecom devices/tools) that support typical societal activities such as learning (e-learning), health (e-health) and government (e-government).

In contrast to the exciting and promising opportunities that ICT offers to DC, in general developing and less developed countries (D/LDC) have not yet fully arrived in the digital era. Most have not yet developed their back office components (i.e., records related to the civil state, to education, to health, etc.), which are a fundamental prerequisite to any e-application. In many situations, e-government systems have been adopted just for appearances' sake, since it is the current standard to have a web portal, an email address and/or social media accounts for governmental agencies. When assessed, it appears that these web portals are ill-equipped for general use (no online services, no localization capabilities, no local/appropriate content, no e-engagement, no precisions, no updates, etc.).

Because of the contrast between DC and D/LDC in terms of ICT's exploitation and proliferation, an important phenomenon has appeared: the digital divide. The digital divide refers to the gap existing between people with effective access to digital and information technology and those with very limited or no access at all.[3] Since the 1990s, many D/LDC have been expressing their intentions to facilitate ICT diffusion in order to contribute to meeting the challenges that their countries face and to fight against the aggravation of the digital divide. These challenges mainly fall into two categories: the need, at the international level, to make the transition toward an information society and its related knowledge-based economy; and the intention, at the national level, to foster human and/or economic development and to improve governance quality to achieve good governance.

---

3   http://en.wikipedia.org/wiki/Digital_divide (accessed June 2009).

Acting on their intentions, many developing countries around the world have established international organizations for the promotion of ICT, focused on assisting technologically struggling nations in catching up, and, as such, preventing the duplication of the already existing economic gap in the area of technology (the digital divide).

Many D/LDC started by modernizing and liberalizing their telecommunications sector in the middle of the 1990s and then proceeded to establish the necessary structures, institutions, policies and strategies to facilitate ICT diffusion in the public sector via e-government projects. These countries adopted national ICT strategies developed by international consultancies, often with the financial support of international donors such as the World Bank and/or the United Nations Development Programme (UNDP). Unfortunately, most of these strategies were simply duplicated from one country to another with no particular attention paid to the local context and associated constraints. The result was of little reward for D/LDC, with very few concrete changes implemented in the field. Many e-government projects that were introduced ended mainly in either partial or total failure. In the few successful cases, e-government projects' deployment remained concentrated at the central government level with a primary focus on government-to-government (G2G) interactions, instead of government-to-citizen (G2C) interactions which did not derive any benefits. Until now, there has been no concrete impact on the daily lives of ordinary citizens in these countries, as evidenced by the almost complete absence of e-government systems at the central and local government level. Most citizen-oriented services, such as medical care, justice, education, safety and municipal services, are still processed and delivered manually without the use of ICT. Citizens need to physically interact with government employees to obtain requested information or services. Government offices still keep data in a paper-based manner, process the data to serve citizens in manual ways, and have one unique delivery channel: face-to-face interactions. Many of these countries have not yet started using ICT to transform their processes, and thus cannot initiate the automation related to the delivery of citizen-oriented services. In developed countries, this state transformation started during the 1960s–70s and ended by the 1970s–80s, which reflects the huge digital divide plaguing D/LDCs.

An increasing number of people, especially from the spheres of civil society and academia, have started to voice concerns and worries:

- Why is state transformation via ICT so slow?
- How can we stop the widening digital divide?
- How is it possible to initiate and accelerate ICT diffusion in local governments through the deployment of e-government systems?

- How could ICT diffusion foster human development (in general) and governance quality (in particular)?
- Could ICT diffusion via the deployment of e-government systems contribute to achieving good governance?

Our research team, the ICT4D Laboratory at Al Akhawayn University in Ifrane, Morocco (AUI), in cooperation with Laval University and the International Development Research Centre (IDRC), both of Canada, decided to carry out research to contribute to this important issue, concentrating our work on Morocco's ICT-related concerns and, specifically, how to use technology in order to enhance good governance in this country.

Morocco's central government promotes the use of ICT in the public sector in order to enhance citizens' wellbeing and good governance (Kettani et al. 2006). However, the development and deployment of e-government systems remains very slow due to socio-political and economic factors such as the high cost of deployment and maintenance, the high level of e-illiteracy among the population, the low level of e-readiness/e-awareness among decision makers and the lack of ICT infrastructures at the local level. Other challenging issues are related to the low levels of acceptability, usability, accessibility and appropriateness of e-government systems (in general), and the lack of formal or structured monitoring and evaluation approaches to address and remedy weaknesses. These interrelated factors influence each other, which creates a vicious circle aggravating the digital divide between Morocco and developed countries. In addition, there is no e-government system deployed for local governments (i.e., local communities at the city level). This is where most of the interactions between citizens and the public administration take place, mostly involving citizens requesting services and documents (e.g., birth certificates, residency certificates and passports). These are the most frequently used and needed services at the community level and the most relevant for any e-government system to target to achieve good governance (Kettani et al. 2010). By far, Morocco is not the worst developing country in relation to its use and dissemination of technology, but it offers a good case study as its e-government projects are typical of the current state of many D/LCD.

As part of its global research mission (ICT for good governance), one of the main projects our research team has worked on is the eFez Project. This project was a true success (see Section IV) and a multi-award winner (see Section IV, Subsection H). It generated a strong set of outcomes, at different levels, along with ideas, knowledge and skills pertaining to both the engineering and social science fields.

Before going into the details of the eFez Project, how it worked, and what results it generated, let us explore the origin and motivations of this project.

Everything started with the personal experience of Driss Kettani, one of the coauthors of this book.

II. The eFez Prolog (Narrated by Dr Kettani)

When I returned from Canada to my mother country Morocco after 11 long years, I was shocked by the so-called "digital divide." Everything seemed to be evolving rather slowly compared to North America, in the airports, schools, hospitals, shops, pharmacies, etc. The use of computers was very limited and mainly focused on creating spreadsheets, word processing, games, chat, etc. The price of a computer was three times higher in Morocco than in North America while the average salary was five times lower! The computer was still perceived and considered to be a luxury item and its use was regarded as limited to the elite.

While this yielded frustration, my inner voice presented the positive side of the situation and insisted that this was a perfect opportunity to contribute to this field (technology) and its application in human and social development! What a gigantic enterprise! Where to begin? How to begin? With whom? With what? All these questions and more plagued me for a long time but I knew that it was clear what I wanted and needed to do.

One day, while preparing my courses in my office, the dean of my school unexpectedly stopped by to inform me about a research project proposed by the British Embassy in Rabat. The project aimed to prove a concept related to a system of e-government. Its schedule (six months) and budget ($20,000US) were too restrictive and I had to politely decline the offer, arguing that I had neither the affinity nor research skills needed to carry out such a project. Furthermore, my wife was shortly expecting a baby, and I told myself that it was poor timing as soon I would be occupied with the new birth. My dean accepted my refusal but asked me to continue to think about it!

A little later, my daughter Lyna was born, and the event was celebrated with joy and happiness. A few days later, the Mokaddam (the field representative of the government) came to my home to remind me of the obligation to register the newborn at the Civil State Office (*bureau d'état civil*, or BEC for short). I was pleased by the Mokaddam's visit and seized the opportunity to ask him the location of this noted office. He smiled and explained that since the baby was born in Meknes (an hour's drive from the small town of Ifrane where I lived), I would have to enroll her at the BEC nearest her birthplace, and that it was not possible to do otherwise or elsewhere. Though I found that strange, I thanked the Mokaddam for the valuable information he gave me and let him go.

The next day, as a responsible citizen, I headed to the city of Meknes looking for the renowned BEC, and, after several attempts, found it and entered. Nobody was there and it appeared that it had been recently and quickly evacuated! I tried to get information from various sources about the situation of this BEC, and discovered that, following a court decision regarding a rental dispute, the BEC and civil registers had to be relocated in a hurry and with no public notice – thus impacting the citizens who would now have to suffer inconvenience due to the bad decisions of their elected officials. Because the BEC administration did not see fit to post a note with the new address, citizens would now need to invest in the difficult task of finding it on their own. Since I am not from Meknes, it was near impossible for me to guess where this office could be! By asking random people on the street, I finally figured out that I must go to the courthouse for this information. Once there, the story of the last-minute evacuation of the BEC was confirmed and I was advised to come back at a later time to find out where the office would be relocated. My attempts to get a relevant phone number and/or a website with the necessary information were futile (I was naive then!) It was clear that this was not how I was going to get the information, and that it would be absolutely necessary for me to make the trip to Meknes again. I returned to Ifrane rather frustrated with the bad luck I had had that day.

I returned to Meknes again, three days later, and went immediately to the courthouse to speak with the same gentleman with whom I had talked before. Unfortunately, the courthouse was on strike and he would not return to his duties until early in the following week. I did manage, however, to share my story with a guard and, after some consultations, he told me that the BEC's new address was at the Congress Palace of Meknes. I arrived there to find, in fact, a huge exhibition center completely unrelated to the BEC. Again, I had to ask a number of people for directions to finally be informed that the BEC was located at the end of a poorly lit and ventilated corridor. When, at last, I found the office, I was surprised to see a huge and random group of people milling about with no semblance of organized order or sequence. It was discouraging! While there, occasionally, I would notice a lucky or privileged person meeting with another individual and then being directed from the queue and served immediately. I wondered what differentiated them from the rest of us.

After a long hour of patience, it was finally my turn. I greeted the gentleman in front of me without reply and he then asked, "What can I do for you, sir?" I explained that I wanted to register the birth of my baby with the BEC, and he cited the long list of administrative documents necessary to do so. Among other things, I would need documents from my own birth and that of my wife. My birth documents are filed in a town that I knew then only by name and my wife's documents were located in a city more than 1,000 km from our residence. I seriously started thinking I would abandon the process entirely as it was getting too complicated and costly!

Once home, I confirmed the list of documents and the procedure with some of my friends and they all agreed that this was inevitable and would require much patience to get through it. Basically, the process consists of preparing and providing the authorities with medical evidence of the baby's birth as well as the original documents related to the birth, residence and professional status of both parents.

After a few weeks, I succeeded in gathering all the documents requested by the BEC officer, but, to my dismay, every time I came back to the officer to provide him with the missing documents, he would routinely ask for more/other documents that he claimed to have forgotten to request the last time, leading to increased delays, costs and efforts from my side. After several iterations, I finally asked why he always forgot to ask for specific papers knowing that this would cause me embarrassment and inconvenience. The man then started to complain relentlessly about his miserable and calamitous working conditions and, in doing so, made it obvious that he had absolutely no care for the dozens of other people waiting in line. The officer made it clear to me, at the end of his long monologue, that he could, in fact, help me (on his personal time indeed!) if I agreed to be "generous" with him, an implication that I readily understood and with which I was not entirely comfortable. After some hesitation, I accepted his offer and did as, I assumed, almost everyone else did. I knew I just committed an act that was unrewarding and against all my moral principles but I found hundreds of thousands of reasons (and even more!) to legitimize it and consoled myself that it was part of the process and, thus, not that bad. I even sympathized with the officer given the horrible stories he seemed to experience on a daily basis in his work. I concluded that the real culprit in the whole story was the system.

Yes, the system is uniquely responsible because it inherently encourages corruption, opacity, inequity and mistreatment. Let us now understand a little more about this system:

The BEC was introduced in the early twentieth century to Morocco by the French protectorate, mainly for French nationals. At the end of the protectorate, Morocco adopted this system with minor/insignificant changes (Arabization, separation of records: Moroccans vs. foreigners, Muslim vs. non-Muslims, etc.) and the structures, functions, methods and tools remained unchanged. Everything was done manually (with no typing or xeroxing!) and every BEC was totally independent, with no interaction with the others, including aspects related to citizens' data stored in the registers. Hence, if someone is born in a city and they currently live in another city, there is no way for them to avoid the trip to their birthplace in order to retrieve an updated copy of their civil state documents (valid for 90 days). It is only when one is very lucky (or rather adept at coping with the BEC environment) that these documents are delivered on the same day and without error. But this is not the general case at all. Manual errors are very common, and are almost inevitable (especially for documents written in French) for various reasons. First, the use of pen and paper to write thousands of documents is inherently prone to errors. Second, the work overload of the officers who might have to write the same act 30 times (for example, when processing candidates for the exam to access military positions) contributes to the tedium and reduces focus. Finally, the terrible environment and professional conditions exacerbate the situation. In the BEC, computer databases, citizen service, efficiency, effectiveness, transparency, fluidity, etc. are considered only concepts, with no applicability or validity in the process context. Of course, over the last 50 years, a few timid attempts, here and there, have decried this archaic system and tried to reform/restructure it, but the political will has never been strong enough to see it through to completion. Thus, until today, the BECs, local in all cities and regions of Morocco, are generally in a dilapidated state – dirty, poorly ventilated, poorly indicated – the list would be much longer if we wanted to describe in more detail these defects. Employees are badly trained, underpaid and often assigned to this service as a professional punishment. Citizens' support and guidance are nonexistent in BECs and nothing is clear, including the procedures, responsibilities, deadlines, costs, etc.

The regrettable state of BECs in Morocco strangely contrasts with the importance and predominance of this service for any Moroccan citizen:

- The BEC is the closest administrative office (physically and functionally) to citizens;
- In the region of 70–80 percent of all public services provided to citizens (school, health, justice, etc.) require evidence emanating from the BEC;
- A very large part of all administrative procedures take place at the BEC;
- The Civil Register is the only repository of any Moroccan citizen identity: it can make or break people and lives.

To return to my personal story with the BEC of Meknes, I eventually completed the paperwork, and had all the necessary papers delivered to me without making any further trips. I now understood that this was the opportunity I was awaiting for my research, to act on the ground and have a tangible impact on the lives of my fellow citizens. As such, I contacted my dean, who, as we remember, had suggested my involvement a few weeks earlier concerning an e-government proof of concept funded by the British Embassy in Rabat. I told him about my story with the BEC office and informed him that I would accept the project he proposed. The dean was delighted and he realized that this project would not be like any other!

I simply proposed to the British Embassy the development of an experimental system to automate, from beginning to end, the Civil State Service, including online requests. I suggested the city of Ifrane as a pilot site, given its proximity and small size. Technically, the project consisted of the development of a portal for the city of Ifrane with two essential components: a static/informational piece (which would allow, among other things, the download of sample forms for administrative procedures, accessing information about the commune services and getting contacts/coordinates of commune staff and administrators, etc.), and a dynamic transactional piece (which would allow the download of administrative documents, requests for online services, etc.). I hired an intern (Asmae El Mahdi, one of the main collaborators in this project) and some masters students (including Houda Chakiri, now president of Enhanced Technologies, a company that develops/commercializes the eFez system in all of Morocco) to work with me on this project. After 12 months of work, the results were excellent and exceeded the British Embassy's expectations. We even received a letter as an official recognition of outstanding achievement from the British Embassy. Several presentations and demonstrations were made for/to various officials and municipal governments and, without exception, they were all delighted to see the improvements in governance (efficiency, transparency, speed, etc.) that the system generated. They were also perplexed and thoughtful in relation to the potential this system could have in the structural reorganization of the registry office.

With the prototype established in Ifrane, we built a channel of discussion with the Ministry of Interior in relation to the ever-pending issue of BEC modernization. The department seemed interested in our approach and design and was "curious" about the piece of software we had developed. But it voiced a strong, valid and challenging reservation, namely that "the system we developed for the city of Ifrane does not reflect what happens in the big cities of Morocco and cannot be considered as a generic example, since the town of Ifrane is too small to be compared to the average Moroccan city and not subject to typical urban problems" (oral communication, June 2003). This was indeed an intelligent and polite way to both thank us and to bring us back to square one.

We needed then to find a way to capitalize on the success of the Ifrane project and to bring the Ministry of Interior back to the discussion table. We decided to work on another experimental site, in a big city this time. We knew that the technical and technological aspects would not present any difficulty for us. What worried us, rather, was the socio-political aspect, which we had little expertise or knowledge in and which seemed insurmountable. We started writing the research proposal before even identifying the potential funders. I was inspired by the initial proposal of the Ifrane project and its results, and requested the help of a colleague who specialized in sociology, in the School of Humanities and Social Sciences of our university.

The integration of technical and social aspects in the same proposal intrigued me a lot and I really enjoyed it. It even motivated me to take all the time needed to refine the initial hypotheses, research questions, project objectives, description of the technical platform, etc. At last, with a fairly well-written and structured project description in hand, I had to find a buyer (i.e., a funding agency).

I started prospecting funding opportunities for research projects in Morocco and quickly realized that most academic research, with an international scope, was financed by the European Union. To gain such funding requires you to be part of well-established research networks and there was virtually no chance for me and my project to go through this channel. As I have dual citizenship in Morocco and Canada, I naturally thought of the Canadian International Development Agency (CIDA). But, although CIDA found my project very interesting and important, they kindly informed me that it does not fund individual projects but only large projects involving the government. As I was deepening my investigations, I realized that finding funding for an isolated research initiative, such as mine, was almost impossible, and I found this to be very unfortunate. So I called back CIDA to express my disappointment at their inability to fund a worthwhile project for administrative reasons. My argument was that the agency must reserve part of its funding for individual initiatives that do not fit into the political machinery and help international relations. My interlocutor did not seem to appreciate my remarks and reminded me that, due to the formal mission and goals of CIDA, they could not grant a positive answer to a request of such nature. However, and in a quite spontaneous way, he informed me of another Canadian agency for international development whose objective was precisely to fund individual initiatives, aside from the diplomatic/international cooperation track: the International Development Research Centre (IDRC). At that moment, I didn't realize that this gentleman had given me the information I was looking for, information that would change a great deal in my life and the lives of other Moroccan citizens. I noted the acronym and hurried to check online to see what I could learn about it.

I read the general description of IDRC: "IDRC is a Canadian Crown Corporation that supports research in developing countries to promote growth and development. IDRC works with researchers and innovators in these countries to find practical, long-term solutions to the social, economic, and environmental problems their societies face. The goal is to bring choice and change to the people who need it most…"

I also read the details on the vision, mission and goals of this organization and I realized that this was exactly what I had been seeking for my research project.

With a lot of hope and confidence, I sent an email to the regional office of IDRC in Dakar, Senegal. A few days later, I got a very brief message back from an IDRC officer telling me that the idea was good and he would like to know more about the project. I immediately sent my research proposal, which was ready a few weeks prior. After six months of discussions (very sharp and sometimes painful!) on the project details, I received the official approval, along with the funding, to finally begin a fascinating adventure: the eFez Project, the main concern and raison d'être of this book!

III. The eFez Project

The eFez Project aimed at developing an e-government pilot and, simultaneously, to refine and enrich our understanding in order to prepare to undertake larger projects. The pilot targeted the development of an online delivery system of citizen-oriented services for the municipal government of the city of Fez. Our guiding intention was to offer easy, efficient, quick and equal service delivery to citizens, in a measurable and replicable way. Accordingly, we paid particular attention to the collection of indicators and the development of measurement techniques to assess the project's outputs with respect to enhancing governance. This allowed us to develop an outcomes assessment framework for e-government systems based on good governance (see Chapter 4 of this book), and to document all the project's steps, actions and important decisions. We thus created an elaborate roadmap related to the development and use of e-government systems as a means to enhance good governance in a country. (See Chapters V, VI and VII of this book.)

In its first phase (the project was two years in duration and was completed in October 2006), the eFez Project concentrated on services delivered by the BEC. These offices have daily and direct contact with the local community, and yet service delivery was (and still is) conducted in a manual paper-based manner. The eFez Project aimed at automating the back office operations (through the digitization of all the BEC's records into a database) and enabling electronic front office service delivery through a multilingual (i.e., Classical Arabic, Moroccan dialect, Berber and French), multichannel (i.e., web, GSM, self-service kiosk and conventional desk service) and multimodal (i.e., vocal instructions, text messaging, etc.) interface. The project also attempted to answer a number of research questions highly significant to national concerns, many of which fall into three main categories: local governance, usage and accessibility issues:

- Local governance: How do e-government services improve local governance? What is the role of local e-government initiatives in furthering and supporting the municipal decentralization process promoted by the central government?

How does such a process influence the local administration? Does increased public information and services lead to greater political empowerment?

- Users and usage of e-government services: How will users employ these services? What are the benefits of these services? How do behaviors change? Is this a form of empowerment? What are the obstacles and challenges to effectively using such services?
- Access to services and technological appropriateness: In order to meet the expectations of the wider Moroccan society, which kinds of political, social and economic strategies can be created and utilized to help a greater number of people access these services, and hence "democratize" their use. Which tools are most apt to ensure the use of such services? Which factors can ensure the sustainability and usefulness of this type of project in the long term?
- How can governments successfully design, conceptualize, develop and implement ICT projects in an effort to foster local good governance?
- Is there empirical evidence on how e-government implementation fosters local good governance in a Moroccan context?
  - If yes, what are the outcomes and impacts generated and produced with e-government implementation?
  - If not, how can we systematically assess results and measure outcomes post-deployment of e-government systems?
- How can governments promote digital culture and ICT use in general society and in the public sector, in particular?

The eFez Project's main research questions were related to its social influence and political implications, as well as to its acceptability, adoption and ways of generalizing and diffusing it all over Morocco.

The first phase of the eFez Project was successfully completed in July 2006 and all initial objectives were successfully achieved, including:

- The deployment of an e-government portal allowing the Fez–Agdal local community to have easy, fast and convenient access to government information. This portal includes a platform enabling the online request and receipt of birth certificates (which is the most requested citizen-oriented document) via a variety of devices including cellphones, PCs and touchscreen kiosks;
- The elaboration of a road map to serve as a reference for the development of e-government systems in other communities. It is aimed at guiding and informing local and national government practitioners about good practices that work toward the successful implementation of e-government systems;
- The proposition of a framework for the assessment of the changes and outcomes generated by the deployment of electronically enabled services at political, organizational, social and governance levels.

Phase one of the eFez Project has been successful, with excellent feedback and noticeable satisfaction expressed by all stakeholders, including city authorities, BEC officers and employees, and responding citizens. A survey of more than five hundred citizens conducted during May and June 2006 showed that 95 percent of them used the kiosk located in the BEC office. The satisfaction rate was exceptionally high: 91.2 percent of respondents were very satisfied (7 percent were satisfied) and 93 percent of respondents qualified service delivery as excellent (3 percent rated it as good).

In official recognition of their outstanding achievements, the project's team was awarded the national prestigious prize "eMtiaz 2006" for creating the best e-government project in Morocco. And, surprisingly, in a country where public activism is not very common, more than five thousand citizens and civil servants of Fez's non-automated BECs signed a public petition to request that the system be generalized. Given the strong level of commitment from the different stakeholders to pursue this project at a national level, a consensus was built to launch the second phase of the eFez Project.

The Scaling-Up Phase (or eFez2 for short) was aimed at generalizing and scaling up the findings and achievements made in the first phase. eFez2 looked at potential methods to enhance stakeholders' readiness and awareness, establish connections between the central government and local authorities, disseminate e-government implementation strategies and models, and refine a national roadmap and an outcomes assessment framework. Specifically, eFez2 built on the findings, achievements and positive outcomes of the first phase in order to:

- Improve the BEC automation capabilities in an effort to enable the electronic delivery of a wider range of citizen-oriented services;
- Generalize (or spatially diffuse) the e-government tools to the whole city of Fez as well as in partner cities and provinces, including Larache, Hajeb and Ifrane;
- Enhance and refine the national roadmap by making it generic and less specific to Fez's local context in order to facilitate the further generalization of these local e-governance systems at a national level;
- Enhance and refine the national outcome assessment method based on a broader and more representative sample of the Moroccan population to ascertain its validity at a national level;
- Enhance e-readiness and e-awareness levels within a broader base of citizens, employees and decision makers at a national level.

IV. eFez Project Global Outputs/Outcomes

The eFez Project changed the face of local public administration in Fez and continues to do so in an increasing number of Moroccan cities. It succeeded in transforming local governance structures by introducing and enabling the online delivery of citizen-oriented services. It raised and investigated a series of research questions related to ways of facilitating and promoting ICT use and appropriation in Morocco. It enabled an accelerated process of ICT penetration and diffusion in the country's governance structures. It influenced guidelines and strategies toward the successful implementation of e-government projects, as well as introducing methods to assess and analyze e-government's socio-political, organizational and governance outcomes.

In the following subsections, we present some important outcomes and results of the eFez Project.

A. *Organizational outcomes*

At an organizational level, the eFez Project revolutionized the functioning of BECs and modernized their internal operations. It introduced ICT and automated service delivery to replace manual processes. Shortly after this deployment, employees started noticing unprecedented concrete improvements. They no longer had to perform tedious and time-consuming tasks when processing citizens' service requests. It now only takes a couple of mouse clicks to enter the identifiers of the requested certificate and print the needed copies. As a result, the service process has become an effortless, instant task, increasing employees' productivity.

Automation has also eliminated common health problems from which employees suffered using the former tedious manual service delivery process (i.e., back pain, shoulder pain, headaches, finger swelling and allergies caused by the regular consultation of dusty volumes of records).

The project also showed that designing and building an e-government system at a local level is challenging not only because of the lack of ICT-related infrastructure and facilities but also because the employees are not qualified to provide the user requirements necessary to determine the characteristics of the e-government system to be implemented without prior formal training in this BEC area. We observed that many of them had received informal, on-the-job training and did not acquire a minimum knowledge and understanding of the regulations and legislations governing the BEC's service delivery. This clearly indicates that building an e-government system requires intense fieldwork to discover, identify and gather the needed requirements. It also entails the design team's patience to adjust, readjust and refine the collected system's requirements over time.

The improvements generated with ICT's introduction communicated the high importance and value of the project and facilitated project appropriation at the organizational level. All employees abandoned the manual process and adopted the electronic one. Their main wish was to extend the project to include other services that were not yet automated.

B. Citizen-related outcomes

At a social level, the eFez Project improved the BEC's governance tools and practice, hence enabling an unprecedented, citizen-friendly service delivery. The eFez Project did not only electronically enable the BEC front office, but also created and diversified electronic delivery channels. These new electronic channels have created for citizens a simplified system for the request/receipt of their needed certificates. Dependency on employees for this process has noticeably decreased thanks to the availability of the kiosk and internet delivery channels.

In addition, citizens now receive printed (as opposed to handwritten) certificates. These printed certificates are more elegant, visually appealing, easy to read, and, more importantly, free of the errors common to manual copying.

Furthermore, the electronic/automated service delivery has provided citizens with instant and convenient access to their needed certificates. This instant access has eliminated queuing, waiting time and repeated physical trips to the BEC.

Finally, the automated service delivery allowed citizens access to BEC services on an equal basis, discouraging the inclination to pay for special privileges (i.e., being served more promptly than others).

C. Policy-making-related outcomes

One major blessing in the project was the high level of cooperation from political figures. The president of the Fez–Agdal arrondissement, Senator Alaoui Titna (see more about how he supported the project in the conclusion of this book), provided much support to the eFez Project. He facilitated the logistics to enable the smooth implementation of the project. His strong political leadership increased the visibility of the project at a local level and also contributed to further the project's visibility at regional and national levels by engaging other influential people, including Fez's mayor and wali (who is appointed by, and is the official representative of, His Majesty the King).

The eFez Project also influenced local policy making. Not only did the Agdal president support the project, but he proceeded to extend BEC automation to include several additional major bureaus at Fez, providing all the necessary resources. This political decision motivated and encouraged citizens and personnel to request the general enablement of the electronic/automated service delivery.

D. Technology-related outcomes

A complete and generic ICT platform for the BEC has been developed. It enables the digitization of citizens' records related to both birth and death events, electronically generates statistics and reports them to Morocco's central planning, and enables the electronic issuance of a wider range of citizen-oriented services via multiplatform delivery channels. The BEC counter is equipped with networked database technology, a touchscreen kiosk with an intuitive graphic user interface (GUI) to accommodate basic/digital illiteracy and the Fez web-portal, accessible via SMS and PDA.

Building and deploying e-government systems at the local level proved to be technologically feasible. It is true that the work had to start from scratch as improving the building capacity of local government via introducing and installing electricity and connectivity infrastructure was a prerequisite for the e-government platform to be deployed.

E-Government is usually defined as "utilizing the internet and the world wide web for delivering government information and services to citizens" (UN 2003b, 1). Deploying an e-government system at the local level allows the web-based delivery of essential citizen-oriented services and provides the local community with online access to these anytime and anywhere. However, building such a system requires, in addition to an electricity and connectivity infrastructure as mentioned above, that data be computerized and digitally accessible, and that the related workflow process be automated. The eFez experience shows clearly that building a functioning e-government system at a local level in a developing country requires the local government to make strides to minimize its digital delay by first completing electricity and connectivity installation, and then proceeding with back office digitization and automation, before enabling the electronic/web-based delivery channels.

The eFez Project revealed that the digital delay is not the only issue for local government to address when attempting to deploy an e-government platform that can function and operate smoothly in the long run. For example, since most municipal employees had never used a computer, it was crucial to offer training programs introducing employees to ICT so that they could acquire the basic knowledge and skills. Such basic and elementary training was vital to help employees become familiar with ICT. Further, the project then offered training programs that were specifically tailored to using the deployed e-government system, crucial for its effective use when serving citizens.

The project extended the technical tailored training programs to the personnel of the commune IT Department. Such "eFez-related training" was the first instruction that the personnel had received since university graduation and, as such, was a golden opportunity for them to upgrade their skills. It was also a unique chance to learn how to smoothly maintain the functioning of the deployed e-government system. With such training programs, the deployed ICT platform was widely used, adopted and maintained. The eFez experience shows very clearly that offering training programs to meet employees' diverse ICT deficiencies should not be overlooked; rather they should be carefully designed and planned to ensure the use and continuous maintenance of the system.

E. E-appropriateness, e-awareness and e-readiness

The term e-government or "electronic government" indicates the combination of technology (i.e., electronic) and society (i.e., government). From this perspective, the government body cannot be just a passive recipient of technology. Rather, it needs to lead the engagement with technology throughout the different phases of building an e-government system to ensure that the technological system is developed to serve the purposes of the local government and the community that it represents. Accordingly, for the whole project duration, the active participation of the local Fez government (politicians, decision makers and employees) was encouraged. Its high level of involvement and participation enabled the system to meet the locals' needs and adjust to Fez's political, organizational and social context. The project's contextualization with respect to local needs and characteristics prevented the reproduction and automation of service delivery faults and inefficiencies, thus enabling the project's acceptability, appropriation and adoption at all levels. For instance, all Fez local civil servants abandoned the manual service processes to adopt the eFez electronic system, an increasing number of citizens have opted to use the electronic delivery channels to gain access to their needed services and a growing number of Morocco's local decision makers have expressed their emergent interest in ICT projects. In this respect, the active participation of the local government facilitated the deployment of an e-government platform as an enabler of political and socio-organizational gains.

The eFez Project indicates that ICT diffusion is not a technology problem; rather, it is a political issue. Our first site visits in Fez revealed that a large number of local decision makers expressed their ignorance of the possible uses of ICT and the related opportunities. In many cases, elected politicians in Morocco lack high literacy skills, let alone digital skills, knowledge and understanding. Accordingly, the typical questions that arose in these site visit presentations included, among other things: "*Chnou had chi?*"

(i.e., Arabic for "what is this?"), "*Achn dirou bih?*" ("what can we do with it?"), "*Aallach?*" ("why?"), "*Ma kentch aaref*" ("I did not know about it"), etc. These questions clearly reflect the lack of ICT awareness among local decision makers. It was surprising to see that even highly ranked politicians with better educational backgrounds asked such questions. Indeed, their questions were more related to the capabilities and utility of ICT than to the technical device itself. Such low ICT-related awareness had many implications. For instance, due to the low level of interest, ICT projects were absent from the political agenda and, thus, no budget was allocated to them. Furthermore, the municipality of Fez (population: 944,376 according to the 2004 national census) had only one IT department with one full time employee. Created in 2003, the department was concerned primarily with the acquisition and installation of computers. There was no application development aimed at launching office automation. By the time the eFez Project started, the available computers were obsolete, nonfunctioning and covered with dust from inactivity.

Despite their lack of ICT-related awareness, the politicians showed a high readiness, involvement and commitment to the eFez Project shortly after gaining an understanding of its objectives and expected concrete contributions to citizens' daily life. This was commonly expressed via supporting statements, such as: "*chouf rahna maakoum*" ("look, we are with you!"), "*ghir goulounna chnou ndirou*" ("just let us know what we shall do to help you!"), etc.

ICT diffusion is also an organizational issue. For instance, the civil servants were usually reluctant to use and adapt to ICT-enabled workflows. The employees' reluctance was usually expressed via fear-based statements such as "*wa hadchi machi dyanna*" ("this thing is not ours!"), "*ghadi ghir yzdeli lmachakil*" ("it is only going to create troubles for me!"), "*Ra ghir mahtout tmma*" ("look at the computer, it is just sitting there with no use!"). These reflect employees' concern for and lack of understanding about the appropriateness and convenience of the proposed e-government system.

Fieldwork also revealed that, at the community level, a large number of citizens had expressed a need for electronic interaction with government offices but complained that their political representatives had not been responsive. They expressed themselves with statements like: "*wha chhal hadi bach bghina had chi walakine maddaha fina hadd*" ("we wanted this facility a long time ago, but nobody cares about us!"). Such a reaction showed us that Fez's citizens were open and keen to have access to ICT facilities despite their low "digital culture" and the intimidation associated with the required new learning. They asked many questions, such as: "*Wach kaddine aala hadchi*" ("do we have the 'power' to use it/ can we use it?") and "*Ghan aarfou kin dirou lou*" ("will we get to know how to use it by ourselves?"). Such questions reflect the lack of basic

ICT knowledge amongst citizens. They also reflect concerns about system accessibility and usability.

F. Roadmap

The transformation of local municipal service delivery and the related implications on local governance were recorded by the eFez Team, but in addition to this, they also created a corresponding roadmap which guides practitioners in successful e-government deployment in other local governments in Morocco.

Within the framework of the eFez Project, the roadmap acts as a reference handbook, presenting the different phases of a typical local e-governance project. Each phase is composed of different steps, identifying specific required inputs, activities, outcomes and human resources. The roadmap includes clear indications about lessons learned, good practices, risks, guidelines, planning, budget, ICT platforms, etc. One of the main characteristics of the eFez roadmap is that it is highly related and sensitive to the Moroccan context in terms of the culture, current business processes (i.e., workflows), locally perceived needs and the values and interests of citizens.

In the course of the eFez Project, we found out that such a roadmap, which communicates the project's experiences in methodological terms, is very useful to government executives and decision makers in Moroccan cities as it provides the needed guidance for deploying and effectively using e-government as a tool to promote good governance. Accordingly, the broader significance of the roadmap is the way it documents and disseminates knowledge acquired throughout the project's implementation. Documenting the methods and mechanisms used to overcome the project's numerous challenges and difficulties, the roadmap becomes an excellent tool for local governments and the central government of Morocco to implement e-government systems elsewhere. The project roadmap is a learning tool empowering government institutions with the skills to create appropriate management and successfully implement similar projects. In this regard, the roadmap contributes to the improvement of the quality of local governance in Morocco, and consequently improves the citizens' quality of life.

Chapters V, VI and VII of this book specifically deal with the issue of documenting and presenting the details of our generic roadmap and its specific application to the eFez Project.

G. Impacts / outcomes assessment framework

A systematic assessment process is a fundamental mechanism of adjustment and improvement in any field. Considering good governance enhancement as the *raison d'être* of e-government systems, and given the noticeable lack of a generic approach to evaluating such a system, our research team took the initiative, within the eFez Project research activities, to develop an original formal assessment framework. Our team focused on assessing what was achieved (the outcomes) and, following the system deployment, generated results through the "outcome analysis method" which we developed. This methodology was used to investigate the relationship between the eFez Project implementation and good governance. People involved in the design, development and deployment of ICT systems (in this case, an e-government system) were able to use this method to assess the broader significance of these systems in relation to normative goals, while using both qualitative and quantitative measurements. The outcome analysis begins with the selection of formal (and generally accepted) definitions of good governance attributes and their underlying characteristics. Then, these general definitions are translated into specific normative goals for the project and discussed with the project's main stakeholders. This translation provides the foundation for identifying anticipated project outcomes. Finally, specifiable (and measurable) project outputs are identified in relation to the expected outcomes.

Chapter 4 of this book specifically deals with the issue of evaluation and assessment and presents the details of our framework.

H. Awards and international recognitions

The back office and front office integration has had highly visible effects, reshaping the relationship between the state and its constituents and enabling eFez to receive innovation recognition and credentials, these include:

- The prestigious African award, 2007 Technology in Government in Africa (TIGA-2007): http://repository.uneca.org/tiga/sites/default/files/TIGA-2007-Announcement-EN.pdf;
- The prestigious, international United Nations Public Service Awards (2007) in the category "Improving the Delivery of Services": http://www.unpan.org/innovmed/documents/Vienna07/28June07/summary_of_innovations.pdf;
- The Best Scientific Paper Award in the Conference of Information and Communication Technologies delivered at the fifth Congress of Scientific Research Outlook and Technology Development in the Arab World (SRO5), organized by the Arab Science and Technology Foundation (ASTF) in cooperation with the Ministry of National and Higher Education, Professional Training and Scientific Research from the 25 to 30 of October 2008 in Fez, Morocco;

- Enhanced Technologies (SARL/Inc.), a social entrepreneurship initiative based at AUI incubator and created as a spinoff of the IDRC-funded eFez Project, led by Houda Chakiri. The project was selected among the top ten finalists of the Sawaed contest (2008–2009), for generating innovative ideas on using ICT to promote Arabic Content in the Arab World: http://www.yabiladi.com/article-economie-2198.html.

V. Why This Book?

As it has already been said, at the end of the eFez Project, a great number of ideas, views and knowledge had been generated. Part of it has been published at different conferences, in journals and book chapters, and the other part was waiting to be revealed at the right moment (since the authors were highly engaged in many activities to ensure the project's success!). Furthermore, most of the eFez publications that have been released are "fractal" and related to a specific aspect and/or lifecycle phase of the project. Finally, the global vision and approach of the eFez Project was never presented as such in a publication, nor was a direct link made between this vision and the specific objectives and/or milestones that were set to be achieved in the project's two phases. Hence our desire to write this book and to present the eFez Project in its entirety, from the initial concept to the present.

This book was mainly the result of two important factors:

1) The success of the eFez Project (Phase 1 and Phase 2) and the authors' realization that the learning and good practices that evolved from this project could be useful to practitioners and decision makers in other developing countries, including the invaluable material and findings that the project generated using a participatory approach in a real-life setting. In fact, the "ingredients and recipe" for this project's success were so simple and accessible that we thought it was worth sharing with others.
2) There is also a noticeable lack of practical books targeting decision makers with respect to principles and good practices guiding the design and implementation of e-government for good governance, and any other sector-specific ICT4D for that matter.

The aspiration to write this book was further strengthened by the intention to design it in a textbook format to be ultimately utilized as material for modular training programs. The authors hope that their experience in ICT4D, in a D/LDC context, will be disseminated to inform, guide and inspire their peers in these countries. They hope that this will contribute to south–south dialogue and emphasize the need to build a "knowledge society" in D/LDC.

More specifically, this book intends to:

- Document and disseminate the eFez Project experience in all its aspects (approach, methodology, test beds, etc.);
- Present the knowledge and skills (roadmap, impact assessment framework, design issues, lessons learned and best practices, etc.) that the authors developed (and published in many journal papers and conference proceedings) due to their involvement in this project and their systematic quest to turn its indigenous experimentations, result and findings into a formal framework to propose to academics, practitioners and decision makers;
- Offer practical supporting material to decision makers in developing countries with respect to ICT4D, and specifically e-government implementation.

VI. Targeted Population

The eFez Project was an action research project where academics, politicians, employees and citizens acted as researchers. The knowledge generated by the different activities of the project is intrinsically of interest to anyone intending to learn more about the reaction and behavioral evolution of these stakeholders, the impacts and outcomes of the implemented system and how to accurately measure these to ensure that the system adheres to its ultimate purpose (i.e., good governance), and finally, how to successfully complete an ICT4D project based on the generic roadmap proposed in this book.

More specifically, we believe that the main readership of this book should be politicians (or, rather, their advisers due to the time constraints on many politicians), decisions makers and project managers. It is intended for those who retain the power to include ICT4D in the national political agenda and have the capacity to allocate adequate resources to it, and those who instruct, manage and implement ICT4D programs. It is important to mention that the research described in this book, and all associated discoveries, recommendations and observations, have been performed in a typical developing country context (Morocco) with all the constraints and constants characterized in such a context. Further, this suggests the inclusion of all organizations (donors/funders, NGOs, international cooperation, etc.) and individuals (practitioners, researchers/academics, people at large, etc.) with a particular interest in development (specifically through ICT) as a potential readership for this book.

This book contains enough original and structured ideas to offer a good reference for teachers in the field of e-government/e-governance. It is designed in a format which is appropriate for dissemination to development organizations. The objective is to provide a practical guide to ICT4D implementation in which the focus on theoretic matters is minimized in order to ensure a balance between rigor and practice.

VII. Book Structure

In Chapter 1, we present the general context and motivations that led to the writing of this book. We also present the eFez Project, its motivations, objectives and outcomes. Particular attention is paid to show the link between the eFez Project and this book.

Chapter 2 of this book presents essential background knowledge that readers need in order to acquire the terminology and understand the concepts related to the main topic of this book: e-government. We consider e-government to globally fall within the context of ICT4D (Information and Communication Technology for Development) applications and, as such, it is important to define ICT4D, how it applies to D/LDC (successes, failures, problems, constraints, etc.) and how it influences the global development process of these countries. We also show that ICT represents a real opportunity for D/LDC to recover and to decrease the digital divide. Unfortunately, due to a number of complex and interlinked factors, this opportunity is not correctly exploited.

Chapter 3 concentrates on e-government systems (goals, strategies, plans, etc.) and shows how they can lead to better governance through the improvement of transparency, efficiency, effectiveness, service delivery, etc. A number of facts and figures are presented to show the link between e-government and good governance.

In Chapter 4, we present the outcomes analysis framework that we developed during the eFez Project. This framework supports our vision of e-government systems being assets in promoting good governance. We think that all stakeholders involved in an ICT4D project should share this vision and act accordingly. Our framework provides a formal way to measure the impacts and outcomes of e-government systems on good governance and provides "hard" evidence to managers and politicians allowing them to fine tune their decisions about the use of ICT4D.

Chapters V and VI present the foundations and main phases of the generic roadmap for the principled development and deployment of e-government systems, while Chapter 7 presents the approach that the eFez Project took, which can be thought of as a practical application of the generic roadmap. More specifically, the first part of Chapter 5 discusses a number of issues that need to be addressed when planning and launching an ICT4D or e-government project and presents our fundamental claim: that ICT4D/e-government projects are transformational processes that should be managed as such.

The second part of Chapter 5 presents the foundations of the transformative approach that we have developed and applied in the eFez Project.

Using the foundations of the preceding chapter, Chapter 6 presents the generic roadmap that we have created to plan, manage and assess the progress of ICT4D and e-government projects in a systematic and principled way. This generic roadmap promotes the principles of good governance and emphasizes the importance of involving all stakeholders when creating the e-government system, it also discusses the need to develop and preserve favorable conditions during the project's duration. The generic roadmap also shows how an ICT4D or an e-government project can be managed as a transformative process with the goal of delivering and deploying an ICT system that will be sustainable in the transformed institution. This chapter is presented in a rather technical way so that project managers might be able to customize the roadmap to the specific needs of their own ICT4D and e-government projects.

Chapter 7 presents the eFez Approach through narrative. Our goal is to illustrate how the generic roadmap has been applied in the e-government project for the city of Fez. Our goal is to present critical events, issues and decisions that occurred during the eFez Project in order to share our experience in a way useful to readers involved in similar projects.

Chapter 8 deals with the main technology concepts and tools of which decision makers should be aware. A successful implementation of e-government systems requires a solid and consistent technological vision across all government departments and services, set by the highest level of authority in any country. This vision should emphasize technology as a means to boost the human and economic development. Three fundamental building blocks should be addressed in this vision: infrastructural issues, integration and interoperability matters and the transformational features of ICT. These must evolve within the right regulatory environment and with the appropriate e-strategy benefiting from good practices and lessons learned in successful e-government projects.

Chapter 9 concludes this book and presents important lessons learned that the authors would like to share with the readers, along with some general recommendations.

Chapter 2

THE TWO FACETS OF ICT FOR DEVELOPMENT

I. Introduction

As we have previously stated in Chapter 1, the contrast between DC and D/LDC in terms of ICT exploitation and proliferation has led to a worrying phenomenon that is known as the digital divide. This phenomenon refers to the gap between countries with effective access to digital and information technology and those with very limited or no access at all. It includes the imbalances in physical access to technology as well as in the resources and skills needed to effectively participate in a digital society. From this perspective, technology has, undoubtedly, two contradictory facets: a "positive" facet enabling the growth of the economy, business and public administration, and a "negative" facet consolidating the digital divide, the isolation of regions/populations and the degradation of living conditions. The digital divide is closely related to the knowledge divide since the lack of access to technology creates a challenge to obtaining useful information and knowledge.

One consequence of these two contradictory facets of technology is that decision makers and politicians in D/LDC countries are left with only two choices: to accept and use technology as an enabler of development and prosperity, or to ignore it and run into the risks associated with the digital divide. Indeed, not making a choice (or trying to keep to the status quo!) is a deliberate action that is equivalent to ignoring technology.

II. A Journey through the Evolution of ICT

Throughout time, humans have invented ingenious calculating machines. One of the earliest was the abacus, about five thousand years ago. As early as the 1640s, mechanical calculators were already being manufactured for sale. Records exist of earlier machines, but Blaise Pascal is recognized to be the inventor of the first commercial calculator, a hand-powered adding machine. Although attempts to mechanically multiply were made by Gottfried Leibnitz in the 1670s, the first true multiplying calculator appeared in Germany shortly before the American Revolution. In 1820, Charles Xavier Thomas de Colman invented the "arithmometer," a machine that could add, subtract, multiply and divide. It was Charles Babbage though, in the early 1800s, who designed a mechanical calculating machine that is the true ancestor of today's computers. In 1943, development began on the Electronic Numerical Integrator and Computer (ENIAC) at Penn State. Work was completed on the ENIAC in 1946. Although only three years old, the machine was woefully behind on technology, but the inventors opted to continue while working on a more modern machine, the Electronic Discrete Variable Automatic Computer (EDVAC). In 1975, the first personal computer (PC) was marketed in kit form. Bill Gates, with others, wrote a BASIC compiler for the machine.

The next year, Apple also began to market PCs, again, in kit form. These included a monitor and keyboard. In 1976, Queen Elizabeth went online with the first royal email message. Subsequently, the personal computer market exploded, and, by 1977, stores had begun to sell PCs. By the seventies, most banks, insurance companies and finance institutions were computer dependent and most scientific discoveries and realizations (including the space exploration race) were made possible thanks to computers. IBM introduced its first consumer PC in 1981 which, in an unprecedented move in 1982, was selected by *Time* magazine as its "Man of the Year!" By the eighties, computer systems and networks had become a social fact, with governmental agencies relying on them to provide their citizens with different services, involving the Civil State Service, education, health and justice.

By the end of the 1980s, most western countries had already developed a very solid infrastructure (telecom, networks, hardware, software, etc.) and achieved their back office digitization. Most G2G and G2B transactions were automated, either partially or totally. On the public side, citizens became progressively acquainted with computers and accepted them as part of their "natural" environment. Currently, it is difficult to imagine our lives without computers. They are simply everywhere, in cars, in phones, in aircraft, in banks, in schools, etc. Several factors have contributed to this invasion and transformed the computer into an indispensable tool, not only for business, but also to support and boost the social and personal activities of individuals. The contributing factors include the appearance of the internet, the integration between informatics devices and telecom infrastructure, the miniaturization of technology and the fact that acquisition cost has considerably decreased. Society's perception of computers has progressively shifted from considering them as purely technical devices to an "all-in-one" support tool for almost all human activities. The term ICT has appeared in order to accompany this shift and is defined as the set of facilities and features (produced in combination with computing machinery, the internet and the telecom devices/tools) that support typical societal activities such as learning (e-learning), health (e-health) and government (e-government). Aronson (2001) surveys the key defining events and features of ICT growth in his article "The Communications and Internet Revolution." The first wave of ICT started in 1843 with the invention of telegraph and grew with the successive inventions of the telephone, radio, television, computers and culminated with the invention of the internet, originally known as the world wide web.

Because of its ubiquitous feature, ICT is being used everywhere to do almost everything quickly and accurately. All the important domains of our modern society have experienced a boost in progress due to the introduction and use of ICT, including: better service delivery to citizens and businesses, better access to information for decision makers, better management of administrative and business structures, better citizens/client records and better information for the community. ICT improvements and related diffusion have led to the launch of what is called the "information revolution." This refers to "the rapid technological advances in computers, communications, and software that in turn have led to dramatic decreases in the cost of processing and transmitting information" (Nye and Welch 2000).

The information revolution has enabled the rise of the "information society," also known as "'the information age,' 'postindustrial society,' 'the services economy,' or 'the knowledge society.'" In the "information society," telecommunication and ICT infrastructure have become far more valuable economic resources than traditional resources and means of production, such as land, capital, factories and labor. Accordingly, wealth is increasingly generated and maximized via flows of information, data and knowledge, as opposed to agriculture and the manufacturing of material goods and commodities that were highly valued in the industrial era. Accordingly, the continuous advances and expansion of ICT has led to structural transformations in the global economic landscape with a main underlying pattern: the "globalization of business." This suggests "a qualitative departure from traditional approaches to doing business internationally" which involves, among other things, "the attempt to set up such [business] entities in various countries, functioning as single, 'seamless' business operations" (Gurstein 2007). In this sense, enabled by ICT, globalization is a process transforming the global economy via new emerging settings and structures, creating "centrally coordinated networks of producers and consumers, of supply chains and distribution networks". Despite this, global inequalities are widening in what is increasingly known as the "digital divide." A study comparing a person's average income in the richest and poorest countries in the world found that global divides almost did not exist two centuries ago, but that, shortly after the industrial revolution in 1913, global inequalities grew. This growth further increased with the IT revolution in 1950, and finally augmented with globalization by 1973 and the internet revolution by 1992. The digital divide refers to the disparity in the degree of penetration of ICT facilities between communities and has acquired increasing significance since its inception. "Twenty years ago, the concern was simply how to get a communications network, generally conceived as the plain old telephone, within everyone's reach. Today the digital divide is not centered on simple telephone access but instead focuses on richer communication and information connectivity via the internet and beyond" (Unwin 2009).

One important fact about the digital divide is that it is not a phenomenon observed between world regions; rather, the phenomenon exists within regions themselves.

III. The Rise of Information and Communication Technology for Development

Several studies also found that the digital divide is interlinked with other human development divides. Interest in linking ICT to development started in 1984 when the Independent Commission of the International Telecommunication Union (ITU) delivered its final report entitled *The Missing Link* and known as "The Maitland Report." The report noted the need to pursue telecommunication reforms to extend the coverage of telephony and its effects, and thereby address the "telecom divide." Progressively, global institutional efforts elevated ICT4D to the forefront of the international agenda.

"Unlike IT and ICT, where the main focus is on what is and what can be achieved, ICT4D is about what should be done and how to do it. ICT4D therefore has a profoundly moral agenda. It is not primarily about the technologies themselves, but is concerned, rather, with how they can be used to enable the empowerment of poor and marginalized communities. This is a shared agenda and involves reflection on behalf of all those who aspire to make the world a fairer and better place" (Unwin 2009).

The term ICT4D has emerged to refer to the application of ICT within the field of socio-economic development. ICT4D mainly addresses issues related to the digital divide and how to overcome these issues through applications that directly or indirectly benefit the disadvantaged population and improve their socio-economic conditions. ICT4D is not about developing the ICT industry or any sector of the economy. It is primarily about using ICT to engender socio-economic and political growth. As already stated, ICT4D emerged in response to international efforts pursuing the connection of ICT to development. The key drivers were the rise of the internet and then the declaration of the millennium development goals (MDG). These coinciding international developments created a dynamic where "the digital technology of the 1990s, then, supplied a new tool in search for purpose; development goals were new targets in search of a delivery mechanism" (Heeks 2008).

Fueled by a sense of urgency to deliver results, there was a general tendency to use quick and accessible off-the-shelf products as a deployment solution in developing communities. One example used amongst ICT4D actors was replicating the US "Telecottage" or "Tele-Centers" program which was designed to provide quick ICT access to poor rural communities during the 1980s and early 1990s. The Tele-Center trend faced infrastructure problems (i.e., power, telecommunication) and was limited in sustainability and scalability. This created a need for more formal evaluative methodology and therefore efforts were made to address the emerging issues and to provide alternatives.

The quest for alternatives and related future trends are discussed below.

A. Basic physical infrastructure and the persisting limitations in electricity supply

This is a major barrier to ICT penetration in countries such as Africa. "All communication systems require a physical infrastructure to be in place to provide energy and to generate and receive signals" (Unwin 2009). This seems self-explanatory and taken for granted but "on more than one occasion, ambitious programs have been developed to introduce computers into schools, only for it to be realized subsequently that the absence of electricity has meant that only a few such schools would actually be able to benefit." Incidences like these occur simply because "much of the inequality in the distribution of the benefits of ICT can be attributed to a spatially differentiated supply of basic infrastructure" (Unwin 2009). This is a serious challenge for Africa as the lack of a basic and reliable electricity supply across much of the continent remains one of the greatest handicaps to its development.

With such an alarming reality in Africa's basic infrastructure and the same dynamic replicated in other developing countries, there is an urgent need for alternatives to address the power issue and to find new solutions to ensure the availability and reliability of power generation, power transmission and power consumption. Unwin (2009) names some of these alternatives, noting that four main scales of electricity supply for ICT4D can be identified: national mains supplies, or the electricity grid; locally produced electricity from solar, wind, water and human energy; generators producing electricity from fuel such as oil or natural gas for specific organizations or institutions; and batteries, both rechargeable and otherwise. Regardless of the difficulties of using such alternative electricity supplies, projects, such as Greenstar in Brazil, Jamaica and Ghana revealed that it is possible to build effective solar-powered community centers that deliver electricity, purified water, health and education information, and a wireless internet connection (Unwin 2009).

B. *From wired technology to wireless technology*

Telecommunication infrastructure (known also as backbone provision) has been evolving. Unwin (2009) reviewed major wired technology that revolutionized our communication capabilities. Until recently, most telecommunication systems used wires as the medium to connect transmitters and receivers using analogue systems. First, phone calls were initiated with telephone lines made of basic material: steel and iron. Then copper wires, evolved with Bell's two-wire circuit in 1881, replaced the steel or iron. Digital subscriber lines (DSL) were in use by the twentieth century, and finally the asymmetric digital subscriber line (ADSL), which augmented data transmission, was diffused worldwide.

Regardless of its affordability, copper cables have had security issues as they are frequently stolen in developing countries (Kaul et al. 2008). Fiber-optic technology was launched first in the 1970s. It has become increasingly competitive with copper wires due to its important data-carrying capacity (technically called bandwidth), coupled with effective/viable data transmission (no noise/loss of data). One main challenge of fiber optic is its expensive deployment cost (Kaul et al. 2008). However, Unwin (2009) suggests that if sufficient funding can be made available, there is a strong case for the poorer countries of the world to install fiber-optic cables from the very beginning in areas that are not yet served, so that they will have the bandwidth capacity for the delivery of services in the future as they become available.

C. *From high-cost terminals to low-cost terminals*

Further to telecom infrastructure, workstation cost is an additional major barrier to ICT access in developing countries. Computer technologies are not new devices but the introduction of circuits and microprocessors only occurred as recently as the 1960s, and that facilitated computer diffusion by the 1970s. The computer has until recently been one of the most powerful tools in transforming the ways in which we communicate, gain information and share knowledge (Unwin 2009). Its uses are widely reported to include:

- "Information gathering (most frequently on the internet, but also from data storage devices such as CDs or DVDs);
- Communication (traditionally via email, but now increasingly through social networking sites, such as Facebook and VoIP);

- Information processing (from basic calculations to image processing and database applications);
- The production of information and knowledge (as in the writing of reports or graphic design and simulations) and,
- Entertainment (in the form of music, films and games)." (Unwin 2009)

There are additional efforts aimed at manufacturing cheap personal computers (PCs). Latest efforts include the One Laptop per Child (OLPC) project, which was launched in 2005 as an initiative by Nicholas Negroponte along with researchers in the MIT Media Lab. The project's mission is to develop low-cost laptops with educational value for African children. The OLPC business model rests on the premise that laptop manufacturing costs could be reduced by using discounted, cheaper parts and, thereby, laptops could be readily available at a price as low as $100. In response, India announced its own endeavor to develop low-cost laptops with prices starting from $45.

Accordingly, "despite 20 years of over-promising and under-delivering – from the 'People's PC' to the Simputer – it seems low-cost terminals will be a central part of ICT4D" (OECD 2010).

D. Software solutions and emerging alternatives

For the hardware to function, software solutions are prerequisites. Corporations such as Microsoft develop and sell software solutions while keeping the coding of programs confidential. Alternatives started emerging as early as the 1980s. The "free software movement" first started in 1983 with Richard Stallman's GNP project, and by 1992, the movement received momentum with the release of the Linux operating system (Unwin 2009).

The movement evolved in the 1990s with the rise of free and open-source software (FOSS). FOSS productions are marshaled by "programmers who generate income from other activities, even working for companies selling proprietary software, and treat their FOSS work as a 'spare-time' activity, thus, in a sense, self-exploiting their labor for the common good" (Unwin 2009). FOSS activities are increasingly viewed as "a new mode of production" that "relies entirely on self-organizing, egalitarian communities of individuals who come together voluntarily to produce a shared outcome" (Unwin 2009). It is increasingly recognized that "the three rules of open source – nobody owns it, everybody uses it, and anybody can improve it – may be the source of endless innovation" (Tapscott and Williams 2006).

One clear example is Wikipedia, known as "the encyclopedia that anyone can edit," and which proved able to compete with the actual "*Encyclopedia*

Britannica" (Shally-Jensen 2011). Another free software movement example is the IBM experience of working with open-source programmers and integrating Apache into its package. In this case, open-source software has enabled IBM to speed innovation and offload tremendous costs. Open-source software is increasingly gaining acceptance as a promising alternative software solution; though debate on proprietary/open-source effectiveness still persists.

E. Increased attention to digital content made available on the web

One finding of ICT4D 1.0 is that access to an internet-connected PC does not provide sufficient value because the web content required to meet poor communities' information and communication needs is not readily available. However, there has been an emerging trend called "open content," which refers to making content freely available to the general public online. Examples of this emerging practice include MIT creating open access to its educational material and lectures via http://ocw.mit.edu, marking the ongoing rise of open educational resources (OER) (Wiley 2006). Unwin (2009) explains that "as with FOSS, discussions concerning OER are similarly charged, and derive from fundamentally different conceptualizations of the world: on the one hand, the individualistic view, where knowledge is seen as a commodity, the purchase of which can give rise to greater earning potential and is thus a good investment; on the other hand, the view that knowledge is a collectively produced social good, that should therefore be shared communally and indeed globally." There are also voices calling for the results of donor-funded projects to be made freely accessible via OER protocol.

F. From paper records to e-records:

Government organizations base their operations on information processing and began record digitization with the advent of ICT. Accordingly, industrialized countries, such as the United States, Canada, Australia and Britain, designed and carried out programs of record computerization and automation as early as the 1980s. Subsequently, developing countries in Latin America (such as Argentina, Chile and Mexico) and Asia (such as Malaysia, India and China) integrated programs of record automation into their public reforms. African countries, however, are lagging far behind. Therefore, the UN's 2008 e-government readiness survey underscored the urgent need to automate backend operations as a prerequisite path to seize ICT opportunities.

To conclude this section, in contrast with the exciting and promising opportunities that ICT and ICT4D can now offer to developed countries,

African countries in general have not yet joined the digital era. Most have not yet developed their back office component (records related to the civil state, to education track, to health, etc.) which is a fundamental prerequisite to any e-application.

ICT4D exists in Africa with several good but unconnected projects and initiatives, but it is mainly perceived as an imported concept or tool due to the lack of readiness, awareness and appropriation by the decision makers and the public.

IV. The Ubiquitous and Pervasive Nature of ICT

Clearly, technology is everywhere, indoors and outdoors, continuously conveying information in an effort to facilitate people's convenience and wellbeing. Technology is permeating daily routines and habits. The pervasive nature of technology is leading toward the "ubicom world" (or "ubiquitous computing"), a term first coined by Mark Weiser in 1988 at the Computer Science Laboratory at Xerox PARC. Ubiquitous computing is defined as "the method of enhancing computer use by making many computers available throughout the physical environment, but making them effectively invisible to the user" (Weiser 1993). Ubiquitous computing (or ubicomp) rests on the idea that there should not be a need for users to seek out computers to accomplish tasks. Rather, computing devices should be embedded in the users' environment and enabled (with sensors) to locate users and serve them. "At their core, all models of ubiquitous computing (also called 'pervasive computing') share a vision of small, inexpensive, robust networked processing devices, distributed at all scales throughout everyday life and generally turned to distinctly common-place ends."[1]

Alan Dix explained that "the defining characteristics of ubiquitous computing are the attempt to break away from the traditional desktop interaction paradigm and move computational power into the environment that surrounds the user. Rather than force the user to search out and find the computer's interface, ubiquitous computing suggests that the interface itself can take on the responsibility of locating and serving the user" (Dix et al. 1998).

Examples of these include: "pen-based technology, handheld or portable devices, large-scale interactive screens, wireless networking infrastructure, and voice or vision technology" (Abowd 2004). Ubiquitous computing looks away from machines to focus on applications. Weiser (1993) explains that "applications are, of course, the whole point of ubiquitous computing.

---

1   http://en.wikipedia.org/wiki/Ubiquitous_computing (accessed June 2009).

For example, ubicomp permits the location of people and objects in an environment." The *Journal of Ubiquitous Computing and Intelligence (JUCI)*[2] explains that "any place/any time/any means; vision of ubiquitous computing has explosive impact on academics, industry, government and daily life. Ubicomp results from research and technological advances in wireless and sensor networks, embedded systems, mobile computing, distributed computing, agent technology, autonomic computing and communication."

Castells, in his book "The Rise of the Network Society" (2000), explains the paradigm shift from standalone mainframes to personal computing to ubiquitous computing. He points out that pervasive computing started with the rise of the internet and its diffusion and infiltration into routines, irrespective of location or context.

Weiser (1993) also points out that "ubiquitous computing names the third wave in computing, just now beginning. First were mainframes, each shared by lots of people. Now we are in the personal computing era, person and machine staring uneasily at each other across the desktop. Next comes ubiquitous computing, or the age of calm technology, when technology recedes into the background of our lives." Figure 2.1 below distinguishes the three computing waves.

Figure 2.1. The major trends in computing (Weiser 1993)

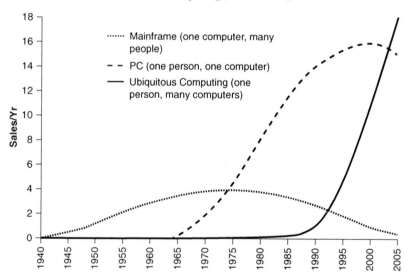

---

2   http://www.aspbs.com/juci.html (accessed June 2009).

Thus, it clearly appears that technology pervasiveness is an ongoing trend toward further advancing technology mediation where "smart" settings are able to locate users and anticipate their needs for service provision.

V. The Transformative Capabilities of ICT

Today's "information revolution" is one uncontested result of the steady diffusion and pervasive use of technology generally, and of ICT in particular. The "information revolution" refers to "the rapid technological advances in computers, communications, and software that have, in turn, led to dramatic decreases in the cost of processing and transmitting information" (Gurstein 2007). With communication technology costs becoming more and more affordable and thus enabling instantaneous contact between people anywhere, the world is becoming "a single place." The underlying resultant characteristics are interconnectedness and interdependence (or "mutual dependence"), which implies that "situations in which actors or events in different parts of a system affect each other" (Gurstein 2007). A UN report noted that the world is evolving toward "an era of environmental, economic and technological interdependence" (UN 2008).

As stated earlier, in Section II, the information revolution led to the "globalization of business" and created a transition in the perception of economic transactional significance. ICT has changed the way business is done. One notable example is Walmart, an American retail store chain which has been a global business phenomenon since the 1980s. Its success certainly results from the integration of ICT applications and capabilities throughout all of its operational cycle, in an effort to connect networks of suppliers and clients around the globe.

ICT's transformative effects on business structures are clearly observed in their managerial and operational practices. Walmart, eBay and UPS are business structures with the common feature of "centrally coordinated networks" operating quite distinctly and unconventionally. Coordination and management are carried out through a highly centralized control system that sets standards and requirements, and these are to be fulfilled within its operational entities, which are located in remote areas around the globe (Gurstein 2007). The main underlying feature of such networks is the ever-advancing ICT infrastructure that seeks further efficiency and effectiveness in operations (to minimize costs and maximize profits); and that enables employees in dispersed operational entities to fulfill their responsibilities and tasks assigned by the centralized control. Employees have contractual relations with such networks and are dealt with as an "electronically mediated 'profile'" (Gurstein 2007). Violating the rules and requirements established by the centralized control leads to a set of electronically enabled measures, such as having the employee "obliterated," which means "removed [from the network] including all historical traces or fragments" (Gurstein 2007). In concrete terms, the network changes the employees' password to prevent him/her from having access to the network's facilities, services and information.

Fukuyama (2004) explains that "information technology, by creating lower transaction costs, has provided the theoretical justification for many firms to flatten their managerial hierarchies, outsource, or 'virtualize their structures'." In this sense, the rise of new structures, such as these centrally coordinated networks, is one notable result of the transformational effects of ICT expansion and pervasiveness.

Not only did ICT pervasiveness change the way firms do business, but it has also altered the way governments serve their constituencies. In the 1990s there was a growing interest in information technology, encouraged by the rise of ICT and especially the internet, and new terms were coined and used (namely e-government and e-governance). ICT diffusion and pervasiveness, respectively, have not only had transformative effects on firms and their operations, but have also triggered "state transformations" and reshaped the way governments interact and serve their organizational peers, firms and public constituents.

Given the importance of the e-government topic for this book and its strong/direct link with the eFez Project, Chapter 3 will address this topic exclusively and in depth.

VI. ICT Is Not an Option: It Is Either an Opportunity or a Threat!

ICT use within government organizations is increasingly driven by a variety of factors, falling into the following broad categorization areas:

A. *Organizational internal pressures including:*

- The high cost of government operations and transactions;
- The increasing challenges of paper record management and obsolete paper booking arrangements;
- A lack of data sharing and the high cost of multiple data collection and verification;
- The high cost of information distribution and dissemination;
- The high rate of errors in the various activities of information processing;
- The limited response capacity due to the low coverage of service provision, and thereby the further reinforcing of existing disparities;

- The constituency's increasing dissatisfaction with service quality;
- The restricted service delivery channels failing to accommodate users' constraints and preferences;
- The perturbing effects of organizational misbehavior such as rent seeking and red tape, which compromise the government's credibility.

B. Nationwide pressures characterized by data sharing difficulties among dispersed stakeholder groups

These include:

- The constituency's frustration with the widening gap between the government's actions and their needs.
- Lack of consultation mechanisms to engage constituents in defining policies that affect their wellbeing and interests.
- Limited taxation performance: Fukuyama (2004) points out that "the rate of tax extraction is, of course, a measure of state scope, particularly for countries with higher levels of per capita GDP, but it is also a measure of administrative capacity (and is increasingly used as a metric by international funding institutions)." Challenges of taxation policy implementation is evidenced in poor taxation collections where countries "cannot monitor tax compliance and enforce tax laws," as this requires inter-agency information sharing.
- Pressing demands on healthcare services which could be mitigated with the dissemination of basic health information and the optimized administration of limited resources.
- Distressing socioeconomic challenges, namely illiteracy complicated with the challenge of extending the reach of learning opportunities to disadvantaged populations, but also the challenge of unemployment and the need to connect job seekers with job opportunities.
- Rising community-based ethnic tensions and the challenge of preserving native languages.
- The rising urgency for environmental policy making that would involve countrywide organizational data sharing, coordination, and collaborative work.
- The increasing need to rethink the public sector, to build and reinforce institutional capacity, and to retool government structures and processes. This urgency is fueled by the reality of the public administration blocking development efforts.

Fukuyama (2004) reports the following: De Soto (1989) had researchers determine the process time for acquiring a small business license in Lima, Peru.

After ten months, eleven offices and \$1,231, they were granted the legal authorization to start a business. The same process in the United States or Canada would take less than two days. The inefficiency of this process was a significant barrier to new business formation, and De Soto observed that it forced poor entrepreneurs into an informal sector. This sector was dynamic and often served as the only source of certain goods and services in poor neighborhoods, but the lack of formal and enforceable property rights reduced the potential investment horizons and prevented small businesses from becoming big ones (De Soto 1989). Such an observation clearly shows that organizational dysfunctions render the public sector an obstacle to development since they constrain income generating ventures and thus block social-uplift opportunities.

C. *International pressures featured by the following realities:*

- Public reforms and ICT integration have become common requirements imposed by international financial institutions.
- Fierce competition with respect to attracting foreign direct investments (FDI); poor institutional effectiveness inevitably means missing out on FDI flows. In fact, "inward FDI can be particularly important to developing countries in providing the necessary capital to achieve satisfactory economic growth and the transfer of technology and employment. That is why many of these countries are willing to offer major tax concessions and other favorable arrangements for new businesses in order to succeed in attracting foreign investment and retain that already acquired" (Jepma 2001).

The ICT exponential expansion is continuously altering space–time factors and is inherently expanding across borders, thus fueling globalization. Careful regulation is important to align ICT to a country's interests, otherwise, national interests would be compromised and the country's institutions simply bypassed. The global economy has become highly information intensive and extremely competitive.

Hanna (1994) points out that ICT has become a "critical infrastructure for competing in an information-intensive global economy." Indeed, ICT-effective applications and integration have become instrumental to survive the threats of the ongoing process of globalization and to seize the opportunities it offers. One notable barrier to a global economy is the so-called "digital divide" which is evidenced by worrying statistical facts. The population of internet users is increasing worldwide. Nevertheless, in 2006, internet users in developing countries represented merely 2 percent of the world's internet population.

In Africa, a continent with a population of over 1 billion, internet users, according to statistics from 30 June 2010, represented merely 5.6 percent of the world's internet population.

Table 2.1 and Figure 2.2 reveal the troubling reality of the digital divide.

Table 2.1. Two continents with developing countries, Africa and Asia, have internet penetration below the world's average

World regions	Population (2010 est.)	Internet users 31 Dec. 2000	Internet users' latest data	Penetration (% pop.)	Growth 2000– 2010	Users % of table
Africa	1,013,779,050	4,514,400	110,931,700	10.9 %	2,357.3 %	5.6 %
Asia	3,834,792,852	114,304,000	825,094,396	21.5 %	621.8 %	42.0 %
Europe	813,319,511	105,096,093	475,069,448	58.4 %	352.0 %	24.2 %
Middle East	212,336,924	3,284,800	63,240,946	29.8 %	1,825.3 %	3.2 %
North America	344,124,450	108,096,800	266,224,500	77.4 %	146.3 %	13.5 %
Latin America/ Caribbean	592,556,972	18,068,919	204,689,836	34.5 %	1,032.8 %	10.4 %
Oceania/ Australia	34,700,201	7,620,480	21,263,990	61.3 %	179.0 %	1.1 %
WORLD TOTAL	6,845,609,960	360,985,492	1,966,514,816	28.7 %	444.8 %	100.0 %

Internet usage and world population statistics are for 30 June 2010 (www.internetworldstats.com).

Figure 2.2. World Internet Penetration Rates (from www.internetworldstats.com)

North America 77.4%
Oceania / Australia 61.3%
Europe 58.4%
Latian America / Caribbean 34.5%
Middle East 29.8%
Asia 21.5%
Africa 10.9%
World, Avg. 28.7%

Penetration Rate

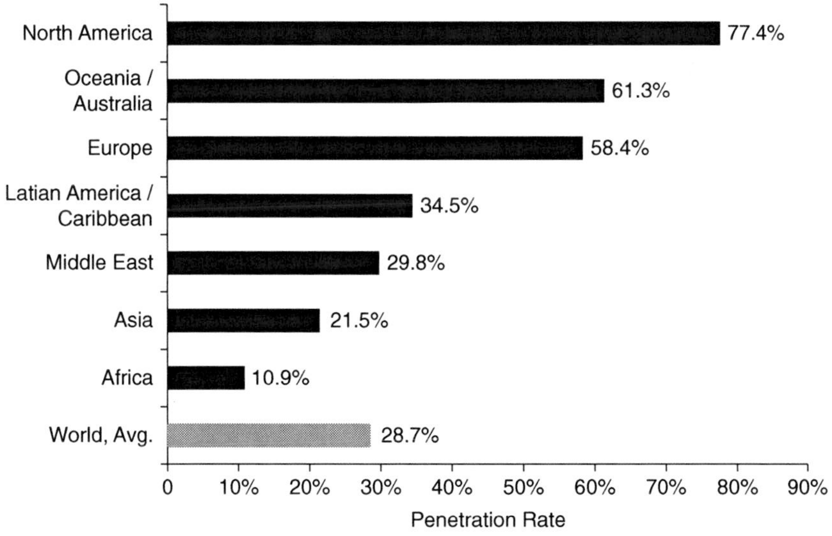

In light of the preceding facts, it is quite clear that ICT integration offers opportunities to effectively respond to pressing issues at organizational, national and international levels. Conversely, when ICT is not adopted and managed seriously, the multilevel pressures remain unsolved and inevitably fuel a variety of threats. Past experience has shown that it often takes a crisis of one sort or another to create the political conditions for major institutional reform.

Consequently, indifference to ICT and inaction is no longer a choice for developing countries. The viable options are limited: they must either make the needed arrangements for ICT integration to harness its power and seize the opportunities that it offers or continue to ignore ICT and consequently assume the human development costs and legitimacy implications.

VII. Leapfrogging as a Mechanism for Developing Countries to Capitalize on Past Experiences and Lessons Learned

It is true that industrialized countries are well ahead technologically; but the process of arriving there has been both painful and costly. They have encountered problems with managing, integrating and interfacing fragmented, incompatible and large legacy systems. The following case study is powerfully informative.

Considering the costly problems attached to the maintenance of legacy systems, developing countries are still lagging behind in ICT integration and mainstreaming; but, arguably, the advantage is that they can always leapfrog by taking on the latest technology, tested and proven at the expense of others, that effectively meet and satisfy their needs and wants.

Learning about past and current experiences and capitalizing on lessons learned is highly advantageous to developing countries' ICT leapfrog. The leapfrogging process will allow developing countries to skip poorly conceived, less efficient, more expensive ICT systems and integrate ICT systems with true transformative capabilities. Existing ICT experiences can help developing countries to carefully outline their plans for ICT integration, thus, a trend has emerged known as "ICT urbanization." This uses a functional framework and a useful analogy is the "city planning concept of IT architecture" (Namba 2007). The analogy emerged in response to the recognition that it is primordial to adopt a global vision, in space and throughout the duration of any project of computerization. This is useful to know because the urbanization approach used to design information systems answers the new requirements rather well. Taking as a starting point the theories of town planning, the urbanization of the information system proposes to define a coherent development plan in phase with the strategy, the trades and the processes. A city is composed of multiple cores of growth which one can describe as "functional": dwellings,

Table 2.2. Developing countries top performers in successful ICT integration (UN 2010)

Rank	Country	E-government development index value		World e-government development ranking	
		2010	2008	2010	2008
1	Republic of Korea	0.8785	0.8317	1	6
2	Singapore	0.7476	0.7009	11	23
3	Bahrain	0.7363	0.5723	13	42
4	Israel	0.6552	0.7393	26	17
5	Colombia	0.6125	0.5317	31	52
6	Malaysia	0.6101	0.6063	32	34
7	Chile	0.6014	0.5819	34	40
8	Uruguay	0.5848	0.5645	36	48
9	Barbados	0.5714	0.5667	40	46
10	Cyprus	0.5705	0.6019	42	35
11	Kazakhstan	0.5578	0.4743	46	81
12	Argentina	0.5467	0.5844	48	39
13	United Arab Emirates	0.5349	0.6301	49	32
14	Kuwait	0.5290	0.5202	50	57
15	Jordan	0.5278	0.5480	51	50
16	Mongolia	0.5243	0.4735	53	82
17	Ukraine	0.5181	0.5728	54	41
18	Antigua and Barbuda	0.5154	0.4485	55	96
19	Mexico	0.5150	0.5893	56	37
20	Saudi Arabia	0.5142	0.4935	58	70
21	Russian Federation	0.5136	0.5120	59	60
22	Brazil	0.5006	0.5679	61	45
23	Qatar	0.4928	0.5314	62	53
24	Peru	0.4923	0.5252	63	55
25	Belarus	0.4900	0.5213	64	56
World average		0.4406	0.4514		

trade, industrial parks, etc. The roadway system connects and serves each core as well as the services which are common and shared like the administration, the hospitals, the schools… The city is in perpetual development. To preserve the overall level of quality of service, the resources and infrastructures are continually adapted, while keeping an eye on the budget!

An information system curiously resembles, at a logical level, the concept of a city. An information system is also composed of functional modules answering special needs, while the overall resources and the communication networks are also shared. And of course, the system evolves/moves permanently.

It is clear that there are tried and tested technology, methods and frameworks. Developing countries need only to capitalize on the available lessons learned, act on the advantage that there are no costly legacy systems to manage and proceed to ICT leapfrogging to catch up with the existing technology in other parts of the world.

The UN 2010 global survey presents a significant example. One developing country, the Republic of Korea, moved ahead of traditional e-government leaders (Canada, US, Norway) and attained first place in the rankings of the UN 2010 e-government survey. "Notable climbers" include Bahrain, Chile, Colombia, Singapore and the United Kingdom, which have all joined the world's top performers in online service delivery.

Table 2.2 above presents a listing of developing countries who are top performers in successful ICT integration.

VIII. Conclusion

In this chapter we presented the two "contradictory" facets of ICT and contrasted the opportunities which ICT offers when used well to promote and foster good governance, and the threat they implicitly engender when ignored and/or inappropriately used. Another important idea of this chapter is that ICT4D is not about buying machines and servers, developing and deploying web pages and/or being present on Facebook (in order to count how many "likes" received at the end of each day!) It is rather about using technology as a means to foster development and to fight against the digital divide.

Certainly, there are different ways to achieve human and social development in countries, but without ICT this challenge is much less attainable due to the huge number of requests, their complexity and the expectation of a high quality of services, particularly in public services. ICT is seen from this perspective as an indispensable enabler, without which not only is it difficult to enhance the situation in developing and less developed countries but, and more importantly, there is serious risk of degradation and isolation due to the digital divide.

Chapter 3

E-GOVERNMENT AND E-GOVERNANCE

I. Introduction

There has been an evolution in the concept of good governance. First appearing in the twentieth century, the notion of good governance began in the discussions of business analysts and economists who were highlighting the structures and strategies of corporate management which succeed in increasing productivity and profits (IDRC 2005).

In the late 1980s, scientists in the field of social and economic development also began to consider the notion of good governance, focusing on the role of government. The World Bank presented good governance as a requirement, at a national level, to enable and facilitate the success of economic development reform (Haldenwang 2004). The UNDP followed, embracing the notion by the 1990s and further extending the idea that good governance would enable countries to achieve human development.

The ascendancy of good governance has occurred through long-term public administration reform. Toffler, cited in Denthardt and Grubbs (2003), proposed that there is a specific chronological order to the evolution of "human organizations," and that this order includes three waves of organizations:

- "First-wave preindustrial organizations," built to serve the preindustrial agricultural societies in their harvesting activities;
- "Second-wave industrial organizations" which developed centralized, hierarchical, bureaucratic mechanisms operating with uniformity principles in order to serve the growing urban populations emerging as a result of the industrial revolution;
- And finally "third-wave decentralized organizations" which had matured from bureaucracy to more flexible structures to address the needs of postindustrial societies.

This means that, over the last three decades, public administration has undergone rapid transformative changes, shifting away from the "traditional administration" model resting on bureaucracy to what is now known as the "new public management" (NPM) model. NPM rests on the conviction that management in public and private sectors should be alike. It argues that, in order to sustain itself, the public administration needs to adopt the principles, management models and related practices established by the private sector (Felts and Jos 2000).

NPM has roots in what are known as "the Westminster-system countries (Australia, New Zealand, the United Kingdom and Canada) and the United States, which is considered the foremost exponent of NPM" (UN 2001). Shortly after NPM started being implemented in these countries, the NPM reform agenda became a global trend. International donors (mainly the World Bank and the International Monetary Fund) implemented NPM reform via the structural adjustment programs offered to developing countries during the 1980s.

II. E-Government versus E-Governance

The public sector reform agenda in developing countries, and its shift toward a governance model, became more concerned with "institutional building" also known as "capacity reinforcement." Capacity building pursues a twofold approach:

• Reforming and improving the structures associated with public administration;
• Developing personnel capable of effectively operating and managing the organizational structures of public administration.

Yet, globalization (and its concomitant technological expansion) continues to shape public sector reform, "capacity-reinforcement must therefore be understood in broad strategic terms as a long-term endeavour, indeed a continual task of shaping, redefining and revamping institutions with the help of evolving technologies and refining human competencies in this light" (UN 2003). This suggests that public sector reform and its related capacity building process should integrate new technologies as enabling tools. In fact, Heeks (1999) notes that "reinventing government is a continuation of existing new public management reform, but reinventing government in the information age should mean two things that are different:

• First, a much greater (i.e., more overt) role for information and information systems in the processes of change;
• Second, a much greater (i.e., more widely employed) role for information technology in the processes of change."

In this sense, globalization and the information age is bringing about "IT-enabled public sector reform": integrating technology to influence and enable NPM reform and related governance principles (Heeks 1999). Consequently, a number of "IT-based concepts" are increasingly used: e-government and e-governance (UN 2003).

Backus defines e-governance as "the application of electronic means to (1) the interaction between government and citizens and government and businesses, as well as (2) to internal government operations in order to simplify and improve democratic, government and business aspects of governance" (UN 2003).

E-Governance consists of three components: "(1) e-administration: improving government processes; (2) e-citizens and e-services: connecting citizens; and (3) e-society: building interactions with and within the civil society" (Heeks 2001). In this sense, e-governance has two complementary aspects: a political aspect, which focuses on enabling democratic participatory processes by engaging citizens, and a technical aspect, which focuses on government operations and processes (Bhatnagar 2004). Addressing a government's technical issues makes e-government "a subset of e-governance." **E-Government** is defined as a process of reform in the way governments work, share information and deliver services to external and internal clients.

The UN describes e-government as "utilizing the internet and the world wide web for delivering government information and services to citizens" (UN 2003). In this regard, e-government occurs when a governmental institution uses ICT to serve citizens and meet their informational and transactional needs. The worldwide expansion and extension of ICT has included its introduction and diffusion within public administrations. Such diffusion has led to the electronic enabling of the three functions of government (although this is of varying degrees), which could be said to reflect a trend toward "state transformation" (Finger 2005). In addition, ICT applications have revolutionized the government's service delivery function. Finger indicates that service delivery is where ICT has, so far, made the most spectacular inroads. For the two other main state functions, ICT use is limited, but there has been an ICT-enabled emergence of e-participation / e-democracy within the policy making arena, and the emergence of e-regulation within the regulatory function (Finger 2005).

In its simplest definition, e-government refers to "the use of digital technologies to transform government operations in order to improve effectiveness, efficiency and service delivery" (Forman 2005). Generally, the more services that are available online and the more widespread their use, the greater the impact that e-government will have. "In addition to the internet, mobile phones offer an even more convenient channel through which to distribute government information. By utilizing text messaging, governments are able to send out region-wide and specific emergency warnings, provide up-to-the-minute information upon request, and in essence make governments accessible to the people no matter where they may be, at any time" (McGuigan 2010).

E-Government involves the automation or computerization of existing paper-based procedures. This prompts new styles of leadership, new ways of debating and determining strategies, transacting business, listening to citizens and communities, and organizing and delivering information; essentially new ways of governing. Hence, this process, which consists of using, enhancing, inventing and managing e-government tools for governance purposes, is called e-governance. The "e" part of both e-government and e-governance stands for the electronic platform or infrastructure that enables and supports the networking of public policy development and deployment.

For the UN, "e-government can be defined as the use of information and communication technologies (ICT) to improve the activities of public sector organizations and their agents. Such efforts may be directed at 'front office' delivery of services to citizens or at modernizing working practices and delivering improvements in operational efficiency within the 'back office'" (2008).

E-Governance is a wide concept that defines and assesses the impact that technologies have on the practice and administration of governments, on the relationships between civil servants and the wider society, and on interactions with elected bodies or outside groups, such as not-for-profit organizations or private sector corporate entities. E-Governance encompasses a series of necessary steps that government agencies need to develop and administer to ensure the successful implementation of e-government services to the public at large. If e-government is thought of as the application of electronic means to the workings and operations of governments, e-governance is the application of electronic means to:

- The interactions between government and citizens and government and businesses; and
- Internal government operations to simplify and improve the democratic, government and business aspects of governance" (Backus 2001).

E-Governance has three aims:

1) "Improving government processes: e-administration;
2) Connecting citizens: e-citizens and e-services;
3) Building interactions with and within civil society: e-society" (Heeks 2001).

As shown in Box 3.1 below, these three e-governance aims seem to match governance processes: implementation (G2G), engagement and consultation processes (G2B and G2C, B2G and C2G).

Box 3.1. E-Government nomenclature (UN 2003)

Government-to-Government (G2G) involves sharing data and conducting electronic exchanges between governmental actors. This involves both intra- and inter-agency exchanges at the national level, as well as exchanges among the national, provincial and local levels.

Government-to-Business (G2B) involves business-specific transactions (e.g., payments with regard to sale and purchase of goods and services) as well as provision on line of business-focussed services.

Government-to-Consumer/Citizen (G2C) involves initiatives designed to facilitate people's interaction with government as consumers of public services and as citizens. This includes interactions related to the delivery of public services as well as to participation in the consultation and decision-making process.

III. E-Government and E-Governance as a Means for Good Governance

Several studies have promoted the use of e-government systems, suggesting that they produce a number of benefits which foster good governance (Nute 2002). E-Government is presented as a way to promote the responsiveness of government institutions to citizens' growing demands. These demands include improved access to public services, public institutional efficiency and more stringent security measures (O'Connell 2003).

The Electronic Government for Developing Countries report (ITU 2008) mentions that: "using ICT effectively to serve citizens online is a struggle for many governments, particularly in developing countries. Government organizations face great levels of uncertainty in developing and providing e-government services because of the complexity of the technology, deeply entrenched organizational routines, and great diversity in the acceptance of technology by individuals."

E-Government requires much more than technical wizardry to develop and operate successful online services. Strategic approaches need to be developed to organize and assemble tangible resources such as computers and networks, and intangible resources such as employee skills, knowledge and organizational processes. Consequently, government organizations need to address two issues in order to achieve success:

- They must have a significant population of citizens willing and able to adopt and use online services; and,
- They need to develop the managerial and technical capability to implement e-government applications to meet the needs of citizens (Hanna 2010).

Bhatnagar (2004) assessed 12 e-government projects in developing countries. These projects provide "examples where e-government has delivered concrete benefits by increasing transparency, reducing corruption, improving service delivery, empowering people and enhancing economic goals of good governance." These examples confirm Heeks' claim that e-governance (including e-government) "is the ICT-enabled route to achieving good governance" (UN 2003).

Yet, it has also been observed that a large number of e-government systems deployed in developing countries fail to enhance governance for a number of reasons (Heeks 2003). Guida and Crow (2007) suggested that several issues might explain this disappointing record:

- The application of inappropriate technologies;
- A field-level disconnection between multilateral banks, donors, other project sponsors and the client governments they serve;
- An excessive reliance on top-down government approaches which do not account for users' needs and citizens' demands.

Guida and Crow (2007) listed other important governance-related factors that contribute to such failures, such as: a lack of transparency and citizen involvement; resistance by entrenched bureaucracy; corruption; regressive policy and regulatory environments; and, unskilled human resources. The issues of the lack of readiness, adoption and use of e-government (ICT and related services and practices) are often grouped together under the term, **e-readiness**. We believe that the e-readiness of all government stakeholders (politicians, senior managers, middle managers and employees) is also an important factor for successful e-government deployment, usage and adoption. E-readiness assessments are performed to determine a country's capacity to use and apply ICT. These are primarily focused on the extent to which governments have the capacity to implement applications and users have the capacity to take advantage of them. They help to determine which types of services can realistically be provided, which barriers are likely to be encountered, and which complementary initiatives are necessary to enhance their impact and sustainability (Hanna 2010).

IV. E-Government Application Areas

Government service delivery is the area "where ICT have, so far, made the most spectacular inroads" (Finger 2005), but in the other two main governmental areas (regulation and policy making) ICT use is reported to still be limited. A UN study (2008) mentions that "this dichotomy between democratic politics and government operations is one that is common in many parts of the world – namely that the executive branch far outpaces the legislative branch of the public sector in terms of investment in new technologies and corresponding openness to digital innovation. The majority of the efforts made by governments in the initial phases of e-government (information and integration) have largely been orchestrated by executive branch officials, both elected and appointed" (Roy 2006b).

ICT artifacts fuelling e-government/e-governance are numerous and continuously evolving. Table 3.1 below intends to provide an overview of how certain ICT transform the government's functions.

Table 3.1. Technologies transforming government organizations (Snellen 2002)

Technology	Explanations
Database technologies	Are applied in three basic forms of information systems: Object registration systems hold a general purpose register of the population, legal entities such as institutions, immovable properties, enterprises, etc. Object registration systems may be maintained by authorized officials, such as a public notary. Object registration systems make (legally) reliable societal exchanges possible. They function as a general purpose register. No concrete transactions are performed by the object registration systems. Object registration systems are for exchanges between bureaucracies and citizens. The administrative identity of the citizen is certified by these types of authentic registers. Sectoral systems assist in the basic transactions in a specific sector of public administration such as social security, healthcare, police, traffic and transport, etc. Control systems perform and monitor the expenditures of financial, human and physical (building and equipment) resources within ministries, other government bodies and subsidized organizations.
Decision support technologies	Serve as an aid to decision making processes, by applying specific rules to individually, or collectively, entered data. Decision support systems can range from fairly simple processing (case-handling) systems, based on a few production rules, to complex advisory systems and knowledge-based systems. As a general rule, one can state that, for the information society, every type of decision that can be put into an algorithm will sooner or later be automated.
Networking technologies	Are rapidly mushrooming. They add the communication dimension to information technologies. As a result of this, time and place are losing their significance. All kinds of services are thereby introduced. Examples of these technologies are: file-sharing, email, websites, navigating, chatting, targeting messages, video conferencing, and the like.

(Continued)

Table 3.1. Continued

Technology	Explanations
Personal identification, tracking, tracing and monitoring technologies	Are becoming increasingly sophisticated and are pervading all spheres of life. General personal identification numbers (PIN) or more specific numbers such as fiscal, social security, healthcare or educational numbers can be used to create general databases. Smart cards, incorporating identification numbers, and other tracing or tracking devices can also be used for identification purposes by public services and to monitor the mobility of people and vehicles. Tracking and monitoring devices are becoming more and more important: they are unobtrusive; they do not require any rearrangement of workflows or routines but can adapt themselves to existing habits; and they are extremely effective for surveillance.
Office automation and multimedia technologies	Are used in the core business of public administration for the generation, handling, rearrangement and provision of information in a retrievable form. Retrievability of information is necessary for all types of audits to which public administration is subjected including legal, political, democratic, managerial and historical auditing. Office automation serves this purpose through the use of text processing systems and other entry devices; storage media such as magnetic tapes, CDs, CD-ROMs or photographic films; electronic mail, electronic data interchange; and document and text retrieval systems. The importance of these forms in office automation is determined by precedent, legal evidence and audits regarding public actions.

In response to the rise of the internet and its steady penetration among people and organizations, governments in developed countries have made an effort to adapt to the trend. Governments started creating new channels mediated by ICT to serve constituents (i.e., citizens and businesses). This was known as the "webification solution" (Riley 2003) and allowed governments to share documents, enabling them to better fulfill their obligation to provide information.

As ICT capabilities increased in sophistication, governments moved from the "webification solution" to advanced "e-solutions" to keep up with constituents' increasing expectations and demands. Respectively, applications such as online tax payment, online job applications and electronic certificate issuance have mushroomed. For instance, 76 percent of Estonia's tax declarations were carried out on the web in 2004 (UN 2008). Table 3.2 below shows the findings of the UN's 2008 global e-government survey with respect to electronic service delivery applications by government sectors.

Table 3.2. Provision of services by sector (UN 2008)

	Health	Education	Welfare	Labour	Finance
Stage II					
Archived information (laws, policy documents, etc)	124	124	107	105	141
Site offers news section	104	118	98	96	118
Databases (web access to / downloadable statistics)	105	104	91	91	123
One-stop shop / single-window	45	61	41	39	34
Stage III					
Downloadable forms	62	62	62	57	71
Submission of online forms	17	19	19	20	34
Audio, video feature	28	31	32	29	25
Electronic signature	7	4	7	6	11
Stage IV					
Personal online account	28	39	31	33	41
Payment by card	5	3	6	6	14
Stage V					
Encouraging citizen participation	32	37	8	24	42
E-mail sign-up option	38	56	38	30	38
Response time frame indicated for e-mails / forms	6	8	6	9	10

The UN's 2008 global e-government survey emphasized one major lesson learned: the effectiveness of government organizations in electronically serving constituents is highly dependent on automating backend operations and building integrated departmental data repositories. Experience reveals that government organizations need to learn from private sector practice; and their developed "business rules." This should inspire public organizations to develop "administrative rules" prerequisite to automating up to 80 percent of government operations and transactions. Online access to departmental data repositories, for example, is vital for sound policy analysis and related action plans.

Figure 3.1 below shows the evolution continuum of government service delivery.

Figure 3.1. The evolution continuum of government service delivery (UN 2008)

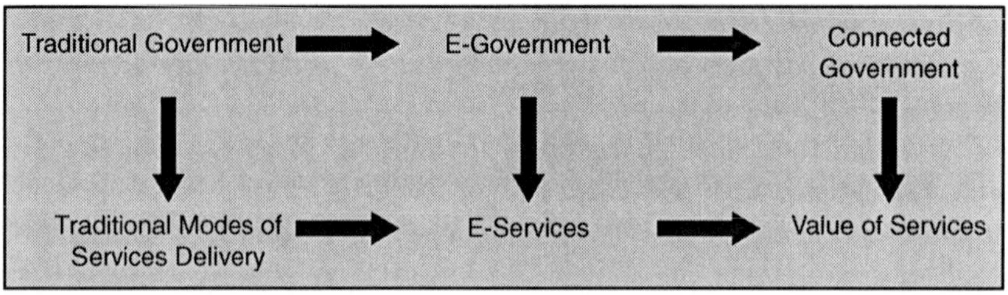

Voting is a mechanism used to allow citizens input in government affairs. Electronic voting (e-voting) was intended to make this mechanism easier and more convenient for citizens. E-voting first appeared in the Canton of Geneva, Switzerland and was first applied nationwide in Estonia in the year of 2004. Nevertheless, the practice is still in its infancy due to a lack of trust in e-voting records and their outcomes.

Table 3.3 below shows the UN's 2008 survey results with respect to the percentage of countries which use various online mechanisms for citizens' engagement.

Table 3.3. The percentage of countries which use various online mechanisms for citizens' engagement (UN 2008)

	Number of Countries	Percent
Government commits itself, formally or informally, to incorporating the results of e-participation into e-decision-making	22	11%
Explicit acknowledgement of received e-opinions, e-deliberations and e-interactions	18	9%
Government sends a 'sent receipt' to citizens after receiving input, including a copy of what was received, by whom, time/date received and estimated response time	12	6%
Officials moderate e-deliberations online	6	3%
Government publishes findings/results of citizen opinions, including e-opinions, on website	23	12%

V. E-Governance Application Areas

A. Electronic engagement (C2G)

There is an increasing interest in ICT applications that facilitate and encourage citizens to effectively contribute to government policy formulation.

Nevertheless, these applications are still limited in practice and results (UN 2008).

As shown in Table 3.4 below, the UN e-government survey findings clearly show the limited use of ICT applications in policy formulation.

Table 3.4. ICT application in policy formulation (UN 2008)

	Number of Countries	Percent
Government provides a clear and explicit written e-participation policy or mission	37	19%
E-mail alerts for e-participation purposes	21	11%
RSS used to update and involve citizens	20	10%
Written calendar listing of upcoming online participation activities	21	11%

B. Electronic consultation (G2C)

To facilitate the interactions of government officials with citizenry and lobbying groups, ICT-mediated channels are increasingly deployed. The rationale is to make it easier and more convenient for constituents to engage in the consultation process when the government is drafting and issuing laws. This application is, however, still in its infancy.

Table 3.5 below shows the UN's 2008 global e-government survey results with respect to e-consultation applications.

Table 3.5. E-consultation applications (UN 2008)

	Number of Countries	Percent
Use of polls to solicit citizen opinion	32	17%
Use of chat/instant messaging to solicit citizen opinion	10	5%
Use of weblogs (blogs) to solicit citizen opinion	8	4%
An open web forum for discussing any topic	26	14%
An open online discussion forum specifically for policy issues	23	12%
The content of past discussions in an online forum is posted	22	11%
Formal online consultation process offering a structured way for citizens to comment on government laws or policy	21	11%
Non-formal online consultation mechanism asking for citizen feedback on policies and activities	18	9%

Though limited in practice and results, it is clear there is emerging interest in applying ICT capabilities to facilitate citizens' engagement processes and to improve deliberative and consultative operations.

C. Electronic controllership (G2G)

Controllership is a set of procedures and mechanisms for internal auditing to monitor matters of organizational functioning such as measures of value chain expense processes (inputs, throughout and outputs), performance and outcomes. With the rise of ICT, electronic means are increasingly deployed to monitor the performance of the telecommunication networks and the content running on top of this infrastructure.

VI. E-Government and E-Governance Benefits

The introduction of ICT applications into government organizations has generated noticeable development gains. One notable lesson learned from the Asian economic crisis during the 1990s, as a result of the application of the World Bank's structural adjustment programs, is that "institutions matter" (World Bank 1991). This new finding suggests the need for improvement, namely in "governance," "state capacity" and "institutional quality." Respectively, in response to the need for institutional capacity reinforcement, there has been an increased emphasis on initiating and leading ICT projects in developing countries, enabling positive results and benefits.

Bhatnagar (2004) assessed the results of 12 e-government projects in developing countries and concluded that they are "examples where e-government has delivered concrete benefits by increasing transparency, reducing corruption, improving service delivery, empowering people and enhancing economic goals of good governance."

Malaysia is increasingly recognized as a developing nation role model that accomplished a major challenge: connecting its e-government implementations with clear development targets; and, thereby, has evolved into an exemplary case featuring project developers "who by effort of visionary policy and nurturing of critical conditions have realized tremendous growth which can be demonstrably attributed to proactive ICT-related initiatives" (John et al. 2005).

E-Government is a means for institutional capacity reinforcement because it retools/changes two complementary components which are prerequisites for the proper functioning of government organizations. These components are:

• The back office (government organizations' backend operations and processes "behind the scenes"), and,

- The front office (organizations' interactions and exchanges with the constituents: citizens and business enterprises)

E-Government owes its transformative capabilities to "information technology [that] carries the prospect of major reforms in governance and public administration through more efficient and effective public management; more accessible and better information for the public; better service delivery; and building partnership for interactive and participative governance" (Bertucci and Alberta 2003). Studies of e-government implementation in developing countries, namely Tanzania, South Africa and China, explain how introducing ICT to government organizations generates concrete improvements.
    "Efficiency gains:

- Governance that is cheaper: producing the same outputs at lower total cost.
- Governance that does more: producing more outputs at the same total cost.
- Governance that is quicker: producing the same outputs at the same total cost in less time.

Effectiveness gains:

- Governance that works better: producing the same outputs at the same total cost in the same time, but to a higher quality standard.
- Governance that is innovative: producing new outputs" (Heeks 2001).

Empirical studies have shown that certain gains are generated by the deployment of e-government systems, such as those listed in Figure 3.2 below.

Figure 3.2. Gains generated by the deployment of e-government systems (UN 2008)

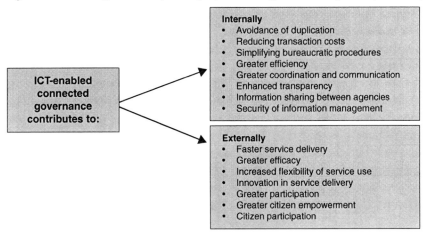

Clearly, e-government influences the value chain of government organizations by:

- Reducing the amount of input resources required (e.g., more limited workforce and less physical effort);
- Reducing throughput time (e.g., reduced service elapsed time);
- Increasing output (e.g., increased number of services), and
- Improving outcomes (e.g., improved service delivery quality).

ICT is therefore proved to be among the most innovative tools for realizing improved capabilities. Used in support of good governance, e-government has tremendous transformative potential. It can significantly change the way governments approach their mandate, solve development problems and interact with citizens and businesses. It can give rise to a new paradigm of governance: one that places citizens at its center, responds to their needs and expectations, and is transparent, accountable and participatory (Sisk 2003).

Indeed, the use of e-government applications in the functions and workings of governmental organizations has increased in popularity in industrialized countries. One significant reason for this is that government operations are mainly "information-based" and ICT have increasingly sophisticated capabilities for capturing, storing, processing and retrieving information. Consequently, ICT have increasingly succeeded in integrating government workings and operations, fulfilling government information needs to serve citizenry and businesses.

Nevertheless, the utilization of ICT applications does not generate development effects immediately. The Philippines, for instance, is open to technological importation and adoption. The Philippines acquired a modern shipping infrastructure and railways as early as 1849 and 1887 respectively. The country has since maintained this acquisition of technology, importing electric trams in 1905 and aircraft in 1924. Technological importation is not problematic in the Philippines, but what is distressing is the failure to harness the power of these technologies for the country's development.

Pertierra (2009) explains that technology in the Philippines mainly benefited metropolitan areas and was controlled by elite interests, and thus had little transformative power in the development of the country as this technology did not enter into the everyday life of most Filipinos. In Luhmann's (1998) terms, technology in the Philippines lacked system integration. It affected external, but not internal, system functionality. Moreover, this lack of "absorptive capacity" (Hanna 2010) prevented the effective utilization of ICT and diminished the likelihood of the emergence of benefits and development. This clearly highlights the critical importance of mainstreaming ICT and facilitating its pervasiveness to generate development ramifications and externalities.

Table 3.6 below shows e-government's multi-user benefits.

Table 3.6. E-Government's multi-user benefits (Guida and Crow 2009)

Target users	Applications	Benefits
Citizens	Information Education Healthcare Benefits transactions Tax payment	A more convenient channel. Lower transaction costs, increased transparency and reduced corruption. Allows for greater democratic participation.
Businesses	Information and guidance Licensing and regulation Tax payment	Faster interactions that reduce transaction costs. Reduced regulatory burden. Reduced corruption.
Suppliers	E-procurement	Improved access to the government marketplace, reduced transaction costs, greater transparency and reduced corruption.
Other agencies of government	Information sharing Data transfer and back office process automation	Greater accuracy and efficiency, reduced transaction costs, better information sharing.

VII. Risk Factors

Several contextual elements put political, legal and organizational constraints on governments, such as public policies, the availability of technological environments and the availability of trained and skilled human capital. Indeed, citizens and government stakeholders (politicians, managers and employees) are varied in their ability to understand government services and in their desire and ability to use digital systems. Hence, governments must develop the knowledge and capabilities needed to respond to these challenges and, simultaneously, to deal with ongoing issues in political, economic and social arenas. These issues generate risks which may limit the government's opportunity to be successful in adopting e-government. Kendal (ITU 2009) provides a list of risks that may limit the success of e-government: laws and public policy, citizen reaction, measuring impact, organizational structure, processes, technology, costs, lack of funding, etc.

Hanna (2010) explains that "for mainly political reasons, governments tend to favour large and expensive ICT projects with high visibility and profile.

This leads to frequent failures, since risk is usually proportional to the size of the project and to the degree of change – technical, organizational, and cultural – that it brings."

This illustrates why large and complex projects often fail, particularly when initiated ahead of learning and capacity building. Hanna (2010) also sheds lights on additional risks to e-government. These include:

- Attitudinal stands of public officials with respect to ICT;
- Organizational practices underestimating the implications of ICT decisions;
- Organizational capacity lacking the capabilities to effectively manage public-private partnerships (PPP);
- Managerial weaknesses;
- Poorly implemented participatory approaches;
- Risks inherent to a supply-driven e-government framework.

The Electronic Government for Developing Countries report (ITU 2008) identified a number of technological issues related to building e-government services to illustrate why government institutions struggle to deal with this process:

- E-Government involves taking computer-based technologies and combining them with human-based administrative processes to create new ways of serving citizens. Organizations have to adapt ICT to business processes and, similarly, business processes have to adapt to ICT.
- ICT exist in a broader context. It is not only challenging for organizations to understand computer systems, it is also challenging to understand the business, legislative and political processes that make up the day-to-day operations of all types of government institutions. Many of these processes involve numerous steps and procedures that have evolved idiosyncratically to conform to legislation, mandates and norms, based on the formal bureaucratic structure and the informal employee practices of each ministry.
- Governments must understand the local context and local practices in which ICT will be used to provide e-government services. Generally, developing countries often adopt ICT and software that are designed in the developed world and introduced to them through technology transfer programs.

Therefore, leaders of e-government projects need to wear two hats at once: a technology hat and a process engineering hat. These managers, typically, must understand how to customize applications that tie together complex computer-based technologies in concert with revamping underlying business processes and organizational structures.

The Electronic Government for Developing Countries report concludes that e-government requires government leaders and managers to answer three main questions:

- How do you take the technologies of the internet and integrate them with existing information systems and existing organizational and institutional processes?
- How do you build e-government applications to meet the needs, capabilities and values of the end user?
- How do you overcome the reality of the organizational, economic, political, technological, legal and local environment that, through complex factors, influences and defines the context of the e-government service?

Another study by the Communication Initiative Network, Branch of Africa,[1] identified factors that led to the failure of e-government deployment in Africa including:

- The lack of agreement within the public administration system: internal resistance by government;
- Inadequate plans and strategies: e-government is introduced in a fragmented and unsystematic fashion;
- The lack of adequate human resources: insufficient institutional and human capacity building;
- The absence of an investment plan;
- A shortage of IT and system suppliers;
- Immature technologies: over-emphasis on technology or technology-oriented deployment; and
- The rapid implementation of e-government without adequate testing and preparation.

The concern is no longer whether e-government benefits public organizations; rather, the concern is on how to effectively design and implement e-government projects to facilitate the achievement of expected organizational improvements. Therefore, there is a need to gain empirical insights on the risk factors and to learn about good practices that mitigate the risk.

---

1   http://www.comminit.com/africa/node/323777 (accessed June 2009).

VIII. E-Government and E-Governance Maturity

It has been observed that e-governance follows an evolutionary maturity model. Backus (2001) presents an overview of such a model which shows that, by the early 1990s, e-governance initiatives started with the creation of a web-based presence, through which a government entity could electronically deliver and disseminate information to the public. The "information" stage was then followed in the mid-'90s by an "interaction" phase, enabling citizens to communicate with a governmental entity via email and to initiate a transaction by downloading the related forms. The transaction then needed to be completed at the office counter. E-Governance initiatives have since advanced in maturity and sophistication and reached the third stage, known as "transaction." Transactions can be initiated, fully completed and finalized online; without any need to physically visit the government office. It is a more sophisticated stage that requires regulatory changes and amendments to legally allow online payment and digital certification. The fourth emerging stage is known as "transformation," "in which all information systems are integrated and the public can complete G2C and G2B services at one (virtual) counter. One single point of contact for all services is the ultimate goal." This is a challenging stage as it requires internal government re-engineering to enable advanced coordination between different government departments (Backus 2001). This four stage maturity model has been criticized as viewing the "online transaction to be the 'nirvana' of e-government, yet nirvana might actually be the proactive completion of the transaction within government or even its elimination" (Heeks 2006). The model describes the experience of e-governance as it emerged and evolved in industrialized, developed countries. As mentioned in the introduction to this chapter, the World Bank defines e-government as "the use of information and communications technologies to improve the efficiency, effectiveness, transparency and accountability of government." E-Government can be seen as simply moving citizen services online, but in its broadest sense, it refers to the technology-enabled transformation of government – a method to reduce costs, while promoting economic development, increasing transparency in government, improving service delivery and public administration, and facilitating the advancement of an information society (World Bank 2006b). In other words, e-government is a means for enhancing governance as it changes both the back office (government's internal operations and relations) and the front office (government's relations with citizens and other external stakeholders) in a way that makes good governance a reality.

Over the last two decades, with the resurgent interest in technologies, and especially ICT, there has been an increasing need to monitor and learn about the different areas and degree of ICT diffusion and penetration in governments worldwide. International organizations conducted global studies to respond to such information needs. For instance, the UN has prepared and released a series of *Global E-Government Readiness* reports (UNPAN 2010). Its first global e-readiness report (released in 2003) defined e-government sophistication levels as depicted in Figure 3.3 below.

Figure 3.3. E-Government sophistication levels (UN 2010)

Stage I: **Emerging**	Government websites provide information on public policy, governance, laws, regulations, relevant documentation and types of government services provided. They have links to ministries, departments and other branches of government. Information is limited, basic and static.
Stage II: **Enhanced**	Online services are enhanced to include databases and sources of current and archived information, such as laws and regulation, reports, newsletters and downloadable databases. The user can search for a document and there is help and a site map is provided.
Stage III: **Interactive**	Government websites deliver enhanced one-way or simple two-way e-communication between government and citizen, such as downloadable forms for government services and applications. The sites have audio and video capabilities and are multilingual. Some limited e-services enable citizens to submit requests for nonelectronic forms or personal information, which will be mailed to their house.
Stage IV: **Transactional**	Government websites engage in two-way communication with their citizens, including requesting and receiving inputs on government policies, programs, regulations, etc. Some form of electronic authentication of the citizen's identity is required to successfully complete the exchange. Government websites process non-financial transactions, e.g., e-voting, downloading and uploading forms, filing taxes online or applying for certificates, licenses and permits. They also handle financial transactions, i.e., where money is transferred on a secure network to government.
Stage V: **Networked**	Government websites have changed the way governments communicate with their citizens. They are proactive in requesting information and opinions from the citizens using Web 2.0 and other interactive tools. E-services and e-solutions cut across the departments and ministries in a seamless manner. Information, data and knowledge is transferred from government agencies through integrated applications. Governments have moved from a government-centric to a citizen-centric approach, where e-services are targeted at citizens through lifecycle events and segmented groups to provide tailor-made services. Governments create an environment that empowers citizens to be more involved with government activities to have a voice in decision making.

The World Summit on the Information Society (Geneva 2003 – Tunis 2005) also decided to monitor progress toward an information society by approving the adoption of the digital opportunity index (DOI) which looks at three indicators (ITU 2006):

- The access opportunity to ICT,
- The infrastructure of ICT, and
- The utilization rate of ICT.

And since then, the International Telecommunications Union (ITU) has conducted global surveys to build and update the world DOI index. DOI's 11 criteria are depicted in the diagram below:

Figure 3.4. The DOI's eleven criteria (ITU 2006)

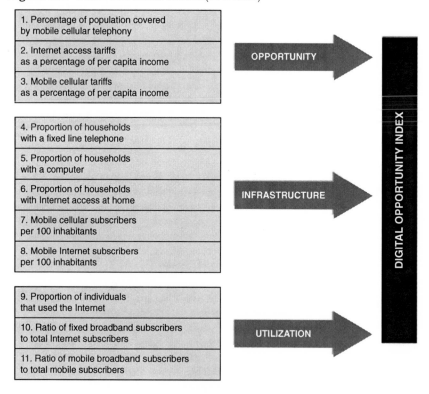

Global measurements of these criteria reveal a clear digital divide. For instance the 2006 DOI reports that "Europe, the Americas and Asia all have average DOI scores higher than the world average of 0.37, while Africa has an average DOI score of 0.20, mainly due to limited utilization and fixed line infrastructure. When compared to other regions, Africa ranks last with an average regional DOI score of barely one-third that of Europe (0.55)" (ITU 2006).

Figure 3.5 below shows Africa's DOI ranking.

Figure 3.5. The DOIs of African countries (ITU 2006)

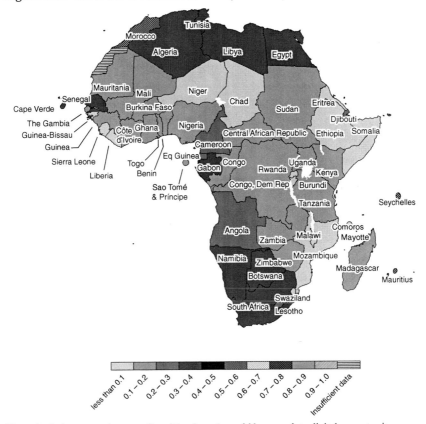

Note: the index ranges between 0 and 1, where 1 would be complete digital opportunity.

Africa's DOI rankings highlight the digital divide; and specifically the disparities in digital opportunities. The ITU (2006) explains that: "From a telecommunication policy perspective, high-ranking countries illustrate the influence of liberalization and competition in promoting opportunity and infrastructure deployment. Most of the North African countries, as well as Senegal and South Africa, have opened their fixed and mobile markets to competition and are rapidly increasing high-speed network deployment. Competition is helping to reduce tariffs and introduce service packages that respond better to the needs of the population."

The UN's 2008 e-government global survey revealed new insights (confirming the widening digital divide), stating that, "there were large differences between the five regions in terms of e-government readiness, with Europe (0.6490) having a clear advantage over the other regions, followed by the Americas (0.4936), Asia (0.4470), Oceania (0.4338) and Africa (0.2739). Asia and Oceania were slightly below the world average (0.4514), while Africa lagged far behind."

These results are depicted in Table 3.7 and Figure 3.6 below:

Table 3.7. The DOIs of the five continents and their subregions (UN 2008)

Region	2008	2005	Region	2008	2005
Africa			Americas		
Central Africa	0.2530	0.2397	Caribbean	0.4480	0.4282
Eastern Africa	0.2879	0.2836	Central America	0.4604	0.4255
Northern Africa	0.3403	0.3098	North America	0.8408	0.8744
Southern Africa	0.3893	0.3886	South America	0.5072	0.4901
West Africa	0.2110	0.1930			
Asia			Europe		
Central Asia	0.3881	0.4173	Eastern Europe	0.5689	0.5556
Eastern Asia	0.6443	0.6392	Northern Europe	0.7721	0.7751
Southern Asia	0.3395	0.3126	Southern Europe	0.5642	0.4654
South-Eastern Asia	0.4290	0.4388	Western Europe	0.7329	0.6248
Western Asia	0.4857	0.4384			
Oceania	0.4338	0.2888			
World Average	0.4514	0.4267			

In fact, no D/LDC is ranked among the top 60 countries in the UN's e-government readiness survey.

The absence of D/LDC countries among the top 60 countries in the UN global survey clearly reflects the e-government readiness divide (see Table 3.8).

Below is the list of the top 35 countries in the UN e-government global survey.

Most e-government systems that are currently deployed in D/LDC fail to enhance good governance for a number of reasons. For example, in the case of Morocco, a developing country with a reasonable growth rate, the

Figure 3.6. The DOI's comparison in the five continents (UN 2008)

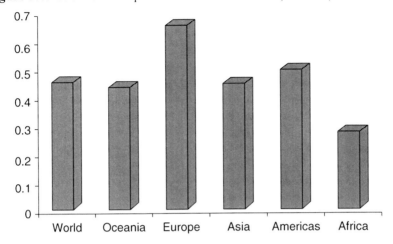

central government promotes the use of ICT in the public sector in order to enhance citizens' wellbeing and good governance. However, the development and deployment of e-government systems remains very slow due to socio-political and economic factors such as the high cost, the high level of poverty in the population and the lack of ICT infrastructures at the local governance level. Other challenging issues are the low levels of acceptability, usability, accessibility and appropriateness of e-government systems deployed for Moroccans (Kettani et al 2008). These interrelated factors influence each other, which creates a vicious circle aggravating the digital divide between Morocco and developed countries.

The e-government readiness divide exists not only between D/LDC and the rest of the world, but also within D/LDC themselves.

As depicted by Figure 3.7, Africa perfectly illustrates the regional/local digital divide.

Studies have shown that government in the developing countries "costs too much, delivers too little, and is not sufficiently responsive or accountable" (Heeks 2001). Respectively, growing emphasis has been put on initiating and leading ICT initiatives, namely e-government and e-governance, in developing countries with the aim of advancing public sector reforms to accomplish a distressing challenge: institutional building.

Accordingly, the UN's 2008 global e-government survey indicates that much of the focus in developing countries has been on leveraging e-government to overcome traditional governance weaknesses, notably an absence of openness, excessive corruption and weak accountability to citizenries as a result (UN 2008).

Table 3.8. Top 35 countries in the UN e-government global survey (UN 2008)

Rank	Country	E-Government Readiness Index
1	Sweden	0.9157
2	Denmark	0.9134
3	Norway	0.8921
4	United States	0.8644
5	Netherlards	0.8631
6	Republic of Korea	0.8317
7	Canada	0.8172
8	Australia	0.8108
9	France	0.8038
10	United Kingdom	0.7872
11	Japan	0.7703
12	Switzerland	0.7626
13	Estonia	0.7600
14	Luxembourg	0.7512
15	Finland	0.7488
16	Austria	0.7428
17	Israel	0.7393
18	New Zealand	0.7392
19	Ireland	0.7296
20	Spain	0.7228
21	Iceland	0.7176
22	Germany	0.7136
23	Singapore	0.7009
24	Belgium	0.6779
25	Czech Republic	0.6696
26	Slovenia	0.6681
27	Italy	0.6680
28	Lithuania	0.6617
29	Malta	0.6582
30	Hungary	0.6485
31	Portugal	0.6479
32	United Arab Emirates	0.6301
33	Poland	0.6117
34	Malaysia	0.6063
35	Cyprus	0.6019

Figure 3.7. Illustration of the regional/local digital divide (UN 2008)

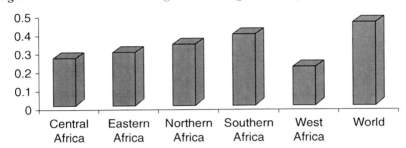

IX. Conclusion

In concluding this chapter, we can say that the debate is no longer on whether e-government could assist in improving good governance conditions. The real challenge, rather, is to determine how to successfully build e-government systems that contribute to the realization of good governance targets (Hagen 2005). This is then related to the procedural and methodological "know-how" required for effective e-government implementation.

Unfortunately, many e-government and e-governance projects in D/LDC have led to failure; either partial or total. We believe that to address these failures, stakeholders must be sensitized to the large gap between project planning and goals and the reality of the public sector in developing countries.

They should be aware of the scope and implications of the e-government system, its direct relation to their immediate environment, and be ready to use it and accept the underlying, inevitable changes that it will engender. They should perceive these systems as their own and not as being imported or imposed, so that a feeling of appropriation will emerge to accompany and strengthen the use and proliferation of ICT.

Furthermore, considering that there is such a high failure rate, there is a need for e-government assessment methods. Identifying/documenting the outcomes/results of e-government implementation projects in D/LDC and disseminating their lessons learned and proposed best practices are paramount for ongoing and future projects, and for decision makers and managers too.

Chapter 4

EVALUATION OF OUTCOMES/IMPACTS ON GOOD GOVERNANCE

I. Introduction

In relation to the assessment of e-government projects in developing countries, Heeks (2003) estimates that:

- "35 percent of projects are total failures: the system was never implemented or was implemented but immediately abandoned;
- 50 percent are partial failures: the major goals of the system were not attained and/or there were significant undesirable outcomes; and
- 15 percent are successes: most stakeholder groups attained their major goals and did not experience significant undesirable outcomes."

More generally, considering software development projects, Sommerville (2006) estimates that:

- Software bugs, or errors, are so prevalent and detrimental that they cost the US economy an estimated $59.5 billion annually, or about 0.6 percent of America's GDP;
- 23 percent of all projects undertaken by internal information system organizations are cancelled before their completion;
- 49 percent of projects cost 189 percent of their original estimates;
- Only 28 percent of projects are completed on time and within budget; and
- Completed projects have only 42 percent of the originally proposed specifications or functions.

The UN Report (2003), *E-Government at the Crossroads*, confirms that despite very limited data on e-government failures, "some analysts estimate the rate of failure of e-government projects in countries with developing economies to be very high, at around 60–80 percent, with the higher rate of failure characteristic of Africa."

Researchers such as Kreps and Richardson (2007) have identified numerous reasons for these failures including:

- Delay in delivery;
- Creeping scope;
- Weak software reliability and robustness;
- Missing core functionalities;
- Lack of integration and ineffective interface with legacy systems;
- Escalating costs;
- Poor user interface;
- Data integrity and confidentiality issues; and
- Lack of suitable training.

"The e-government primer" (InfoDev 2009) also examines failure, and its potential causes, in ICT4D and e-government projects and suggests that it is caused by a variety of factors:

- Gaps between information system design and users' needs and capabilities;
- Poor planning;
- Unclear goals and objectives;
- Objectives changing during the project;
- Unrealistic time or resource estimates;
- Lack of executive support and user involvement;
- Failure to communicate and act as a team; and
- Inappropriate skills.

With such a high failure rate, several authors agree that there is a crucial need for systematic assessment methods for e-government systems. Systematic assessment includes, among other things, a process of monitoring and evaluation. Monitoring refers to the ongoing process through which self-reflective individuals and organizations regularly check their progress against intended outcomes, so that they can improve the quality of their performance (Unwin 2009). Evaluation refers to the "mid- or end- point assessment of a program against its original objectives, and should normally involve external evaluators" (Unwin 2009).

Systematic assessment is essential for organizational learning and to gain insight into how to adjust and improve the following issues:

- Facilitating and ensuring the project progression toward the materialization of its objectives;
- Tackling staffing matters;

- Assessing users' capacity;
- Fostering institutional capacity development; and
- Communicating e-government results and effects as they emerge.

As part of the research of the eFez Project, our team developed the "outcome analysis method," which is a formal assessment framework that investigates the relationship between the project outcomes and the enhancement in good governance that followed its implementation. Our intention was to base the success of e-government projects on whether they led to or promoted good governance. We were motivated to develop this framework given the noticeable absence, in literature and in practice, of generic approaches able to evaluate whether e-government implementation promotes good governance.

In this chapter, Section II presents a number of measures (indexes) and methods that have been proposed to assess the success e-government. Section III then reviews some definitions of good governance and a number of indicators (attributes) that may be used to assess it. Section IV expands on the method impacts assessment that we developed, through examples and illustrations from the eFez Project. Section V concludes this chapter with some salient issues that need to be memorized and systematically recalled when developing e-government systems.

II. E-Government Evaluation Approaches

Garridon (2004) presents an exploratory study on the current stage of frameworks that evaluate e-government projects. There are two main evaluation approaches: a theory-based approach, in which evaluation is structured around a theoretical and conceptual body of knowledge; and a program-specific approach, where evaluation is structured around the program's objectives and goals. Garridon (2004) notes that "e-government evaluations are currently mostly program-specific and question-based" since they use a set of ad hoc questions, are context dependent, and do not refer to a formal structured evaluation framework. Moreover, Garridon highlights the need to promote and develop e-government theory-based evaluation and indicates how academic entities (universities) can play a vital role.

Garridon (2004) presents four e-government evaluation frameworks:

- The E-Government Index is an evaluation framework implemented by the United Nations Division for Public Economics and Public Administration and the American Society for Public Administration (ASPA). The E-Government Index measures the readiness for and implementation status of e-government in 144 UN member countries. The index relies on two main methodologies: a content analysis of a country's websites to determine its progress using the e-government stage-based model; and a statistical analysis to determine whether the country has the necessary telecommunication infrastructure and the available human capital.

- Cost–benefits analysis is an e-government evaluation framework implemented by the Public Affairs Centre (Bangalore) and the World Bank Group. This framework assesses the user-related benefits generated throughout the project's implementation. It relies on the "report card methodology" which "is based on feedback from users of public services about quality, efficiency and adequacy of services, and the problems they face in their interactions with service providers" (Garridon 2004).
- Cost–benefits analysis and impact analysis are evaluation frameworks that were implemented by the World Bank Group to assess the FRIENDS Project (fast, reliable, instant, efficient network for disbursement of services) in Kerala. This framework relies on two methodologies: a cost–benefits analysis to measure the project's efficiency gains; and an impact evaluation to assess how the project is influencing and impacting its stakeholders.
- The capabilities approach to human development is an evaluation framework implemented by the Department of Information Systems, the London School of Economics, to assess three e-government projects in India. It rests on Sen's approach (1999) and identifies five freedoms: political, social, economic, security and transparency of operations. This evaluation framework relies on the interpretive case study method. This method involves the researcher undertaking a "longitudinal research design in order to trace the dynamics and long term implications of e-governance projects in India" and attempting to analyze each of these elements: "the e-governance continuum, partnerships, viable business models, skills and education, facilities and resources, and social capital" (Garridon 2004).

Heeks (2006) also reviews evaluation frameworks which assess e-government performance. They fall into two categories: input/process focused and process/output focused. The latter is found to be more practical and includes two specific evaluation areas:

- "Information systems evaluation: treating the e-government system as an information system and evaluating it according to the CIPSODA checklist (capture, input, process, store, output, decision, action) which refers to the information-related tasks in e-government";
- "Data quality evaluation: again treating the e-government system as an information system, but evaluating it according to the CARTA checklist."

Table 4.1. Kearns' indicators for e-government's public value

Value Domain	Indicator	Description
Service Delivery	Take-up	The extent to which e-government is used
	Satisfaction	The level of user satisfaction with e-government
	Information	The level of information provided to users by e-government
	Choice	The level of choice provided to users by e-government
	Importance	The extent to which e-government is focused on user priorities
	Fairness	The extent to which e-government is focused on those most in need
	Cost	The cost of e-government information/service provision
Outcome Achievement	Outcome	E-Government's contribution to delivery of outcomes
Trust in Public Institutions	Trust	E-Government's contribution to public trust

CARTA stands for "completeness, accuracy, relevance, timeliness and appropriate presentation of the information it produces" (Heeks, 2006).

In addition, Heeks (2006b) presents an "outcome-focused approach" which parallels a method used in Canada to assess service delivery in e-government projects. The Canadian method includes 11 "evaluation indicators" of successful service delivery organized into three categories:

- Citizen/client-centered government: convenience, accessibility, credibility;
- Improved, more responsive service: critical mass of services, take-up, service transformation and citizen/client satisfaction;
- Capacity for online delivery: security, privacy, efficiency, innovation.

The "change-related" evaluation (Heeks 2006) is another approach used regularly to measure the progress of e-government projects over a period of time and allows us to see how the measured indicators are changing, for better or worse.

The "public value" related evaluations see public value as a variety of outcomes caused by measurable factors (Kelly and Muers 2002). In this case, services can be measured by customer satisfaction and perception of fairness, when trust, legitimacy and confidence can be measured by perceptions of the overall performance of government.

Alternatively, Heeks (2006) and Kearns (2004) present two other distinct ways to evaluate e-government's public value. Kearns' approach assesses public value in terms of three value elements:

• Service delivery;
• Outcome achievement; and
• Trust in public institutions.

Above are Kearns' measurable indicators for e-governments' public value (Table 4.1).

The E-GEP approach (Heeks 2006b) measures e-government's public value in terms of three value areas:

• Efficiency: organizational value;
• Effectiveness: user value; and
• Democracy: political value.

Below are Heeks' measurable indicators for e-government's public value (Table 4.2).

It is notable that in the above review, none of the e-government assessment approaches specifically concern themselves with the overall impact of implementation on the mode of governance itself. Rather, they focus on the effectiveness, acceptance or efficiency of the specific application being implemented. We instead intend to highlight and assess this relationship between an e-government application and its impact on the attributes and modalities of e-governance (presented in Section IV).

III. Defining and Measuring Good Governance

The notion of governance has been defined in different ways. The World Bank defines governance in terms of how "power is exercised through a country's economic, political and social institutions" (2006). This definition presents governance as the result of the activities and processes which shape the use of power within the institutional units of a national state.

In this respect, the World Bank is mainly concerned with governance with respect to government institutions and how they control their internal processes. The United Nations Development Programme (UNDP) defines governance as "the exercise of economic, political and administrative authority to manage a country's affairs at all levels. It comprises mechanisms, processes and institutions

Table 4.2. E-GEP indicators for e-government's public value (Heeks 2006b)

Value Domain	Indicator	Sample Measures
Efficiency: *Organisational value*	Financial Flows	Reduction in overhead costs Staff time saving per case handled
	Staff Empowerment	% staff with ICT skills Staff satisfaction rating
	Organisation/ IT Architecture	Number of re-designed business processes Volume of authenticated digital documents exchanged
Effectiveness: *User Value*	Administrative Burden	Time saved per transaction for citizens Overhead cost saving for businesses (travel, postage, fees)
	User value/ Satisfaction	Number of out-of-hours usages of e-government User satisfaction rating
	Inclusivity of Service	E-Government usage by disadvantaged groups Number of SMEs bidding for public tenders online
Democracy: *Political Value*	Openness	Number of policy drafts, available online Response time to online queries
	Transparency and Accountability	Number of processes traceable online Number of agencies reporting budgets online
	Participation	Accessibility rating of e-government sites Number of contributions to online discussion forums

through which citizens and groups articulate their interests, exercise their legal rights, meet their obligations and mediate their differences" (UNDP 1997).

The UNDP's definition of governance thus highlights the two main players: a country and its citizens. In this regard, governance refers to the sum of interactions within a governmental structure and includes those who make up that structure. Specifically, it refers to the way governments (as well as civil society and other actors in this context) organize their internal functioning and how citizens are empowered (or not) to interact with and influence this functioning.

The notion of good governance has become the central theme of several approaches aimed at reforming and updating government and governance systems in D/LDC (Backus 2001; Song 2006).

There has been an evolution in the concept of good governance. First appearing in the twentieth century, the notion of good governance began in the discussions of business analysts and economists who were highlighting the structures and strategies of corporate management which succeed in increasing productivity and profits (IDRC 2005). In the late 1980s, scientists in the field of social and economic development also began to consider the notion of good governance, focusing on the role of government.

Good governance was mainly presented by the World Bank as a requirement, at a national level, to enable and facilitate the success of economic development reforms (Haldenwang 2004). The UNDP also embraced the notion by the 1990s, further extending the idea that good governance would enable countries to achieve human development.

For the World Bank, good governance (or the good use of governmental power) is "epitomized by predictable, open and enlightened policy making; a bureaucracy imbued with a professional ethos; an executive arm of government accountable for its actions; and a strong civil society participating in public affairs, and all behaving under the rule of law" (World Bank 2006).

For the UNDP (1997), good governance is described as being: "among other things, participatory, transparent and accountable. It is also effective and equitable. And it promotes the rule of law fairly. Good governance ensures that the voices of the poorest and the most vulnerable are heard when allocating development resources, and that political, social and economic priorities are based on broad consensus among the three stakeholders – the state sector, private sector and civil society" (UNDP 1997).

A. Attributes of good governance

Good governance is quite dependent on the context in which it is assessed. It is up to a society to decide which characteristics are most important within each context, and hence, which ones require intervention toward improvement (UNDP 1997).

However, the UNDP managed to establish eight general characteristics of good governance: it is participatory, consensus oriented, accountable, transparent, responsive, effective and efficient, equitable and inclusive, and follows the rule of law. It assures that corruption is minimized, the views of minorities are taken into account and that the voices of the most vulnerable in society are heard during decision making. It is also responsive to the present and future needs of society. These characteristics and their role in good governance are further explained below:[1]

---

1   http://www.unescap.org/pdd/prs/ProjectActivities/Ongoing/gg/governance.asp (accessed June 2009).

- Participation: participation by a diverse demographic of society's constituents is a key cornerstone of good governance. Participation can be either direct or through legitimate intermediate institutions or representatives. It is important to point out that representative democracy does not necessarily mean that the concerns of the most vulnerable in society would be taken into consideration when decision making. Participation needs to be informed and organized. This means freedom of association and expression on the one hand and an organized civil society on the other hand.
- Rule of law: good governance requires fair legal frameworks that are enforced impartially. It also requires the full protection of human rights, particularly those of minorities. Impartial enforcement of laws requires an independent judiciary and an impartial and incorruptible police force.
- Transparency: transparency means that the decisions made and their enforcement is done in a manner that follows rules and regulations. It also means that information is freely available and directly accessible to those who will be affected by such decisions and their enforcement. It means that enough information is provided and that it is provided in easily understood forms.
- Responsiveness: good governance requires institutions and processes to serve stakeholders within a reasonable timeframe.
- Consensus oriented: there are several actors and many viewpoints in any given society. Good governance requires the mediation of different interests in a society to reach a broad consensus on what is in the best interests of the whole community and how this can be achieved. It also requires a broad and long-term perspective on what is needed for sustainable human development and how to achieve the goals of such development. This can only result from an understanding of the historical, cultural and social contexts of a given society or community.
- Equity and inclusiveness: a society's wellbeing depends on ensuring that members do not feel excluded from mainstream society. This requires all groups, but particularly the most vulnerable, to have opportunities to improve or maintain their wellbeing.
- Effectiveness and efficiency: good governance enables processes and institutions to produce results that meet the needs of society while making the best use of the resources at their disposal. The concept of efficiency in the context of good governance also covers the sustainable use of natural resources and the protection of the environment.
- Accountability: accountability is a key requirement of good governance. Not only governmental institutions, but also the private sector and civil society organizations must be accountable to the public and to their institutional stakeholders. Who is accountable to whom varies depending on whether

decisions or actions are internal or external to an organization or institution. In general, an organization or an institution is accountable to those who will be affected by its decisions or actions. Accountability cannot be enforced without transparency and the rule of law.

The World Bank views governance as a "political and economic conditionality" (Weiss 2000). It considers "public sector management, the reduction of transaction costs and contract enforcement" as the primary elements which enable good governance (Weiss 2000). These elements are credited with being the building blocks of establishing and maintaining sustainable human development.

In contrast to the World Bank, the UNDP emphasizes empowerment. This refers to the act of facilitating local participation by making institutions, processes and mechanisms of democracy available and accessible to the general public. As a result, the UNDP emphasizes the political and civic aspects of governance. It works on improving areas such as "human rights, legislative support, judicial reform and corruption" (UNDP 2000).

The World Bank views these latter concerns, emphasized by the UNDP, as secondary elements that further a country's development in terms of "efficiency and growth" (UNDP 2000). Since good governance is most often associated with the promotion of local participation in the decision making process, it seems that the UNDP's approach is closer to the generally accepted definition of good governance than the World Bank's approach.

The priorities and concerns of good governance have shifted. Its advocates are increasingly downplaying concerns related to economic growth and instead want to establish "governance policies and institutions that best promote greater freedom, genuine participation and sustainable human development" (Weiss 2000). This suggests that the political and civic aspects of good governance are increasingly being emphasized at the expense of the economic aspect.

Good governance has become a common conditionality that international donors require before providing development aids. Specifically, international donors have been pushing country aid recipients to review and reform government structures and institutions to integrate good governance values. The objective is to "get institutions right first" and the underlying premise is the view of "better run public institutions as the most important instrument for fostering economic growth and reducing poverty" (Brinkerhoff and Goldsmith 2005).

Similarly, reform-minded players in governmental and nongovernmental structures have increasingly viewed and promoted the need to improve governance quality in order to facilitate development and build an environment attractive to investment opportunities (Kaufmann et al. 2005). In addition, it is increasingly recognized "that aid flows have a stronger impact on development in countries with good institutional quality" (Kaufmann et al. 2005).

As such, there is a growing demand for the regular monitoring and assessing of countries' governance. For instance, Kaufmann (Kaufmann et al. 2005) has been monitoring the governance performance of approximately "209 countries and territories" between 1996 and 2004, using measurable indicators for "six dimensions of governance:

- Voice and accountability: measuring political, civil and human rights;
- Political instability and violence: measuring the likelihood of violent threats to, or changes in, government, including terrorism;
- Government effectiveness: measuring the competence of the bureaucracy and the quality of public service delivery;
- Regulatory burden: measuring the incidence of market-unfriendly policies;
- Rule of law: measuring the quality of contract enforcement, the police, and the courts, as well as the likelihood of crime and violence; and
- Control of corruption: measuring the exercise of public power for private gain, including both petty and grand corruption and state capture."

Kaufmann's studies show that during the eight year period of regular monitoring, countries' governance quality and performance changed either positively or negatively. As far as the African region is concerned, governance performance is poor in many countries.

Heeks (2001) explains that "government in the developing nations costs too much, delivers too little, and is not sufficiently responsive or accountable". Indeed, structural problems need to be addressed and actions need to be taken to facilitate the adoption and achievement of good governance.

B. Measurements of good governance

Supporters of e-government systems claim that they produce a number of benefits which foster good governance. However, there is a lack of empirical evidence to build upon such a hypothesis (Kettani et al. 2006). Confirming whether e-government systems effectively enhance governance is an issue of increasing importance in developing countries, as they strive to find technology able to bridge the gap in development. E-Government applications have swept the functions and operations of government organizations due to government operations being mainly "information-based." ICT have increasingly sophisticated capabilities for capturing, storing, processing and retrieving information. Consequently, ICT have progressively integrated into government operations and advanced their capabilities, serving citizenry and businesses to a greater extent.

The link between e-government and good governance has been suggested and investigated by several authors through different conceptual and theoretical studies. They believe that both concepts share the same objectives such as administrative efficiency, quality of public services and democratic participation (Haldenwang 2004; Waema and Adera 2011). They suggest that the relationship between good governance and e-government stems from the latter's "dualistic approach to state modernization: it combines an internal focus on administrative reform with an external focus on state–citizen (or state–customer) relations." In other words, e-government is a means for creating good governance as it improves both the back office (government internal operations and relations) and the front office (government relations with citizens and other external stakeholders) in such a way that makes good governance a reality. In recognizing this potential, e-government has become part of the agenda in several multilateral development-oriented institutions. For example, in 1995, the World Bank set up the Information for Development Program (INFODEV), and the UN created the United Nations Online Network in Public Administration and Finance (UNPAN) in 2003 (Haldenwang 2004).

Several tools have been developed in order to measure the quality of governance within a society. Weiss (2000) lists some of these tools: notably, the Human Development Index (HDI), which was developed to enhance the methods of evaluating societal good governance. The HDI shows that "economic wellbeing and human progress are not synonymous" (Weiss 2000): two countries might have different HDIs regardless of equal per capita incomes thus illustrating the significance of higher quality governance (Weiss 2000). The UNDP produces the annual Human Development Report to gauge governance through statistically highlighting the living conditions of people, in particular, those of poor countries.

The World Bank has also developed the Index of Governance Quality (GQI), which is designed to measure the quality of governance (Shah and Hurther 2005). The GQI is composed of four indices:

- A citizen participation index (CP) assessed through political freedom (PF) and political stability (PS);
- A government orientation index (GO) evaluated through judicial efficiency (JE), bureaucratic efficiency (RT), and lack of corruption (CO);
- A social development index measured through human development (HD) and whether income distribution is egalitarian (GI); and

- An economic management index (EM) calculated by outward orientation (OO), central bank independence (CB) and inverted debt to GDP ratio (DB).

An overall index of governance quality (GQI) is calculated by multiplying the four indices together. Table 4.3 below shows the elements of the GQI.

Table 4.3. The elements of the GQI (Shah and Hurther 2005)

	Index Name		Component Indices
CP	Citizen Participation Index		
		PF	Political Freedom
		PS	Political Stability
GO	Government Orientation Index		
		JE	Judicial Efficiency
		RT	Bureaucratic Efficiency
		CO	Lack of Corruption
SD	Social Development Index		
		HD	Human Development
		GI	Egalitarian income distribution
EM	Economic Management Index		
		OO	Outward Orientation
		CB	Central Bank Independence
		DB	Inverted Debt to GDP Ratio

Sets of attributes have also been identified that assess governance within local government. The Global Development Research Centre (GDRC) has provided a list of good governance attributes. These are:

- Accountability;
- Responsiveness;
- Management innovation;
- Public-private partnerships;
- Local government-citizen interaction;
- Decentralized management; and
- Networking and human resource development.

To assess the quality of governance, the presence of these characteristics can be assessed through the measurements of an associated set of indicators: financial and political decentralization, local government (institutions), predictability, responsiveness, empowerment, effectiveness, equity, accountability and transparency, strategic vision, participation, private sector, civil society and management. In this way, each of these indicators can be measured using a set of variables.

Additionally, the GDRC goes on to recognize the top 12 urban governance indicators which identify successful local governance and are provided in Box 4.1 below:

Box 4.1. Top twelve urban governance indicators[2]

1) Consumer satisfaction (survey/complaints)
2) Openness of procedures for contracts and tenders in municipal services
3) Equity in tax system
4) Sources of local government funding (taxes, user charges, borrowing, central government, international aid)
5) Percentage of population served by services
6) Public access to stages of the policy cycle
7) Fairness in enforcing laws
8) Incorporation of excluded groups in the consultation process
9) Clarity of procedures and regulations and responsibilities
10) Existing participatory processes
11) Freedom of media and the existence of local media
12) Autonomy of financial resources

By assessing urban governance through these indicators, an "effectiveness indicator" can be established by the degree of user (i.e., citizen) satisfaction measured through surveys and complaints. The planning and predictability indicator can be obtained by evaluating the openness of procedures for contracts and tenders for municipal services. The responsiveness indicator can be measured by determining the percentage of the community served and the population's access to the policy making process. Accountability and transparency can be evaluated by assessing which laws are fairly enforced and the clarity of procedures, policies and responsibilities. The equity indicator can be obtained by judging the accessibility of the consultation process to marginalized social groups and the degree of impartiality in the tax regime. The empowerment indicator can be estimated by identifying and quantifying

2   http://www.gdrc.org/u-gov/indicators.html (accessed February 2014).

the channels available for participation in local decision making. Participation can be assessed by the presence and scope of freedom in local media.

Indeed, the rise of evidence-based policy making emphasized the importance of assessing and evaluating projects, specifically those which have development goals. Evaluation has increasingly shifted the attention from the project inputs and activities to the project's results and impacts (Picciotto 2003). Evaluation is an instrumental tool that enables readjustment of the project process to improve its capacity to reach its goals. It is also essential to identify the lessons learned in e-government projects which help to inform practitioners and possibly to influence policies (Picciotto 2003).

IV. The eFez Method for Assessing Good Governance

The eFez Project was a technology implementation and deployment project undertaken to facilitate the transformation of local governance. Additionally, it was aimed at assessing the results, outcomes and effects of the deployment of an e-government system on governance and, overall, the transformation of a previously completely manual municipal service delivery process.

The outcome analysis methodology that was developed and used in the eFez Project provides a means to assess the broader significance of ICT systems (i.e., e-governance systems) in relation to normative goals, while using both qualitative and quantitative measurements. An outcome analysis begins by selecting formal (and generally accepted) definitions of good governance and by identifying their underlying characteristics (attributes).

These general definitions are then refined to create project-specific definitions which can be translated into specific normative project goals, identified through collaboration with project stakeholders. Finally, these normative goals are related to anticipated project outcomes and specific measurable outputs.

A. A general presentation of our outcome analysis method

Notably, this approach can be applied to a variety of normative goals in the different domains (technology, organization and service delivery) affected by the project's implementation, and to a variety of applications.

In our outcome analysis method, the identified project outcomes were directly linked to attributes of good governance. It was decided that the UNDP list of good governance attributes was sufficiently complete and easily understood by stakeholders. Starting from these definitions, a set of working definitions were developed based specifically on the requirements of the city of Fez and tailored to the eFez Project.

Figure 4.1 illustrates the method applied to determine these attributes.

Figure 4.1. eFez outcome oriented progress assessment

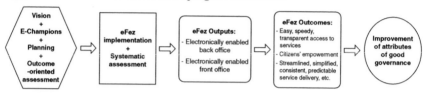

Selected measurable indicators were then associated with these working definitions to enable the team to practically determine the relationship between the project's activities (automating service delivery) and the project's outcomes toward enhancing the attributes of good governance.

In order to assess and measure the project's outcomes, five major outcome categories were identified for evaluation:

- Technology-related outcomes;
- Organization-related outcomes;
- Citizen-related outcomes;
- Regulation-related outcomes; and
- Good-governance-related outcomes.

With regard to good governance, a systematic approach was used to link the eFez Project's outcomes to the nine UNDP attributes by developing project-related definitions of good governance:

- Transparency: creating visibility in the service workflow for citizens through an automated service delivery
- Effectiveness and efficiency: enabling the optimal use of resources for citizens in service delivery
- Participation: empowering citizens to legally control service delivery to their advantage
- Equity: citizens receive service on an equal basis
- Rule of law: ensuring that the laws and regulations governing service are applied impartially
- Accountability: creating standards against which individuals providing service and service delivery can be held accountable
- Responsiveness: serving all citizens consistently and predictably
- Consensus orientation: not applicable to this project which is primarily concerned with service delivery
- Strategic vision: also not applicable to the project

Once the system is operational (being actually used by citizens), the outcomes identification process of our evaluation framework started. This process consisted of reviewing the project activities, identifying the generated outcomes and inspecting these to determine the appropriate link to each working definition. The selected outcomes were then reviewed and revised based on their applicability and fit in the broader context and objectives of the new e-government system in the city of Fez. The revised definitions were:

- Transparency: a workflow that has become visible, transparent and accessible for citizens via automated service delivery
- Effectiveness and efficiency: can be identified as enabling citizens' optimal use of resources in the delivery and utilization of public services
- Participation/empowerment: occurs when citizens are empowered to legally control service delivery to their advantage as a result of minimizing superfluous intermediate roles in the process chain of service delivery
- Equity: is realized when all citizens are served on an equal basis
- Rule of law: is achieved when laws and regulations are applied impartially
- Accountability: is achieved when standards are in place to assign responsibility to the appropriate individuals, due largely to a routine service delivery method
- Responsiveness: when all citizens are served consistently and predictably

The table below summarizes the eFez Project outcomes related to good governance.

Furthermore, four main stakeholder groups were identified for which good governance attributes needed to be assessed:

- High-level decision makers (politicians)
- Middle-level managers
- Employees
- Citizens

For each of these stakeholder categories, good governance attributes must be instantiated into relevant indicators that can be effectively measured. Indicators need to be measured before and after the deployment of the e-government system.

Indeed, the development of these working and operational definitions took into account the context and specifics of the project environment. They enabled the identification of specific project outcomes and thus created the ability to track the project's progress in relation to the broader

Table 4.4. Good governance attributes, their related outcomes and measurable outputs (Kettani, Moulin et al. 2005)

Good governance attributes (UNDP)	Attributes' definitions (for the eFez Project)	Related project outcomes	Measurable indicators (outputs)
Transparency	Visibility of workflows for citizens.	Visibility of workflows for citizens via eFez portal and kiosk.	Online availability of workflow descriptions of relevant public services.
Effectiveness and efficiency	Optimal use of resources for citizens to obtain BEC services.	Optimal use of resources for citizens to request and obtain BEC services.	Citizens saving time/money/effort when requesting and obtaining BEC services.
Responsiveness	Fez's e-government system has no negative effects on the local community.	Usable, accessible and acceptable graphic user interfaces (GUI).	Increased number and types of citizens using Fez's portal and its related kiosk.
Equity	Citizens served with increased equity.	Citizens request and receive BEC services with equity.	Decrease in bribery incidents.
Rule of law	Visible/explicit administrative rules.	The transition from tacit rules and procedures to explicit ones.	1) Documented administrative procedures; 2) Static component of the portal; 3) Number of information pages published on the portal.
Accountability	Clear information on who is responsible for what (a chain of responsibility).	Citizens' access to chain of responsibility available online and via the kiosk.	1) Access to government organization charts; 2) Public officials' names and contact information

definition and requirements of good governance. In turn, this allowed us to characterize and document the manner and the degree to which the project was supporting the achievement of good governance within a particular service delivery (BEC operations) and in a particular institutional context (the city of Fez).

B. Data / evidence gathering method

The next stage of our outcome analysis method was to identify appropriate methods of measuring the selected indicators and then possibly developing procedures and software to collect relevant data.

We were inspired by the results-based management approach (RBM) which proposes an assessment strategy by which an organization ensures that its processes, products and services contribute to the achievement of clearly stated results (UNDP 2002).

Such an approach is based on a continual and systematic process of:

- "Collecting and analysing data to measure the performance of interventions toward achievement of outcomes;
- Conducting effective outcome monitoring;
- Establishing baseline data;
- Selecting outcome indicators of performance; and
- Designing mechanisms that include planned actions such as field visits, stakeholder meetings and systematic analysis or reports" (*UNDP 2002*).

Indeed, the eFez Team paid special attention to the changes caused by the project's implementation. The selected indicators were aimed at assessing the results and outputs of the project. At this stage, fieldwork was carried out in order to determine how the service delivery changed after the eFez system's deployment. In order to collect baseline data before the system's deployment, the existing procedures of service delivery were observed, investigated and analysed. After the eFez system deployment, the automation of service delivery became effective. The resulting service delivery was again observed and analysed to map the emerging changes. Fieldwork tracked the identified indicators before and after the system's deployment and revealed significant value changes.

The eFez Team used various research methods to investigate the community (i.e., citizen) side of BEC service delivery.

Data gathering related to social issues started a few months after the eFez Project launch, in 2004. Accordingly, during periodic site visits, a team member observed how citizens interacted with the BEC personnel to request and receive their life event certificates. Citizens visiting the BEC were interviewed in this context. These steps enabled our team to gather information on the social side of BEC service delivery.

Indicators related to the citizens' experience were identified by the research team, including:

- The facility of the request/receipt process;
- The waiting time;
- The citizens' effort (i.e., physical trips to the BEC office, standing in line, queuing) required to receive processed certificates; and
- The quality of delivered certificates.

These indicators were further discussed and refined by the research team. Focus group discussions were organized with citizens to review this list of indicators in an effort to gather and capture more in-depth information. Citizen-related data gathering, including further focus group sessions, also took place in Fez's other BEC offices. The underlying motivation was to capture as much information as possible on the citizen side of the BEC's service delivery.

One main finding confirmed in these focus group discussions was that the BEC service delivery was not citizen-friendly because it did not use ICT and had only one delivery channel: face-to-face. Citizens had no choice but to physically interact with BEC employees to submit their requests and return to claim the requested certificates. Thus, the eFez Team took this finding into consideration in the first stage of the eFez Project (referred to as the TPP Phase in Chapter 5) and proceeded to develop a prototype version of the eFez system to be deployed as a pilot, offering diverse electronic delivery channels to citizens (at the employee's desk, using a multilingual kiosk, using the web portal).

This system was deployed in the Agdal pilot BEC by November 2005 and the eFez Team resumed data collection activities including:

- Data gathering to track citizens' usage patterns of the deployed delivery channels (2006 onward)
- Data gathering to investigate how BEC service delivery indicators changed after eFez deployment

i. Data gathering on the eFez system usage patterns

The eFez Team tracked usage patterns via qualitative and quantitative data gathering research methods. The team periodically observed and conducted in-depth interviews with employees and citizens on how citizens used the deployed electronic delivery channels.

The main finding of the qualitative data collection was that almost all citizens requested their services by approaching the BEC employees. This revealed that the online and kiosk delivery channels were badly underused. Starting in March 2006, the eFez Team launched a survey consisting of questionnaires which was completed by those requesting BEC services. An assistant was available on site and helped each citizen to complete the questionnaires. In these questionnaires, respondents indicated, among other things, the mode they used to request their needed services (i.e., approaching the employee, requesting online or using the kiosk) and their impressions of the newly deployed electronic delivery channels.

To respond to the kiosk underuse during the first four months of its deployment, the eFez Team started to investigate ways to promote the kiosk use. They observed that kiosk underuse had been a disturbing problem since the kiosk channel has been deployed as a means to mitigate the digital divide evidenced by Moroccans' low access to ICT, PC and the internet, and to avoid socially excluding illiterate people.

To solve this important problem the eFez Team collaborated with ordinary citizens (including illiterates) between February 2005 and February 2006, to iteratively design a new kiosk interface that would satisfy their needs and that would be easily usable by both literate and illiterate people. As suggested by citizens, the new version included clear voice instructions formulated in Morocco's dialect to guide the user step by step. The kiosk also included culturally sensitive illustrative images to represent the different BEC services. The kiosk's graphic user interface (GUI) was designed to mimic a cellphone, because even illiterate people are often familiar with the use of these devices.

Once the kiosk had incorporated these adjustments, the eFez Team tested it with approximately 70 illiterate men and women of a range of ages. These tests proved the ease of completing requests using the new version of the kiosk interface. They revealed that all the participating illiterate people were able to conduct a kiosk request by themselves after light training in kiosk usage.

Nonetheless, new measurements showed that the kiosk usage rate remained unsatisfactorily low after the deployment of this new version. The eFez Team again investigated reasons behind this low usage rate. New observations and in-depth interviews were conducted. The investigation revealed that Fez citizens of the local community were not aware of the presence of a touchscreen kiosk in the BEC. They knew about bank ATMs but did not know that a kiosk was available in their BEC. Hence, it was decided to launch a communication campaign targeting whoever arrived in the Agdal BEC to request BEC services. In addition, an assistant was hired and trained to welcome citizens arriving in the BEC and to inform them of the kiosk availability, invite them to try to use it, and assist them when needed. She also helped them fill in questionnaires to assess the changes of BEC service delivery.

As a result of this iterative method, the kiosk daily usage rate increased dramatically. A new survey carried out in March 2006 showed that more than 90 percent of daily citizens' requests were carried out via the kiosk, with a high degree of satisfaction!

To conclude, it is interesting to observe that the data gathering and assessment process of the system usage patterns had a strong influence on the eFez system development and its adjustments, due largely to the active participation of end users (i.e., citizens).

It is important to note that if the eFez Team had not carried out the outcome analysis and the related data collection from the earliest stages of the project, it could have been judged a failure at the point where the under-usage of the electronic delivery channels (the kiosk and online) was observed. Decision makers would have been quick to conclude that the technological change was too expensive for very little results. This would have strengthened the initial resistance to change that most BEC officers and some city managers voiced during the first year of the eFez Project. However, through this careful outcome analysis, the eFez Team was able to diagnose the reasons behind the kiosk underuse and quickly adapt the project's course of action to involve citizens in the GUI design.

This participatory approach was a key element of the success of the new system. This experience also shows the importance of considering the human side of the transformation that is triggered by the deployment of e-government systems. The communication campaign, along with the presence of the assistant who was responsible for welcoming citizens and introducing them to the kiosk, was a simple course of action that contributed greatly to the success of the project among Fez's population.

ii. Data gathering on BEC service delivery indicators

After addressing the eFez usage issues during the transitional period following the eFez system deployment (during 2006), the eFez Team redirected the data gathering effort to investigate service delivery indicators. These indicators had been identified and assessed before the eFez system deployment. Accordingly, team members periodically spent several working days in the pilot BEC office, during which they observed the process of how citizens request and receive services. They interviewed citizens on the change in service delivery after the eFez deployment and held periodic focus group discussions organized around service delivery indicators. They also used quantitative research methods for data gathering, such as surveys to assess citizens' perception of the newly deployed service delivery. The surveys were conducted via on-site, written, self-administered questionnaires completed by literate citizens and face-to-face interviews conducted with illiterate citizens to gather their input and response to questions. The sample of the respondents' level of literacy breaks down into the following percentages:

- 7.9 percent illiterate
- 6.4 percent with only primary education
- 32.9 percent with secondary education
- 6.4 percent with junior high school
- 45 percent with university education

A thousand questionnaires were completed via convenience sampling, targeting citizens who were requesting BEC services at the Agdal BEC from April to June 2006:

- When asked "How many times do you request BEC certificates on an annual basis?" survey respondents indicated numbers ranging between once a year to 39 times a year; accordingly, BEC certificates were requested by a respondent an average of 9.05 times a year. This reflects the importance of BEC certificates in citizens' daily lives.
- When asked "In previous visits or at another BEC (where there is no use of ICT), how much time did you have to wait on average to request and receive BEC certificates?" responses ranged from between one hour to 2448 hours, with an average waiting time of 40.33 hours among respondents.
- When asked "How did you request the necessary birth certificates? (e.g., via the kiosk or via the desk)" responses showed that 97 percent of respondents used the kiosk located in the BEC office.
- When asked "Today, how much time did it take you to request and receive the necessary birth certificates?" responses ranged from 1 minute to 60 minutes, with an average of 4 minutes waiting time. The satisfaction rate was exceptionally high: 91.8 percent of respondents were very satisfied and 7 percent were satisfied. Most respondents qualified service delivery as very fast/instant, with 92.1 percent agreeing and 6 percent rating it as fast. With regard to the quality of the BEC certificates received, 93.9 percent of respondents indicated that they were excellent and 3 percent felt they were good.
- When asked "What are the advantages and facilities of the new way of service delivery?" 93.49 percent indicated that it saved them time, 84.77

Table 4.5. Good-governance-related results and outcomes of the eFez automated service delivery (Kettani et al. 2008)

Governance attributes	Measured indicator	Value before automated system deployment	Value after automated system deployment
Transparency	Visibility of workflows for citizens via automated service delivery.	No Since the BEC back office is completely manual, subprocesses of making BC requests, processing the request, and filling out the needed copies are carried out separately (often by differing employees). The citizen cannot see or monitor the processing progress (e.g., the length and possible reasons for a delay in processing are neither accessible nor visible).	Yes Since the BEC back office is electronically enabled, subprocesses of making BC requests, processing the request and printing the processed BCs are merged into a single process and carried out in real time. This secures the principle of first-come-first-serve.
Effectiveness and efficiency (as a citizen user)	Optimal use of resources for citizens to request and obtain BCs.	No Requesting and obtaining BCs is costly for citizens: extended waiting time several trips to BEC need to "tip" (or use social connections)	Yes Citizens saving time/money/effort in requesting and obtaining BCs electronically: no waiting time one trip to BEC no "tip"
Effectiveness and efficiency (as tax payer)	Efficiency and effectiveness when using scarce public resources.	No To deliver BCs, the BEC needed three full-time employees (at low and moderate demand periods). During high demand periods (June to Sept.): All BEC employees (10) stop processing their respective tasks to process BC requests. To keep up with the demand, they take BC requests home to be processed (which is illegal).	Yes: (i.e., casual calls on employee time with the elimination of three full time employees): No full time employee to process BCs (employees can instantly process BC requests while completing other BEC-related manual tasks). With the kiosk, no employee is needed to process the requests.
Equity	Citizens served in equitable manner.	No Usually queuing/waiting creates motives and conditions for bribery incidents. Citizens find themselves obliged to tip the employee in charge in order to be served, especially when they are in a hurry to meet the tight deadlines of submitting paperwork.	Yes ICT eliminates the need for citizens to tip in order to be served. All citizens are served in a timely and consistently professional manner (regardless of social class).

Rule of law	Laws are applied impartially.	No Equity is violated and violations are perceived as normal. Many violations of law as people pay for special privileges (queue jumping).	Yes Eliminating value and opportunity for tipping reinforces the rule of law.
Participation/ empowerment (i.e., citizens are empowered to legally control the service delivery to their advantage)	Citizens' active participation in BEC services.	No Citizens not participating actively in the service delivery process (with possible negative consequences arising from issues occurring in the workflow).	Yes Citizens through the kiosk or online service delivery actively participate in the process, reducing the possibility for negative consequences arising from difficulties in the workflow.
Minimize superfluous intermediate roles in the process chain of service delivery	Dependency on bureaucracy: Dependence of citizens on the employees' good will.	Yes Citizens are at the mercy of employees to be served.	No Citizens through the kiosk or online service delivery have control and ownership of the process and are not at the mercy of employees.
Accountability: standards in place to assign responsibility to the appropriate individuals, due largely to a routine service delivery method	Existence of standards to hold individuals accountable.	No No standards because of the opaque and inconsistent system.	Yes Visible/transparent/consistent system with implicit standards available against which to hold BEC accountable.
Responsiveness	Consistency in the relationship between input and output.	No The service delivery is not predictable. The citizen cannot legally influence the system to be predictable/responsive.	Yes The system (i.e., automated service delivery) is by definition/design consistent, responsive and predictable.
Consensus orientation	Not Applicable.		
Strategic vision	Not Applicable.		

percent marked that it saved them expenses (their related traveling expenses back and forth to the BEC office), and 90.51 percent felt that it saved them the effort of standing in line.

The questionnaire asked for suggestions, but many respondents chose not to answer. However, the collected responses fell into two main categories:

- Suggesting extending BEC automation to other BEC offices in Fez and outside of Fez; and,
- Suggesting extending automation to municipal services (other than BEC certificates).

iii. Results of the measurement of indicators

Based on the gathered qualitative and quantitative data before and after the deployment of the eFez System, citizen-related outcomes were able to be assessed. As an illustration, Table 4.5 shows the main citizen-related governance attributes measured.

Columns one and two present the governance attributes and the corresponding indicators that measure them. Columns three and four specify the indicators' values obtained before and after system deployment, respectively. Note that in this table, BC stands for "birth certificate."

V. Conclusion

Considering the high failure rate of software development projects and e-government systems in particular, we suggest that there is a crucial need for a systematic e-government assessment framework. We propose an outcome analysis method, which provides a means to assess the project's results in relation to its goals and activities. Interestingly, such a method not only grounds the assessment in the main stakeholders' expectations and primary goals, but it also presents the process of project assessment as a means to orient the planning and adjustment of a project's development as it proceeds. This enables decision makers to have a clear understanding of the way the project and the system contributed to the overall development (in this case, the contribution to the project's goal to enhance good governance).

Our outcome analysis method is an important phase of the eFez roadmap (see Chapter 7) and of the generic roadmap that we propose for the development of ICT4D/e-government systems (See Chapter 6).

The systematic assessment of projects identifies lessons learned and best practices. Sharing lessons learned can be enlightening and provide guidance to stakeholders, designers and project managers, and can assist ongoing projects to adjust their implementation. They can also provide insights to policy makers to help them to effectively decide on ICT policies (Garridon 2004). E-Government evaluation is also needed to disseminate success stories. Such dissemination "can ignite confidence and bring other stakeholders to the table, especially in programs where different actors compete for resources" (Garridon 2004).

Chapter 5

ADOPTING A TRANSFORMATIVE APPROACH IN E-GOVERNMENT SYSTEMS DEVELOPMENT

I. Introduction

Several studies concerning e-government systems have suggested that they produce a number of benefits which foster good governance (Norris 2001; Nute 2002; O'Connell 2003). E-Government is presented as a method to promote the responsiveness of government institutions to citizens' growing demands, which include improved access to public services, public institutional efficiency and more stringent security measures (O'Connell 2003). But many challenges must be addressed before e-government can improve this responsiveness, as emphasized in several recent documents such as the *Electronic Government for Developing Countries* report. This report suggests that "using ICT effectively to serve citizens online is a struggle for many governments, particularly in developing countries. Government organizations face great levels of uncertainty in creating and providing e-government services because of the complexity of the technology, deeply entrenched organizational routines, and great diversity in the acceptance of technology by individuals. E-Government requires much more than technical wizardry for developing and operating successful online services. This includes developing strategic approaches for organizing and assembling tangible resources such as computers and networks and intangible resources such as employee skills and knowledge and organizational processes" (ITU 2008).

We think that adequately managing intangible resources is one of the most important challenges of ICT4D/e-government projects, especially in developing countries. The issues of preparedness, adoption and use of e-government (ICT and related services and practices) are often grouped together under the term "e-readiness." For over ten years, our experience with ICT4D/e-government system development and deployment in Morocco has shown that the readiness of all government stakeholders (politicians, senior managers, middle managers, employees and citizens) is a critical factor for successful e-government creation, deployment, usage and adoption.

A large number of e-government systems deployed in developing countries fail to enhance governance for a number of reasons (Heeks 2002). The UN report, E-Government at the Crossroads, indicates that "some analysts estimate the rate of failure of e-government projects in countries with developing economies to be very high, at around 60–80 percent, with the higher rate of failure characteristic of Africa" (UN 2003). This can look like a staggering figure, but even in industrialized countries the success rate of e-government projects is low. Gartner Research suggests that about 60 percent of e-government projects fail. While the Standish Group estimates that only 28 percent of all ICT projects in the US, in 2000, in both government and industry, were successful with regard to budget, functionality and timeliness. In fact, 23 percent were cancelled in the US and the remainder succeeded only partially, failing on at least one of the three counts" (UN 2003).

With these statistics in mind, the next two sections of this chapter have several objectives:

- To make decision makers and managers aware of several issues that need to be addressed when planning and launching an ICT4D/e-government project in a developing country.
- To show that some approaches and lessons learned in the development of ICT4D/e-government systems at a national level can be adapted and applied at the local governance (municipal and regional) level (Traikovik et al. 2011). This adaptation is the main focus of this book.

Influential critics including Unwin and Hanna have recently advocated the use of a "holistic approach" for the introduction, creation and deployment of ICT4D/e-government systems in developing countries. This approach emphasizes the requirement of a fundamental transformation of government in terms of governance and strategies, thus reforming institutions and interventions nationwide.

Hanna (2010) defines this e-transformation as "a second generation development strategy for a smart, holistic, inclusive and participatory development." He also emphasizes that "governments of developing countries face daunting challenges, demanding broad, deep and sustained transformation from public institutions: severe financial constraints, poor infrastructure and public services, largely unmet basic needs and expectations, widespread corruption, fragile democracies, high inequalities and information poverty. This calls for transformational change [...] Policies, institutions, and leadership are central to creating the enabling environment for the effective use of ICT in government and society at large. Understanding the stakeholders and the political economy of reform is essential to reform e-policies, build ICT governance, and induce transformation." Hanna envisions a holistic approach to the ICT-enabled transformation of government and society that requires the creation of a number of "infrastructures" (systems and communication infrastructure; technological infrastructure; institutional infrastructure; human infrastructure, policy and legal infrastructure) as well as the building of awareness, commitment, leadership and strategic thinking.

We fully agree with this vision and confirm that it equally applies at a local governance level. We also agree that ICT4D/e-government projects are transformative processes that should be managed as such to ensure the successful transformation of the institutions in which they are implemented. Sections IV to VII of this chapter present the foundations of the transformative approach that we developed and applied in the eFez Project and related projects. In the next chapter, we will present a generic approach (roadmap) for the development of ICT4D/e-government systems, building on the notions and concepts presented in this chapter.

The literature on ICT-based development and e-government approaches is huge. However, most decision makers do not have time to read it and get a clear idea of what is appropriate in their context of intervention. In the next section, we will discuss some important issues and answer typical questions that decision makers and project managers raise in the context of deploying e-government in developing countries. A complementary objective of this chapter is to acquaint the reader with guidelines and experiences that can be found in the prolific literature on ICT4D and e-government projects. Since we wish to give credit to the authors that have already shared their knowledge and experience in published articles and books, we often quote them verbatim in order to transmit their original thoughts to the reader. In this way, we also wish to show that many experiences and lessons learned can be fruitfully shared across different areas of ICT4D and e-government projects, be they at the national, regional, municipal or local levels (Traikovik et al. 2011).

II. Fundamental Questions Asked when Starting ICT4D/E-Government Projects

A. Why do so many ICT4D/e-government projects fail?

Hanna (2010) explains that, for mainly political reasons, governments tend to favor large and expensive ICT projects with high visibility and profile. This leads to frequent failures due to the risk usually being proportionate to the project's size and the large degree of change needed at the technical, organizational and cultural levels. Guida and Crow (2007) indicate that several issues might explain the disappointingly high failure rate of ICT4D/ e-government projects:

- The application of inappropriate technologies;
- A field-level disconnection between multilateral banks, donors and other project sponsors and the client governments they serve; and
- An excessive reliance on top-down government approaches which do not account for users' needs or citizens' demands.

Guida and Crow (2007) also mention other important governance-related factors that contribute to such failures such as a lack of transparency or citizen involvement, resistance by an entrenched bureaucracy, corruption, regressive policy and regulatory environments, and unskilled human resources. In Chapter 4 of this book, we mentioned a number of important reasons behind the failure of e-government systems in developing countries.

Taking a positive stance, we tend to consider the causes of these failures as important factors (some considered risks, others constraints) that should be identified, managed and monitored by decision makers and project leaders of ICT4D/e-government projects to ensure the success of their own projects. We observed that these constraints and risks are omnipresent in developing countries.

B. The "knowledge barrier"

Several contextual elements put political, legal, organizational and technological constraints onto governments, and these include: the technological environment, human capital and public policy. In addition, citizens and government stakeholders (politicians, managers and employees) are very diverse in their abilities to understand government services and their desire and ability to use digital systems. Hence, governments must develop the knowledge and capabilities to respond to these challenges and, simultaneously, to deal with ongoing issues in political, economic and social environments. These issues generate risks which may limit the government's chances of being successful in adopting e-government.

As an illustration, let us mention a significant cause of difficulties (and even failures) in the creation and deployment of ICT4D/e-government systems in developing countries. Governmental institutions (especially at the local governance level) do not have human resources that are sufficiently knowledgeable about software system development practices (analysis and design method, project management, development tools, standards, etc.)

to effectively implement their e-government systems. Consequently, implementing a system without proper planning, analysis and design usually yields an e-government service that is unsatisfactory to the user, and causes the system to ultimately fail (Kendall and Kendall 2008).

C. What kind of critical challenges are faced by ICT4D / e-government projects in a developing country?

The *Electronic Government for Developing Countries* report (ITU 2008) identifies a number of technological issues that illustrate why government institutions struggle to build e-government services:

- E-Government involves taking computer-based technologies and combining them with human-based administrative processes to create new ways of serving citizens. Organizations have to adapt ICT to business processes. Similarly, business processes have to adapt to ICT.
- ICT exist in a broader context. It is not only challenging for organizations to understand computer systems but also to understand the business, legislative and political processes that make up the day-to-day operations of all types of government institutions. Many of the processes involve numerous steps and procedures that have evolved idiosyncratically to conform to legislation, mandates and norms, based on the formal bureaucratic structure and informal employee practices of each ministry.
- Governments must understand the local context and local practices in which ICT will be used to provide e-government services (Walsham et al. 2007). Generally, developing countries often adopt ICT and software that are designed in the developed world and introduced to them through technology transfer programs. [...] Organizations need to have skilled human resources with the ability to creatively adapt new technologies and global practices to the local context and also manage the whole process of implementation (Macome 2003).

We observed the relevance of these issues at all levels of government and especially in the context of municipal governance. Due to a lack of knowledge of system analysis and design methods, most decision makers and project managers in developing countries were not aware that the success of automation is deeply dependent on a clear understanding of business processes and on their careful reengineering which takes into account the organizational context and constraints, as well as the possibilities offered by ICT. Therefore, leaders of e-government projects should be able to wear two hats at once: a technology hat and a process engineering hat. These managers, typically, must understand how to customize applications that tie together complex computer-based technologies while also revamping underlying business processes and organizational structures (this process is often called "business process reengineering"). Let us emphasize that such people are extremely rare in developing countries.

The authors of the *Electronic Government for Developing Countries* report (ITU 2008) conclude that e-government requires government leaders and managers to address three main issues:

- How do you take the technologies of the internet and integrate them with existing information systems and existing organizational and institutional processes?
- How do you build e-government applications to meet the needs, capabilities and values of the end user?
- How do you overcome the reality of the organizational, economic, political, technological, legal and local environments that, through complex factors, influence and define the context of the e-government service?

D. Should we adopt a centralized or decentralized approach?

This is another critical issue since it has often been observed that developing countries tend to adopt ICT-based approaches that are fostered (and often strongly encouraged) by the central government. Considering national strategies for e-government planning, Hanna (2008) distinguishes two main approaches:

- An integrated top-down strategy that is tied to broader economic and development goals
- A decentralized, bottom-up approach that fosters entrepreneurship and allows agencies the independence to launch their own programs

In the context of developing countries, "top-down" and "bottom-up" strategies should be respectively interpreted as "centralized" and "decentralized" strategies.

Indeed, Hanna's discussion takes place at a national level and concerns central government bodies such as agencies ("ministries"). However, at a local level, a governmental institution is often composed of several departments. We observed that implementing ICT4D/e-government systems at a local level involves overcoming similar challenges as those at a national level. Hanna indicates that each strategy has factors that support success, as well as risks that may lead to failure. He suggests that most countries experiment with a hybrid approach that combines features of both the top-down and bottom-up approaches.

In the context of this book, it is worth considering the success factors and risks associated with these strategies since many of them also apply in the context of local governance, the main focus of this book.

A **top-down (centralized) approach** is driven by a governmental body especially mandated for coordinating ICT4D/e-government initiatives in different governmental agencies and constituencies. In such an approach, the cultural change, reengineering and training involved are thought to be best achieved through central oversight and guidance. Scaling up beyond the Pilot Phase and transferring lessons learned in e-government from one governmental constituency to another is also thought to be best facilitated by a central strategy that fosters information exchange, joint project planning and common business processes (Hanna 2008).

Below is a list of important key success factors[1] in a top-down approach:

- Political leadership and commitment: Perhaps the most important factor for success is strong and sustained leadership that is able to articulate the need for change, create momentum in the early stages and push for reform during implementation.
- High-level oversight: Oversight, coordination and planning are the keys to successful deployment of e-government. Central to this effort are policy-guided reengineering and the reform of government processes, followed by sound technological planning for infrastructure services.
- Integration and standardization of data sources: All government processes depend on easy access to data sources, which in turn requires interoperability and the sharing of data, as well as appropriate software architecture.
- Change in government culture: The success and sustainability of e-government applications depend on changing government culture, through comprehensive communication campaigns and change management initiatives, as well as relevant and well-planned training. This process can encounter big challenges in the public sector which generally has weak incentives to improve the delivery of public services and low levels of awareness regarding the transformation process of ICT.
- Sequencing and prioritization: A sound and global strategy can guide the implementation of e-government by careful sequencing and prioritization, focusing on applications that can produce a quick, visible impact on revenue generation and services for citizens and businesses. Sequencing and phasing

---

1   This list is based on the work of Hanna (2008). Note that for conformity, we changed several of Hanna's terms: (1) "national strategy" to "sound and global strategy"; (2) "agency" to "governmental constituency"; and (3) "national" to "global."

also allow the necessary time for organizational learning (learning to reengineer processes, restructure the organization and manage the human factors involved).

- Rationalization of financial and resource planning: A sound and global strategy which provides guidance and the framework to plan the resources and budgets for e-government.
- Integration into a national e-development strategy: E-Government will thrive only if it is part of a sound and global e-development strategy, which puts into place the elements critical to its success. E-Government services rely on: (1) human capacity to access affordable and reliable ICT infrastructure; (2) the ability of citizens and businesses to interact with government through online channels; and (3) the ability to implement and sustain e-government programs through adequately trained IT professionals, IT-aware managers and political leaders.

Let us emphasize that all these factors are also applicable at the level of local government (i.e., cities). Indeed, the city administration has a relationship (involving guidance, coordination, budget allocation, general orientations, centralization/decentralization) with its constituencies (counties, districts, etc.), which is similar to the relationship of a country's central government with the governments of its states or provinces, or with the different agencies of the country. Hence, the same problems, issues and challenges apply, but on a different scale.

The reader will certainly be interested in a list of important risk factors that Hanna (2008) relates to the top-down approach, including:

- Political problems: Strong leadership and political commitment are required for e-government to succeed. Where dramatic political shifts occur, e-government goals can be held hostage by political agendas typically seeking quick wins rather than long-term sustained efforts.
- Lack of space for local initiative: Rigid rules and top-down plans might constrain local initiatives and innovation. Strategic direction is essential to guide local initiatives toward interoperability and enterprise-wide architecture. But too much control is inhibitive and can reduce support among middle-level public administrators, leading to a resistance to change and poor use of new processes and systems.
- Unrealistic sequencing: Many governments have been unrealistic in creating strategies and investment plans, often overestimating the e-readiness of their constituents (the availability of necessary staff capacity, infrastructure and content). E-Government programs may fail when they impose an unrealistic pace of implementation, not sequenced with capability development, change management and without the necessary infrastructure.

- Supply-driven program: A top-down strategy also runs the risk of promoting a "supply-driven" e-government program without carefully assessing whether citizens are ready to interact with the government online, or[2] whether government staff are ready to adopt and use the ICT-based solution and implement new ways of performing their tasks.

Indeed, a centralized approach must be managed with care and with the local context in mind. The issue of citizen and government staff readiness is critical. For example, during the past 15 years, the central government of Morocco has tried to initiate, without definitive success, several projects to automate the service delivery of Moroccan municipalities (Kettani et al. 2009). We think that too much centralization, imposed software solutions, lack of sensitization and involvement of the local constituencies can explain the failure of these attempts, at least partially.

Indeed, we observed that similar risks are faced at the local governance level as at a national level and they are equally as challenging. One important issue is the political, organizational and cultural context of the institution and the engagement of local decision makers, managers and employees in the "transformation process" resulting from the adoption and deployment of ICT.

A bottom-up (decentralized) approach fosters entrepreneurship and allows agencies to launch their own programs. Hanna (2008) indicates that easier implementation and a more immediate payoff are the primary advantages of this approach. Fewer stakeholders are involved. Institutional and process changes only affect the local government's constituencies. The success of small, focused projects builds momentum and excitement within government and provides a "showcase" example that may motivate other constituents to follow. Awareness grows and lessons are learned over time. Entrepreneurial zeal is unleashed, champions are created and coalitions formed (Hanna 2008).

Our practical experience with the eFez Project showed that the bottom-up approach works well in the initial stages of an ICT4D/e-government project because it is a good way to capitalize on existing forces that are favorable to the transformation created by the implementation of such systems. However, once the level of interest in implementing the ICT4D/e-government system was established and the transformative process underway, it was more efficient for an institution to adopt a combination of the centralized approach, for coordination, supervision and general guidance, and the bottom-up approach, to capitalize on the local initiatives and resources, to foster interest and adapt the approach to local constraints.

---

2   This list is based on the work of Hanna (2008), but the end of this sentence is the addition of the authors of this book.

According to Hanna (2008) the bottom-up approach also involves risks due to the lack of central direction and oversight. These include:

- Slow diffusion: A decentralized strategy has often led to visible, but isolated successes because innovations were not diffused and replicated widely enough to have a substantial impact.
- Limited scale-up: With no central vision or direction, there is a risk that governmental constituents may invest in duplicate databases, infrastructure and systems. The capacity to scale up is limited by the project's small, isolated progress and lack of ability to integrate.
- Mismanagement of resources and people: A decentralized strategy may lead to resources being spent on duplicative or suboptimal investments, rather than the most strategic and promising ones.
- Interoperability problems and expensive integration: Local solutions developed without regard to government-wide information and technology architecture can lead to problems such as interoperability, barriers to information and data sharing and, later, to expensive integration remedies.
- Poor maintenance and sustainability: Quick, apparent successes may be short-lived and gained at the cost of creating solutions to more widespread systemic problems. Local champions may initiate new websites and pilot systems, but then fail to maintain and sustain them as they often require central supporting infrastructure and the sharing of resources. Lack of budget, experienced IT project managers and professionals, and resource planning at the global level leave the local constituencies with knowledge gaps that inhibit their ability to sustain solutions.
- Lack of targets and metrics: Lack of global monitoring and evaluation leads to problems in evaluating development impact and progress toward the integrated delivery of client-focused services.

Our experience gained through the practical development and deployment of ICT4D/e-government systems at the local governmental level (i.e., cities and municipalities) (Kettani et al. 2009) shows that most of the issues present at a national level are also relevant at the local level, and that numerous similarities can be observed when trying to apply either the top-down or the bottom-up approaches (Traikovik et al. 2011). We also observed that key success factors and major risks are also relevant at both the national and local levels. Our understanding is that the creation and deployment of ICT4D and e-government systems is a kind of "fractal process" that faces the same strategic, human, cultural, organizational, capacity building, financing and technical problems regardless of the scale (or extent) of the institution (or set of institutions) engaging in the transformation process that is inevitably triggered by the adoption and use of an ICT4D/e-government approach.

III. Important Management Issues for ICT4D/E-Government Projects

Different authors and organizations have raised a number of important issues concerning the management of ICT4D/e-government projects at the national level. We present, in this section, the issues that we believe are also applicable at the local governance level.

A. The main elements of a high-level strategy for ICT4D/e-government projects

Over the last 15 years, numerous countries have applied national strategies that share many common elements for the development of ICT4D/e-government. These common elements are provided in the interesting reference document, "The E-Government Primer" (InfoDev 2009). These elements are shown in Table 5.1 and should be considered in the planning of any ICT4D/e-government project.

Table 5.1. Common elements to national and subnational e-government strategies (InfoDev 2009)

	Composite of a High Level Strategy
The DESTINATION	• Vision
The WHY	• Mission and Rationale
The WHAT	• Networked Society
	• Public Service Delivery – Improving Access and Services
	• Citizen Participation, Engagement, and Inclusion
	• Technology Capabilities and Infrastructure
	• Contribution to Social and Economic Development, Competitiveness
	• Capacity Building, e.g., E-Government Building Blocks
	• E-Government/CIO leadership roles, structures, responsibilities, and whole-of-government assets
	• Training and development of politicians, public sector policymakers, broad employee base, and ICT, E-Government practitioners
	• Information, Intelligence, and Knowledge Management
	• Enabling Environment – Legislation, Business Model and Architectures, Policies, Security, Controls
	• Government structures and organizational developments, e.g., shared services, Centers of Excellence
The HOW	• Priorities, Principles, Methods, and Funding (incl. PPPs)
	• Implementation Plan
By WHEN	• Measurement and Reporting Timeline
The WHO	• Coordinating and Collaborating Structures, Relationships, and Accountability

B. Providing leadership, building partnership

Hanna (2010b) indicates that political and managerial leadership is required in the transformation of government via ICT. It requires leadership from senior executives and legislative officials to enable change, innovation and integration. To support the organizational change, leaders must promote a managerial culture that focuses on innovation and client-oriented service delivery. Hanna also mentions that "to overcome organizational silos, it is often necessary to anchor ownership at the highest levels in a dynamic, proactive executive leadership team. A transformative e-government strategy requires a widely shared long-term vision and sustained institutional reform."

"The key to effectiveness for any public–private partnership is to capitalize on the strengths of each partner. The role of government is that of a leader, a catalyst, and, most important, a domain expert who knows their business. Government alone can resolve legal and procedural problems in implementation, bring together rivals to discuss potential means of competition for the larger public good, decide the terms of competition and regulate them where required by setting standards, and providing public infrastructure for the e-government environment. The private sector can provide investments, the latest technology, expertise in delivery and execution, global knowledge, and best practices. The recipe for success in implementing an e-government strategy is to bring out the best elements of each partner and weave them into a cogent strategy" (Hanna 2008).

These critical issues of leadership and partnership equally apply at the local level of governance in developing countries.

C. Capacity building and training

Capacity building is a critical factor for the successful adoption, development and deployment of ICT4D/e-government systems. Hanna (2008) describes a multilevel ICT training program for e-government and emphasizes that, with e-government being a new way to deliver services and communication, it requires new skills and a different, faster-paced culture. Trained civil servants are needed to manage electronically mediated and networked administrations. Employees need to be equipped with new skills, competencies and capabilities to fulfill new roles and to create, use and deliver new e-services. These skills include contract negotiation and management, project management, relationship management, system security, the ability to share best practices, electronic auditing, IT skills training and internet use. A system of rewards and recognition is needed to cultivate a culture that fosters an e-savvy and e-enabled workforce.

We observed that capacity building and training are the most essential and challenging requirements in the implementation of ICT4D/e-government projects for local governmental institutions in Morocco, and in other developing countries.

D. Guidelines for the design and implementation of e-government projects

"The E-Government Primer" (InfoDev 2009) provides guidelines for the design and implementation of e-government projects. Once the overall e-government strategy and master plan are in place, a set of core initiatives must be identified, funded, designed and implemented. These initiatives may be outlined in the form of a national action plan or roadmap and may include key success factors such as the availability of skilled resources, a range of management disciplines, stakeholder engagement and user training. Overall, the main issues considered in these guidelines are:

1) Project governance
2) The managing of responsibilities
3) The design and reengineering of the project, which is a primary objective
4) Change management
5) The training and development of government (leaders and civil servants)
6) Creating awareness, promoting the project and educating customers

These issues are discussed in the rest of this section.

Project governance: It is often emphasized that the governance and management of ICT4D/e-government projects developed in the different agencies of any given country need to be consistent with (and possibly complementary to) a national strategy and action plan. A number of countries have adopted international standards for project and program management to ensure a consistency of approach which provides a greater likelihood of success (an example is the PRINCE2 process model, 2009). Establishing and recruiting the project team is also a fundamental step. Depending on the size and nature of the project, the project manager should have an experienced team comprised of people with skills in policy development, business analysis, process reengineering, architecture, IT (various domains), communication and marketing, stakeholder management, training, finance and budget control, administration and reporting.

Mastering a structured approach to reengineer business processes while also designing and developing software systems is a critical success factor for ICT4D/e-government projects. The methodology that is selected for individual e-government projects can vary according to a range of factors: the category of project (e.g., service, infrastructure, etc.), the number of involved agencies, policy and process complexity, and the level of technology which is required. The range of potential development lifecycle methods includes:

- Waterfall is a traditional sequential development approach where one phase is completed before moving forward onto the next.
- Spiral combines elements of design and prototyping. It engages both a top-down and bottom-up approach.
- Agile promotes adaptive planning and evolutionary development on an iterative basis through collaborative cross-functional teams.
- Iterative, which is an incremental development method that follows a process of planning, doing, checking and then acting at each stage of a project. It is an improvement cycle and allows for accommodation and back-tracking (Dyba 2008; Petersen and Wohlin 2009).

In addition, related management disciplines (such as those associated with risk and issue management, quality management, sourcing and procurement, financial management, stakeholder management and change management) strengthen the e-government project's implementation and integration process. International standards can be adopted rather than designing a system from scratch, although much effort is required to learn and apply adopted disciplines or processes in institutions in developing countries. Many resources and books are available that propose methods and advice for change management (see Kotter 1996; Kotter and Cohen 2002; Cohen 2005).

The objective of the next two chapters in this book is to propose a structured approach that can be effectively used in, and tailored to, ICT4D/e-government projects.

E. Managing responsibilities

Experience has demonstrated that concentrating e-government responsibility in only one centralized unit will not build ownership and grow understanding or capacity in the whole organization. Many countries are now pursuing a decentralized model for project implementation, within a "controlled environment" that has been centrally defined, agreed upon and facilitated (e.g., principles of design using process reengineering, whole-of-government procurement, compliance with enterprise architecture principles and technology standards, and regular reporting on performance and progress).

Keeping these elements in mind might be useful when dealing with ICT4D/e-government projects at a local level of governance.

F. Design and reengineer first

Effective implementation of e-government often requires the simplification of regulatory requirements, the streamlining of processes and cross-agency integration. Costs may vary greatly and bring to light other institutional inefficiencies which will further impact overall project expenses. A good "rule of thumb" is that only 30 percent of the overall costs should be technology-related with the remainder allotted to the nontechnological processes such as training and organizational changes.

Investing resources and time in stakeholders' engagement and in the design phase of the project has proven to deliver the greatest likelihood of project success. The process of designing e-government projects, like the process of developing an overall strategy, does not start with the technology. It begins with defining the needs of the intended users and the end objectives of the institution. Therefore, government leaders responsible for e-government projects should first examine the objectives and policy outcomes required by the task or operation to which they want to apply ICT. By considering the end-to-end process, they can identify the areas where reform is necessary and feasible. This is known as business process reengineering. The idea is to build a synergy between processes, policies and ICT implementations. An emerging trend in e-government is to take a holistic approach to any given area of public administration (for example "tax collection"), including the harmonization of reporting across government agencies and the establishment of a comprehensive administrative process.

G. Change management

Hanna (2008, 99) emphasizes that "e-government requires strategic direction from the political leadership as well as active partnership with the private sector and civil society. Government needs to act as a catalyst, bringing together the different [key] actors[3] to create information infrastructure and deliver ICT-enabled citizen services. Since e-government involves transforming established ways of doing things, it can achieve maturity only if serious attention is given to change management and new ways to relate clients and partners."

Decision makers and project managers should keep in mind that change management is a continuous process and that it is wise to effectively deal with the transition from the beginning of the project since it will be applicable throughout the development, implementation and deployment

---

3 Hanna speaks about 'leading private actors': for generality's sake we prefer the term 'key actor'.

of the ICT4D/e-government project. The reluctance or inability to manage change appropriately is often one of the key reasons for the failure of technology-enabled and e-government projects. The discipline of change management identifies and addresses the leadership, human resources and organizational factors that can drive or obstruct transformation. Since the planning and implementation of e-government involves a series of complex reforms, sponsors, planners and project implementers can benefit from integrating formal change management processes into the project management cycle.

Insufficient attention to people, or "soft factors", in an e-government project can have unintended consequences with personnel, including a loss of productivity, low morale, high turnover rates, rising costs, increased absenteeism and poor adoption of the technology. In some cases, civil servants and key stakeholders may feel threatened by e-government, either because they fear the transparency and loss of individual power that can come with the introduction of new processes and technology, or because they fear that they will be replaced by computers or private service providers. Responsible senior government officials need to understand and deal with their concerns, to provide education and training opportunities, and possibly build incentives and rewards for positive behavioral change.

H. Training and development of government leaders and decision makers

Leaders, managers and staff throughout the network of organizations and government agencies involved in national e-government projects are affected by many changes to their daily routine. Breaking through the internal "digital divide" takes significant time as well as comprehensive and integrated programs that both educate and encourage a culture of change through performance targets and mainstreaming ICT awareness. Senior politicians and decision makers will be more likely to support e-government initiatives and drive them effectively if they have a basic understanding of ICT, their role in economic and human development, and the essential building blocks of ICT policy. They should also be aware of specific strategic issues such as the role of interorganizational collaboration, donor solicitation, public–private partnerships and process reform. Hence, developing training and development courses for politicians, executives and staff is critical.

Crucial to the acceptance and adoption of new technologies are targeted education and training programs that define e-government, introduce new ways of working and using the new tools and systems, and engage people at each level of decision making and operation.

I. *Awareness, promotion and education of customers*

A significant dimension of e-government implementation involves preparing the customers (citizens and businesses) for the rollout of e-services. In order to enjoy the benefits of e-government, citizens, including small business owners, must have access to the internet or to a mobile phone, and be both literate and e-literate.

Publicity and communication campaigns and educational efforts aimed at end users can raise awareness of new e-services in advance of their launch. Such programs can notify citizens of the practical benefits of e-government, encouraging them to take advantage of these in their daily lives. Involvement of the customers or users throughout the design and implementation process can enhance communication and marketing programs.

As a conclusion to this section, let us emphasize that the different sources quoted throughout agree upon a set of critical issues that need to be addressed to successfully manage ICT4D/e-government projects at a national level. The principles that we will adopt for the creation of a road map for the development of ICT4D/e-government projects at the local governance level (city level) address a similar set of issues which are relevant to developing countries.

IV. ICT4D/E-Government Projects Are Transformation Processes

Indeed, in a large number of developing countries, most local governmental institutions operate manually in an archaic context (without the use of ICT or with outdated equipment and software).[1] Let us consider in simple terms the primary situational characteristics that are usually encountered in such local governmental institutions, mainly at the city level. We emphasize these because they reflect some of the main problems that decision makers hope to resolve by adopting ICTD/e-government approaches. We will also discuss some important issues that should be considered in the decision makers' situational assessment of their institutions and the possibility of launching an ICT4D/ e-government project. This is the context in which we will characterize, in simple terms, the transformation process that results from the introduction of ICT4D/e-government projects in these institutions. Let us first consider the typical operational situation for these institutions.

---

4   In this chapter, we use "institution" as a generic term to refer to any governmental body. We prefer to use the term "organization" to refer to the organizational part of the institution.

A. Typical non-automated situations in developing countries

The institutions that we consider here are operated manually using archaic systems to record data such as hand-written registers and records. Employees and middle managers are unfamiliar with the use of computers ("computer illiteracy") and service delivery to customers (i.e., citizens) is carried out manually. The institution's operational procedures are informal and require the direct and continuous supervision of employees by middle managers to ensure that work is carried out in a proper and timely manner. High-level managers and their superiors (i.e., politicians) rarely use computers and instead apply informal governance principles (i.e., what they feel is right in their management context). The institutions do not use any ICT, and/or have had bad experiences with ICT imposed by external institutions and, thus, ICT has often been rejected in the past.

In the following subsections, we address a number of questions that frequently arise for decision makers when considering the eventual launch of ICT4D/e-government projects.

B. A key question: should we really use ICT?

This is of primary concern to the top decision makers and managers of these institutions. It has been practically demonstrated in a large number of cases that ICT can greatly enhance the operations and governance of institutions operating manually, but it has also been observed that attempts to introduce ICT into these environments often fail without proper management and full adoption by stakeholders.

Let us suggest that most of these failures can be explained by the fact that the introduction of ICT to such institutions triggers a profound transformation which may fail if not properly managed. The first step to properly managing and controlling this process is to make all critical stakeholders aware of the profound transformation that will take place and to enlist their overall support by leading them through appropriate and timely actions and attitude changes.

C. Who are the critical stakeholders of these institutions?

Our experience showed that it is critical to encourage full engagement in the transformation's importance, resulting from the introduction of ICT into institutions and the following people:

- Top managers and their superiors (politicians) in the institution (thereafter called the "target institution")
- Middle managers and skilled/motivated employees

- The managers of other institutions that support the transformation of the target institution financially and politically
- External institutions, such as universities and companies, which have the skills and knowledge to support, assist and advise the target institution during its transformation process

D. How do top managers usually regard the introduction of ICT?

Top managers often regard ICT as like any other commodity, such as furniture or equipment. Their assumption is that once it is purchased and installed, the employees will use it naturally. They take for granted that everything will be done properly, which is often the case, and then, subsequently, neglect to follow up on the employees' ICT operations. They are not aware that ICT are complex technologies that need to be tailored to the institution's needs and culture and that they must be installed, customized and operated by properly trained personnel.

E. Why does such a view fail?

We think that the explanation is simple, yet seldom understood by managers in developing countries:

- Computers and software are complex systems requiring that users be properly sensitized and trained, that they adapt to the technology and associated methods, and that they change their work habits and practices accordingly.
- The introduction of ICT triggers profound changes in the institution at the individual and the organizational levels as well as at the financial and budgetary levels. These changes must be explicitly and carefully managed.
- Proper actions should be undertaken by all the involved stakeholders in the institution in an adequate and timely way.
- The introduction of ICT and related practices should be considered a complex project (or a series of projects) in itself, and managed as such.

Failing to understand and seriously take into account these elements generally results in the failure of ICT4D/e-government projects, as reported in literature and experienced by a large number of institutions, especially in developing countries.

F. Managing change

Hanna (2008) mentions that implementing a nationwide e-government strategy is similar to introducing a disruptive technology into an extremely traditional system. He states that, "indeed, it turns the traditional model of government on its head. That model is centered on the agency providing the service – with service levels, timing, payment mechanisms, and procedures built around the agency. E-government makes the citizen the center of all activity – government services must be available any time the citizen demands them, anywhere the citizen wants to receive them, and through whatever medium the citizen wants to use."

Hanna also emphasizes that the biggest challenge in implementing this model is to help the institution to adopt it and to effectively cope with associated change management issues. "This single factor almost always separates the successes and failures in implementing e-government. So beyond ensuring a clear political intention, there must be serious assessment of political and administrative mechanisms to ensure that they have the depth and maturity to manage the change that any process of implementing e-government will create. The system must also have the capacity to cope with the hard choices and trade-offs that it will encounter, such as fundamental reengineering of business processes, skill changes and staff redeployment. [...] Moreover, both the political and the civil service leadership need to understand and accept all the trade-offs before they embark on the e-government journey. Finding the right people to lead change in the civil service is another big challenge. Change management is critical to overcoming resistance and avoiding duplication of delivery channels."

We fully agree with Hanna that change management is a very critical aspect of the implementation of ICT4D/e-government projects, especially in developing countries, but we suggest going a step further by precisely defining "change management" and "transformation."

G. Change Management

The term "change management" is often used in academic literature to characterize the process that enables managers to supervise and possibly control changes that occur in their institutions. In this book we define "change" as "what occurs in the institution and triggers the transformations that are occurring in it."

We say that change happens, whether managed (controlled) or not! In unstructured institutions and societies, change often happens in unexpected ways. Hence, in this view, change management is quite a reactive process: managers try to facilitate/control change to the best of their knowledge, understanding and capabilities.

However, as we will discuss in the next section, change management can be proactive if managers are able to harness the forces that are involved in the change impetus that drives the transformation in their institution. We will refer to this as "transformation management." Adopting such a view, we claim that it is important to understand that *ICT4D/e-government projects are transformation processes*. Hence, we need to incorporate a principled and systematic approach to managing these projects in order to favor a successful conversion (i.e., transformation) of the institutions in which they are implemented.

In order to explain the transformation process related to the introduction of ICT and new business procedures, we will present in the next sections a simple, yet well thought out, vision of the process mentioned above.

V. A Biological View of the Transformation Process

We define "transformation" as an evolutionary process that makes an institution or an individual progressively modify their internal state and both internal and external interactions to reach a new state of internal and external equilibrium. In this view, a well-managed transformation process enables an institution, or a person, to seamlessly and harmoniously absorb and integrate changes that occur both internally and around it in response to the changes occurring in the institution's environment.

In order to explain why managing transformation processes is critical to the success of ICT4D/e-government projects, we adopt a biological view of institutions, their social and organizational characteristics and the transformations they undergo.[5] Hence, we view an institution as a living organism.

An institution, like a living being, aims to "survive" in its environment. There are internal structural forces that keep it as a whole, functioning entity which reacts to and interacts with its environment. In turn, the environment produces external forces that influence the institution.

An institution can be thought of as a complex system composed of interacting parts which can be also considered as subsystems which themselves, in turn, are also composed of interacting parts. The institution's structure, or organization, results from the relationships established by its component parts and the exchanges that take place between them when the institution is behaving as a whole.

The institution interacts with other institutions, considered as its partners, and individuals or groups of people, its clients, who are located in its environment. These interactions may take place in a more or less formal

---

5 Our view takes some of its inspiration from Kim Lewin's theory of *force field analysis* (1951), which postulated that social systems continuously seek equilibrium between forces favoring change and those opposing change. He also suggested that successful change rests on an institution's ability to "unfreeze" the equilibrium by altering the dynamics of forces.

setting which characterizes the type of exchanges that can take place between the institution and its partners and clients. The degree of formalization of its structure and these internal and external exchanges are related to the degree of organizational maturity (awareness) of the institution.

Figure 5.1. Equilibrium of an institution

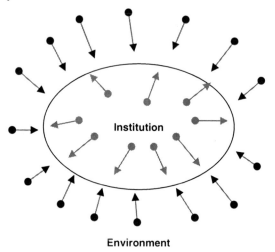

As a living organism, there are tensions that mediate the interactions between the institution's component parts (we call them internal forces and represent them as arrows within the oval in the following figure) as well as other interactions (we call them external forces and represent them as arrows outside the oval in the figure) between the institution and its partners and clients. As illustrated in Figure 5.1, when the institution reaches its equilibrium (it is said to be in homeostasis), the forces are balanced both internally and externally. The institution adequately responds to the external needs and to its internal needs, and to corresponding tensions.

However, social and living systems are dynamic systems and transformations (changes) occur both inside and outside the institution. Usually, the institution, like a living entity, tries to preserve its internal structure as well as its interactions with its environment and its external appearance (that we call its "shape"): it tries to "stay in good shape." This mechanism can be thought of as resulting from an "inertia principle" which tries to "preserve" an established equilibrium. This is often called the status quo in institutions.

But, change forces tend to "deform" the institution, pushing it out of equilibrium. In the next figure, the clear initial elliptical shape of the institution becomes bumpy as a result of the antagonism between internal and external forces at the periphery of the institution. At some point, the change forces (solid line arrows in the next picture) become increasingly stronger whereas the "structuring internal" and "external interaction" forces are fading (dashed arrows). The institution can potentially reach a point where its equilibrium is broken down.

Figure 5.2. Impact of change forces

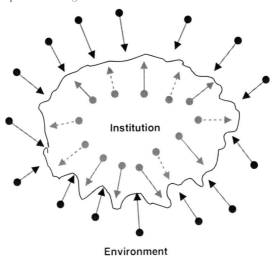

For example, tensions between workers and the institution's top management (for social or salary reasons) may lead to a point at which strikes are called by workers, resulting in a disruption of services. At national levels, recent years have witnessed, in some countries, public insurrections that overthrew apparently well-established leaders and governments who had not adequately assessed the change forces (people's expectations) that built up in the environment of their governmental structures.

In order to avoid reaching such breaking points, we claim that a conscious transformation needs to occur in the institution, in the sense that its managers need to become aware that the institution's survival is in danger, and act accordingly to balance the new forces that apply, both internally and externally.

VI. Toward a Principled Approach to Manage the Transformation

Let us consider three alternative scenarios that can be observed in an institution which tries to preserve its equilibrium and may choose to enact different strategies.

A. The first scenario

We call this the "plaster scenario" (or "status quo scenario") and it is commonly observed in a large number of institutions, both in developed and developing countries. The institution tries to put in place forces (measures) that try to antagonize or neutralize the change forces locally. This might work for a certain period of time, but there is a danger that the local measures aiming to preserve the good shape (or appearance) of the institution will simply mask the signs of the "change-provoking forces" to the external observer (the outside world). Nevertheless, the change-provoking forces usually continue to grow in the background, although they might not be apparent until reaching a critical point where the breakdown occurs suddenly in the institution. There are examples of this scenario found in almost every institution or society.

B. The second scenario

If the need for change is strong, the change-provoking forces will increase, escalating the pressure on the institution (and its shape) accordingly. The "plasters" (local measures aiming at preserving the old equilibrium as discussed in the first scenario) will no longer be able to neutralize the pressure and the shape of the institution will increasingly "deform." The institution may see some of its parts "cracking" until it breaks down (or even explodes). If the institution's managers become aware of the urgency of the situation, they will certainly be willing to act in an effort to avoid the breakdown, and move to the third scenario (hopefully not too late).

C. The third scenario

In what we call a "conscious" institution, a conscious and responsible management becomes aware of the change forces and the pressure that they create. Managers also become aware of the dangers of not acting (maintaining the status quo) and of not trying to reach a new equilibrium state as soon as possible. Under the leadership of its management, the conscious institution will devise and carry out modifications of functioning (often called reforms) to "reshape the institution" so that it can absorb the change, and hence bring back all forces to equilibrium. In this way, the institution will manage its transformation as smoothly as possible.

Let us emphasize that transformation management must be understood in terms of a carefully managed transformation process.

From now on, we will consider the third scenario and suppose that the institution's management becomes aware of the need and urgency to deal with change-provoking forces and to manage the transformation in a cautious way. We suggest that the cautious way of managing transformation in an institution relies on the following principles:

- Start with a Pilot Project and create a structure in a selected and limited part of the institution where the transformation will be managed under favorable conditions.
- Monitor and assess the results of the transformation taking place in this part of the institution (the "incubator") during the Pilot Project.
- Decide if the resulting transformation process should be adopted, abandoned or modified before scaling up (propagating transformation to the whole institution).
- If the results of the transformation in the incubator are positive, propagate the transformation to the whole institution according to a strategy that must be adapted to its particular context (political, managerial, organizational, social or financial). Decide how the scaling up will take place (e.g., at what rate of transformation, in which parts of the institution, using which schedule, etc.)
- Monitor and continually assess the progress of the transformation to make any required adaptation of the transformation process in an adequate and timely way.
- Be aware of the importance of good communications and interactions with all stakeholders as well as communicating the project's results throughout the institution in a timely and adequate way.
- Officially acknowledge the end of the transformation process when the changes are fully absorbed by the institution (and people) and no longer appear as changes.

In the following section, we discuss some critical issues related to this principled approach of managing the institution's transformation.

VII. Managing a Transformation Pilot Project

A cautious way of managing a transformation is to experiment in one part of the institution where "favorable conditions" can be sustained.

The selected part of the institution is considered to be a "safe haven" which can be isolated from the forces that pressure the institution and in which the experiment can be carried out without any disruption. In our biological metaphor, this can be pictured as an isolated cell whose "abstract boundary" is composed of the favorable conditions (see Figure 5.3).

Figure 5.3. The pilot cell in a change environment

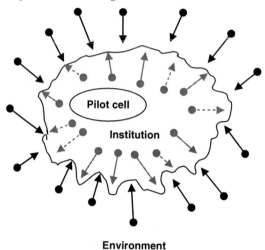

Environment

We call this the "pilot cell," with the objective of creating a solution that will support the transformation as a Pilot Project. The pilot cell can be thought of as a test bed with the aim of helping the institution change by testing the transformation process. In the pilot cell, the institution will be able to carry out the experiment called a Transformation Pilot Project (TPP).

Let us discuss some important steps of a TPP:

• Top decision makers must decide to launch the TPP in the first place
• Top decision makers must identify clear goals for the TPP and create favorable conditions for its operation
• Top decision makers must create the pilot cell and assign people to it (officially assign them with responsibilities and adequate means/resources), hence creating the Pilot Team
• Top decision makers must officially announce the launch of the TPP and the creation of the Pilot Team, as well as its goals and operating conditions
• Top decision makers must designate a champion and assign him/her the responsibility of managing the TPP and the Pilot Team
• The TPP champion manages the TPP, reports to top decision makers and ensures that favorable conditions are preserved

Let us now consider a number of issues that are critical to successfully managing the TPP.

A. The importance of champions

Any transformation is a creative process toward the development of a solution that will enable the institution to undergo change in a well-managed and thoughtful way. Hence, managing an institution's transformation requires that key people cultivate a vision of the future situation in which the institution can find a new equilibrium internally and externally. These key people are called champions. They are found at all levels of the institution. Indeed, the institution needs one or several champions among the top decision makers. They are the visionary people who are aware that the institution must experience a transformation and who have a vision (or develop a vision) for the future of the institution (see Box 5.3).

Box 5.1. The role of local governments in promoting and supporting ICT projects

Local governments (mainly at city levels) cannot just be passive recipients of technology and directives sent by agencies from the central government. For example, several past modernization initiatives failed in Morocco as a result of the low involvement of local governments in this kind of process. Rather, the local government needs to be active in the process of modernization and to take the lead throughout the different phases of building an ICT4D/e-government system to ensure that the system is developed to serve the aims of the local administration and governance and the local community that it represents. In the eFez Project, we invited and encouraged the active participation of Fez's local government. Its high degree of involvement and participation in the project enabled the deployed eFez System to meet the locally perceived needs and to be adjusted to the local political, organizational and social contexts which thus enabled the project to be regarded as acceptable and appropriate, and to be readily adopted at every different level. In this respect, it is critical to involve the right level of decision makers at the local and more global levels of government to put the emphasis on the enhancement of governance and the need to define these enhancements with the concerned decision makers.

Top decision maker champions must have enough power in the institution to launch the TPP and to sustain it by creating favorable conditions. The support of top decision maker champions is compulsory throughout the duration of the transformation process, including during the

TPP, but also throughout all the subsequent phases of the transformation process until the institution has fully appropriated and integrated the changes at all levels. Failing to get the continuous support of top decision maker champions generally ends in the failure of the transformation process (see Box 5.1).

Top decision maker champion(s) must identify and involve some key collaborators (usually middle managers) that we call champion managers, who will also be champions of the Transformation Project. The champion managers are then asked to create the pilot cell, the Pilot Team and favorable conditions in their areas of intervention alongside preparing the launch of the TPP. At their level, champion managers identify and involve some key collaborators (usually skilled and motivated employees) that we call champion employees who will be key actors in the TPP. They are officially assigned to the Pilot Team and given the proper means to fulfill their mission (assigned goals) and tasks. *Hence, the first key success factor for the TPP and the whole transformation process is the setting up of such a "structure of champions" in the institution.*

Favorable conditions are critical and correspond to the second key success factor for the TPP, as well as for any transformation process in an institution. Champions must create and maintain favorable conditions during the TPP and the whole Transformation Project. Let us emphasize that currently technology is not a critical issue. Maintaining favorable conditions relates primarily to the people's willingness to change and to support the project. Important critical success factors that enhance this inclination are:

1) Finding ways of securing and maintaining strong support from influential champions
2) Maintaining a widespread willingness to adopt the transformation within the institution
3) Securing sufficient budget allocations
4) Creating an initial group of skilled and enthusiastic persons within the institution (the champion managers and employees)
5) Building an experienced development team
6) Creating a clear and widely adopted and supported project vision.

Favorable conditions are different from one project phase to another, and they can even change during a given phase. For instance, during the TPP, the strong support and continuous involvement of influential top decision maker champions are critical to build momentum. Then the involvement of key persons (managers and employees) at the different levels of the institution's hierarchy also becomes critical. In parallel, the creation and refinement of a clear and shared project vision (during the TPP) contributes to build a consensus-based approach to the project and to strengthen the involvement and support of all these key persons, which in turn strengthens the favorable conditions. The favorable conditions are dependent on various circumstances emanating from outside and inside the institution and may be threatened by political pressure, financial constraints, the resistance of certain persons, conflicts of interests, power fights, etc.

Unfavorable conditions may appear from anywhere within (and possibly outside) the institution at any time and, most likely, from unexpected sources. Hence, monitoring and maintaining favorable conditions are continuous, intensive endeavors that may call for several team members (including champions) to be involved in different critical parts of the institution. Hence, the presence of champions and supportive stakeholders is a must since they best know the institution and are able to operate within it: they should be able to detect impending unfavorable conditions at their earliest appearance. Unfavorable conditions may not be detected immediately and may build up. The longer they go undetected by the Pilot Team or its supporters, the worse the potential damage. Consequences may range from the complete reactivation of a project step to the loss of staff and/or data, and even to the creation of a bad representation within the institution or outside it (see Box 5.2). Exercising vigilance on these matters is a key success factor. This requires a significant amount of energy from the champions and the Pilot Team.

Hence, the second key success factor for the TPP is to maintain favorable conditions.

Box 5.2. An example of unfavorable conditions detected during the TPP of the eFez Project

> After the successful automation of the Agdal Arrondissement's *bureau d'état civil* (BEC), the authorities of the city of Fez wanted to proceed rapidly and start the automation of other BECs. The newly formed Fez Technical Team was pressed to equip some chosen BECs with the required hardware and networking gear. This was done and a team of young people (internally called the "national promotion team") was recruited to begin digitizing citizens' records from the paper registers using the digitization system built by the eFez Project's development team. Proper training was given to the national promotion team who started the digitization process. Due

to a lack of resources, it took some time to locate and sufficiently train enthusiastic BEC officers assigned to the task of checking the digitized records. When this checking process was launched, it rapidly became apparent that a large percentage of the already digitized records were incorrect.

An investigation into the situation led to the conclusion that some members of the young digitizing team were not meticulous enough: they were more interested in completing a great volume of digitized records (let us emphasize that they were paid by the number of input records) than they were in inputting correct data. Once the situation had been diagnosed, proper actions were quickly taken and favorable conditions reinforced, but it was at the expense of a great deal of time and work invested and many digitized records had to be discarded. In this particular case, the Pilot Team had delegated the task of managing the digitizing process to Fez's newly formed Technical Team. This new team had not anticipated the problems due to a lack of experience and, as a result, had too hastily launched a process for which the BEC's officers were not yet trained.

Developing a shared vision for the project is crucial. ICT4D/e-government projects involve substantial changes to the way employees perform their tasks and the way services are delivered to clients through the use of ICT. Hence, moving an institution from an archaic manual mode of operation to a fully automated one providing e-government services requires visionary people who are able to picture the future state of the institution in which most operations will be automated. This eventually results in a new way of doing business and requires the reorganization of employees' tasks and workflows. This mental picture is called the project vision (see Box 5.3) and should be formalized in terms of clear documents (i.e., vision statement and possibly mission statement) that are used to share and discuss the project vision among all stakeholders. The Pilot Team, the institution's champions and their advisors should be aware of the importance of establishing, updating and maintaining a shared vision of an ICT4D/e-government project because all decisions made during the project should be aligned to this vision.

Hence, the third key success factor for the TPP is to establish, share and update a shared vision of the ICT4D/e-government project among all stakeholders.

Box 5.3. Vision statements, mission statements and values[6]

Vision: Defines the desired or intended future state of an institution or enterprise in terms of its fundamental objective and/or strategic direction. Vision is a long-term view, sometimes describing how the institution would like to see the world in which it operates. For example, a charity working with the poor might have a vision statement which reads, "A world without poverty."

Mission: Defines the fundamental purpose of an institution or an enterprise, succinctly describing why it exists and what it does to achieve its vision.

It is sometimes used to set out a "picture" of the institution in the future. A mission statement provides details of what is done, answering the question: "What is it that we do?" For example, the charity might provide "Job training for the homeless and unemployed."

Values: Beliefs that are shared among the stakeholders of an institution. Values drive an institution's culture and priorities and provide a framework in which decisions are made. For example, "Knowledge and skills are the keys to success."

Strategy: Strategy corresponds to a combination of the ends (goals) for which the organization is striving and the means (policies) by which it is seeking to get there.

Institutions sometimes summarize goals and objectives into a mission statement and/or a vision statement. One can also begin with a vision and mission and then use them to formulate goals and objectives. While the existence of a shared mission is extremely useful, many strategy specialists question the requirement of a written mission statement. However, there are many models of strategic planning that start with mission statements, so it is useful to examine them here.

A ***mission statement*** explains the fundamental purpose of the institution. It defines its customers and critical processes. It prescribes the desired level of performance.

---

6 Adapted from http://en.wikipedia.org/wiki/Strategic_planning (accessed October 2013).

A ***vision statement*** outlines what the institution wants to become, or what the world in which it operates will resemble. It concentrates on the future. It is a source of inspiration and provides clear decision making criteria. An advantage of having such a statement is that it creates value for the people exposed to the statement, especially for managers, employees and even sometimes customers. Statements create a sense of direction and opportunity. They are an essential part of the strategy making process.

Many people mistake the vision statement for the mission statement, and sometimes one is simply used as a longer-term version of the other. *The vision should describe why it is important to achieve the mission.* A vision statement defines the purpose or broader goal of the institution's existence or business and can remain the same for decades if crafted well. A mission statement is more specific to what the institution can achieve by itself. Vision should describe what will be achieved in a wider context if the organization and others are successful in achieving their individual missions.

The mission statement can galvanize people to achieve defined objectives, even if they are stretch objectives, provided it can be elucidated in SMART (specific, measurable, achievable, relevant and time-bound) terms. A mission statement provides a path to realizing the vision in line with its values. These statements have a direct bearing on the bottom line and success of the organization.

Features of an effective vision statement include:

- Clarity and lack of ambiguity
- Creation of a vivid and clear picture
- Description of a bright future
- Memorable and engaging wording
- Realistic aspirations
- Alignment with organizational values and culture

To be effective, an organizational vision statement must (the theory states) become assimilated into the institution's culture. Leaders have the responsibility of communicating the vision regularly, creating narratives that illustrate the vision, acting as role models by embodying the vision, creating short-term objectives compatible with the vision and encouraging others to craft their own personal vision compatible with the institution's overall vision. In addition, mission statements need to be subjected to an internal assessment and an external assessment. The internal assessment should focus on how members inside the organization interpret their mission statement. The external assessment, which includes all of the business' stakeholders, is valuable since it offers a different perspective. Discrepancies between these two assessments can give an insight into the institution's mission statement effectiveness.

Another simple approach to defining vision and mission is to pose two questions. Firstly, "Which aspirations does the organization have for the world in which it operates and where it has some influence?" and, following on from this, "What can (and/or does) the organization do or contribute to fulfill those aspirations?" The succinct answer to the first question provides the basis of the vision statement. The answer to the second question determines the mission statement.

B. Managing the TPP as an experiment

Because it is an experiment in which the Pilot Team seeks a solution for the institution's transformation, the TPP may fail, be a partial success, or even a total success. Everyone must understand that the TPP may fail eventually and if that happens, the failure must be considered positively as a way to better understand the conditions under which the institution operates and the reasons for the failure. Managing the TPP as an experiment in the pilot cell is a good way of minimizing the risks inherent to any transformation, to carefully monitor the costs and to become more familiar with the internal and external forces that drive the ongoing change. If an experiment is a failure and if the reasons of the failure are well analyzed and understood, nothing prevents top decision makers from launching further experiments to find an appropriate solution. Remember that managing an institution's transformation is a creative process in which people seek a good solution to facilitate the transformation. Failure or partial success is a good way to learn on the path to finding the appropriate solution.

Hence, managing the TPP as an experiment is the fourth key success factor for the TPP.

C. The Monitoring and Assessment Process (MAP)

Adopting such an experiment-based approach implies that any TPP must be associated with a Monitoring and Assessment Process (MAP) that aims to observe the TPP from an external point of view. The MAP should usually be carried out by an advisory team external to the institution. This External Advisory Team (EAT) is composed of knowledgeable and experienced experts able to provide advice and possibly guidance to top decision makers, the TPP champion(s) and the Pilot Team.

The MAP is a very important process that is carried out in parallel with the TPP. Since the TPP is an experiment toward finding a solution to the transformation that the institution plans to undertake, the outcomes of the TPP must be assessed as well as the transformation process that takes place throughout the TPP. Everybody agrees that the results of a Pilot Project must be assessed, but very few managers acknowledge the importance of assessing the TPP when it occurs. This is unfortunate, since observing, monitoring and assessing the TPP process at all levels (political, organizational, managerial, technical, financial and social) provides a wealth of critical information on the way people, groups and institutions react to the changes that are taking place. Monitoring and assessment are also very useful in identifying (and confirming the involvement/commitment/enthusiasm of) the internal and external people who are the key actors (champions) in the success of the TPP (as well as for the transformation process as a whole).

In practice, even in ICT-mature institutions, the MAP is not carried out in all the Transformation Projects (ITU 2008b), and this would help to identify the key reasons that Transformation Projects often evolve in unanticipated ways, exceeding budgets and schedules.

In developing countries and especially in ICT4D projects where the skills and budgets are not locally available, the funds and projects are monitored by external international agencies that usually require the setup of an MAP. This is fortunate and a good practice to be put into use even for non-externally funded projects (see Box 5.4).

Hence, setting up the MAP is the fifth key success factor for the TPP.

Box 5.4. The MAP and outcome analysis approach

In the eFez Project, it was decided to base the monitoring and assessment process on a scientifically proven approach allowing for the assessment and measurement of the project's outcome: the *outcome analysis* method (Kettani, Moulin et al. 2005). This method enables people involved in the design, development and deployment of ICT4D/e-government systems to assess the broader significance of these systems in relation to normative goals set up with the main stakeholders, using both qualitative and quantitative measurements. The proposed outcome analysis begins with a characterization of *good governance* (GG) in relation to the project context (such as cities in the case of local governments) and the selection of formal definitions of "attributes" associated with GG. For example, the attributes identified for city-related good governance are: accountability, decentralized management, networking, management innovation, responsiveness, public–private partnerships, local government–citizen interaction and human resource development (for more details, see www.gdrc.org/u-gov/indicators.html).

In the context of the eFez Project, we identified four main groups of stakeholders in which GG attributes needed to be assessed: high-level decision makers (i.e., politicians), middle-level managers, employees and citizens. For each of these categories of stakeholders, the GG attributes had been translated into relevant indicators that could be effectively measured before and after the development and deployment of the e-government system. The definitions of GG attributes have also been translated into normative project goals (as identified in collaboration with the project's main stakeholders) which provide the ground to identify anticipated project outcomes. Finally, specifiable (and measurable) project outputs have been identified in relation to the expected outcomes. In the eFez Project, we identified five major outcome categories that needed to be assessed: technology, organization, citizen, regulation and good governance (Kettani et al. 2006). Using such categories ensures that the proposed outcome analysis method provides the appropriate means to assess the project's results in relation to its goals and activities.

Interestingly, such a method not only grounds the project assessment in the main stakeholders' expectations and in the project goals, but it also considers the process of project assessment as a means to orient the planning and adjustment of a project's development as it proceeds. This enables decision makers to have a clearer understanding of the way the project and the ICT4D/e-government system contributes to achieve the objective of enhancing governance (see Chapter 4).

D. The External Advisory Team (EAT)

In ICT-mature institutions, the EAT mainly plays an advisory and accompaniment role. However, in developing countries and especially in ICT4D projects, the EAT will often play a more active role during the TPP and the other phases of the project. Some of its members might even participate in the management of the Pilot Team. The Pilot Team may also be comprised of external advisors as well as employees and middle managers of the institution. Pairing skilled and motivated employees with knowledgeable and experienced external advisors provides a great opportunity for the employees to learn new techniques and methods and to develop new skills, especially in relation to the transformation that is taking place in the institution. They also gain much confidence in the transformation process by relying on the experience of their advisors.

Hence, the EAT members may have to play various roles in an ICT4D/ e-government project: advice giving, teaching and training, coaching and accompaniment. Indeed, decision makers and managers of local governmental institutions generally acknowledge the need for the advice of the EAT. But very often, especially at the project's start, they do not grasp the interest (or criticality) of many actions initiated or carried out by the EAT. Top decision makers of such institutions are often politicians who want "quick, visible results" to show to the public. They usually consider assessment processes as mere academic exercises. Hence, the EAT needs to gain credibility at all levels of the institution and to convince the different stakeholders of the importance of carefully managing the transformation process in a well thought out and structured way (see Box 5.5). The different phases and steps of the transformation process should be presented and explained to the main champions and stakeholders of the institution to make them aware of its interest and importance. Consequently, a certain amount of time and energy needs to be allocated to this sensitization and education of champions relative to adopting a structured way of managing projects (methods, monitoring and assessment techniques, etc.).

Box 5.5. The EAT and outcome analysis in the eFez Project

In the context of the eFez Project, it is worth mentioning that, at the start, local authorities did not understand the need to carry out an outcome analysis for the project and viewed it as a mere academic exercise. They were mainly driven by the "thrill and challenge" of starting a "technological revolution." Undeterred by such arguments, the eFez EAT painstakingly carried out all the steps and indicator measurements needed for the outcome analysis before and during the system development as well as after its deployment. The set of indicators (organized according to four main groups of stakeholders and to five major outcome categories) and their ongoing measurements provided the team with a kind of dashboard against which each important strategic, tactical and operational decision was assessed.

This approach enabled the team to always present, to the various stakeholders, the actual stakes of the different available options in precise and well-documented terms that clearly emphasized the impacts of potential decisions with respect to the selected good governance attributes. Considering the volatility of certain situations encountered in such projects (due to various factors such as political, emotional and time pressure), this careful approach enabled the eFez EAT to present strong arguments against certain would-be decisions, thus avoiding costly mistakes. On several occasions, several weeks after the decisions were made, local authorities recognized the merits of the advice of the EAT, and, as such, implicitly recognized the value of this "academic assessment approach."

Hence, the sixth critical success factor is setting up a credible EAT that can effectively communicate the importance of carefully applying a well thought out and structured transformation process to the various involved stakeholders.

E. The External Development Team (EDT) and the development of ICT4D solutions

In a large number of ICT4D projects, the institution's employees and managers do not have the technical education, training and means to develop a solution that will sustain the transformation process. It is, thus, necessary that the design and development work (for both business processes and software, as well as for the setup of the hardware infrastructure that will support the new solution) be carried out by a well-trained External Development Team (EDT). This team must be comprised of experts equipped with the know-how to create solutions according to set budgets and schedules. The EDT is usually supervised by the EAT in collaboration with the institution's TPP champion, who reports the TPP progress to the institution's top managers.

Hence, setting up efficient advisory and accompaniment teams such as the EAT and the EDT and making them work harmoniously with the institution's personnel is the seventh key success factor for the TPP.

F. Completing the TPP and communicating its results

The activities of the TPP may take a variety of forms which depend on the nature of the transformation that the institution will undergo. As we already mentioned, it is crucial to set clear goals and deadlines when launching the TPP.

If deadlines cannot be met, the institution's decision makers, the project's champions and the Pilot Team, the EAT and the EDT need to receive valuable information regarding difficulties that had not been anticipated at the TPP start. A variety of reasons (political, budgetary, delays from other parties, inertia of certain persons, etc.) might explain such delays. However, it is a concern for managers when a TPP's deadlines have not been respected, since they can then anticipate that similar difficulties may arise, potentially exacerbated, during the remainder of the development of the project. Hence, missed TPP deadlines should also be considered as a valuable source of information for the project management. The causes of delays should be precisely assessed and explained, and possible remedies should be proposed in order to ensure that the project will not be impaired by similar obstacles during the Scaling-Up Phase.

In any case, the results of the TPP must be assessed in relation to the initial goals of the experiment. The TPP may lead to a variety of results: a software prototype to demonstrate the proposed software solution, the installation of hardware and the activation of their operation, changes in procedures and personnel's organization of work (i.e., workflows), data collection and recording in databases, etc. These results are presented to the main stakeholders and then documented in a report by the TPP champion, the Pilot Team and the EAT (in collaboration with the EDT for the technical aspects). Recommendations are proposed as a conclusion of the TPP report, including possible follow-up actions.

The results and recommendations should be presented in meetings (or workshops, depending on the extent of the work carried out in the TPP) in which all stakeholders and decision makers can participate. It is most critical to broadly communicate the results and to discuss them with all involved stakeholders, as well as the alternative strategies that can be considered as follow-ups. It is important to share and update the vision of the project, and to ensure that everybody understands the possible impacts and challenges of the envisioned transformation of the institution. This is also a good time to assess the criticality of acting toward such a transformation to emphasize the importance of maintaining favorable conditions and to enable the stakeholders to renew their support for the project.

Hence, communicating a clear and objective report on the TPP results and the recommendations and getting the feedback from all the main stakeholders is the eighth key success factor for the TPP.

VIII. Conclusion

In this chapter, we discussed a variety of challenges that should be tackled when launching and managing ICT4D/e-government projects, especially in developing countries. We showed that several causes might lead such projects to failure or partial success. Unfortunate outcomes usually result from a lack of awareness and anticipation of problems that inevitably arise in such projects at all levels: financial, political, managerial, human, technological and educational levels. We also showed how well-managed and well-targeted ICT4D/e-government strategies and systems can improve governance at all levels of government and improve the sustainability of governmental systems and their capacity to deliver adequate and appreciated services to citizens in both the short and long term.

Taking advantage of our experience in developing ICT4D/e-government systems in developing countries, we suggested that lessons learned at national levels can inspire the creation of e-strategies and the development/deployment of ICT4D/e-government systems at local governance levels. We showed how complex and numerous the issues are in an ICT4D/e-government project in the hope that this discussion will increase awareness of a variety of critical elements that must be addressed in such projects. Broadening the understanding of the reader on a variety of important issues is one of this book's goals.

We also emphasized that ICT4D/e-government projects should be managed as transformative processes in order to favor a successful transformation of the institutions in which they are implemented. We discussed several key issues that must be considered by project managers and decision makers to carefully bring about such a transformation, especially during the first phase of such projects that we called the TPP. The TPP is the cornerstone of the generic roadmap that we propose in the next chapter. We expect that the discussions and numerous quotations that we introduced will save some time for the reader trying to orient himself/herself in the jungle of documents written on ICT4D and e-government systems. This was also an occasion for us to introduce key notions, to outline some principles and to propose some guidance as a summary of the main challenges and issues in managing ICT4D/e-government projects. These principles will guide us when we present a roadmap for the development and deployment of ICT4D/e-government systems based on good governance applied to local governmental institutions in the next chapter.

In addition, the appendix to this book offers a detailed list of important elements that influence the transformation affecting a governmental institution when it adopts and integrates new business policies and practices based on ICT4D/e-government techniques and good governance principles. Such a list might be useful to decision makers and project managers when developing project plans and tailoring project management and development approaches (such as the generic roadmap that we present in Chapter 6) to the peculiarities of their projects.

The appendix is presented as a set of tables which organize the list of elements into five general themes:

- Managing the context of the ICT4D/e-government project
- Good governance (GG) and leadership in ICT4D/e-government projects
- Vision and capacity building in relation to the ICT4D/e-government project
- Governance and management of an ICT4D/e-government project
- Ensuring the sustainability of the transformation

Chapter 6

A GENERIC ROADMAP FOR ICT4D/E-GOVERNMENT PROJECTS

I. Introduction

In the preceding chapter, we showed that ICT4D/e-government projects are transformation processes that should be managed as such to favor a successful transformation of the institutions in which they are implemented. We emphasized the importance of launching a Transformation Pilot Process (TPP) to:

• Involve all stakeholders;
• Help decision makers identify clear goals and create favorable conditions for the project;
• Create a Pilot Team and assign its members clear responsibilities and adequate resources;
• Involve champions at all levels of the institution to support the transformation process;
• Find a solution and implement it in a part of the institution which is welcoming to the transformation (the pilot cell); and
• Develop initial methodological guidelines in order to prepare the institution's transformation at a larger scale.

If the TPP has been successful and well received by all stakeholders, the institution might want to spread the transformation to the whole institution. This is often called the "scaling-up" of the solution. Spreading the transformation to the whole institution can be thought of as a project in itself (or even a series of projects) that must also be carefully managed.

In developing countries, the additional important challenge that arises is to make the transformation sustainable (Kendall 2010). Indeed, a large number of ICT4D projects are developed with external help and support (international funds, external teams such as the External Advisory Team (EAT) and External Development Team (EDT)) that will not be available after the project's completion. A large number of e-government projects fail at this stage (InfoDev 2009a). Being aware of the main pitfalls that might arise in the course of spreading the transformation and having a well thought out, principled method (often called a "roadmap") and schedule to manage the transformation process might provide managers with better tools to enact a successful and sustainable transformation of their institution. In this chapter, we provide an overview of such a roadmap.

Section II presents an overview of the generic roadmap and its five phases. Section III presents a common pattern of these phases referenced in the other chapter sections in which each phase is presented in detail.

Section IV presents the first phase of the roadmap, the TPP which initiates the transformation process and mainly aims at:

• Understanding the challenges faced by the institution;
• Developing a common vision;
• Finding a practical solution to these challenges through a Pilot Project;
• Demonstrating the feasibility and applicability of the proposed solution; and
• Sensitizing and engaging key stakeholders in the transformation process.

The Pilot Project is usually carried out in a small part of the institution so that favorable conditions hold during the development of the solution.

Section V presents the Local Solution Development/Deployment/ Assessment (LSDDA) Phase in detail. If the TPP experiment has been successful and if the institution's top managers decide to go on with the transformation process, the LSDDA Phase is launched. Inspired by the TPP's results and taking advantage of lessons learned, the LSDDA Phase aims at developing a solution in a significant part of the organization according to the envisioned transformation. The LSDDA solution may be significantly different to the TPP solution because it involves a larger part of the institution that may raise new challenges. New lessons are learned which prepare the institution for the next stage of the transformation process, which is often called the Scaling-Up Process.

If the LSDDA is successful and the institution as a whole is ready to adopt the solution, the next phase is triggered: the Global Solution Development/ Deployment/Assessment (GSDDA) Phase which is presented in detail in Section VI. The GSDDA Phase aims to deploy the solution developed during the LSDDA Phase to the whole institution. In Section VI, we discuss the particular challenges faced during this Scaling-Up Phase and propose some advice.

As we already mentioned, a big challenge of ICT4D/e-government projects is to deliver sustainable solutions to the institutions that undergo major transformations. To mitigate the risk of failure, the proposed roadmap contains a phase which is particularly devoted to managing the transition of the institution by autonomously supporting and sustaining the solution.

This is the Transition to Autonomy (TTA) Phase, presented in detail in Section VII, with the main challenges, advice and lessons learned. The TTA should start as soon as possible and run in parallel with the GSDDA Phase.

II. A Generic Roadmap

In this section, we present the generic roadmap that we propose to support the e-transformation process in diagrammatic form. This roadmap is composed of five main phases that lead to different organizational situations dependent on whether they are successfully completed or not. Figure 6.1 provides an overview of these phases and the resulting organizational situations. We comment on them briefly in this section.

The diagrammatic conventions are indicated in the figure's legend. Big pointed rectangles represent the phases of the transformation process. Rounded rectangles correspond to the institution's observed situations or to the situations obtained after the completion of a phase or after an important decision. Decisions are represented by diamond shapes, followed by two arrows that lead either to another phase or to a resulting situation. Usually, an arrow exiting a diamond with the GO annotation represents the acknowledgement to go on with the next phase; the other arrow (with the NO-GO annotation) represents the contrary and leads to a certain situation that is characterized in the figure.

A. The first phase (Ph1)

This first phase corresponds to the Transformation Pilot Process (TPP) that we discussed in Chapter 5. It starts at the initial situation (represented as the first rounded rectangle in the top left corner of Figure 6.1) that is generally based on a manual archaic organizational system which often seems fossilized. The governance practices are informal and frequently do not apply the "good governance principles" that are sought after in ICT4D/e-government projects. As we already mentioned, launching the TPP is the result of the formal decision of the institution's top management. This is represented by the GO branch in the first diamond that triggers the first phase (to signify this, the diamond is connected to the rounded rectangle representing the situation). If favorable conditions are not met, meaning that managers are not convinced of the urgency of the current situation, the TPP cannot be launched successfully and the institution stays in its initial situation, corresponding to the NO-GO branch in the first diamond.

After the completion of the TPP (Ph1 rectangle in Figure 6.1), two situations may arise. Either: 1) the experiment is assessed as being successful and the

Figure 6.1. A schematical representation of our roadmap

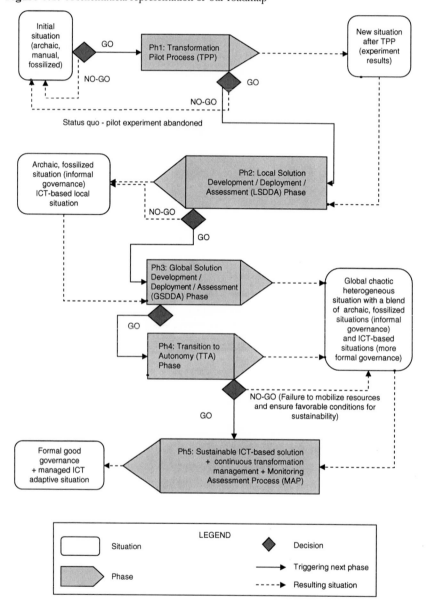

institution's top management decides to go on with the transformation process (the GO branch of the diamond associated with the Ph1 rectangle); or 2) the top management does not think that it is time to trigger the transformation in the organization (the NO-GO branch of the diamond associated with the Ph1 rectangle) and the institution as a whole stays in the archaic manual situation with informal governance. But a local ICT-based situation remains for some time in the part of the institution that we called the "pilot cell." This situation is represented by the rounded rectangle called the "archaic fossilized situation/ICT-based local situation." The details of this first phase will be presented in Section IV.

B. The second phase (Ph2)

This second phase corresponds to the Local Solution Development/ Deployment/Assessment (LSDDA) Phase. It starts from the new situation after TPP (rounded rectangle at the top right corner of Figure 6.1). The aim of this phase is to take advantage of the results of the TPP to create, deploy and assess the new ICT4D/e-government system and associated organization (called the "local solution") in a significant and well-chosen part of the institution that we call the LSDDA sector of the institution. Usually, the LSDDA Phase is carried out in the same institution sector in which the TPP has been performed to capitalize on the momentum gained during the TPP and because there are already active and supportive champions in this sector. Moreover, it is easier to extend the Pilot Team with new employees of the same sector who are eager to be part of the transformation process.

The LSDDA Phase is managed by the LSDDA champion (in most cases, the same person who played the role of TPP champion) in collaboration with the supporting teams (EAT and EDT) that are also extended if deemed necessary. We must emphasize that, even if the LSDDA solution is developed in the same sector in which the TPP was carried out, the LSDDA Project Team (LSDDA champion, EAT and EDT) should be careful not to try to reproduce the TPP solution as such in the LSDDA sector without assessing its suitability for this part of the institution. Indeed, different strategies have been explored during the TPP to find a solution to the institution's problems. Since the experiments have been carried out in the pilot cell, a small part of the institution, certain unconsidered factors and issues may arise when dealing with a larger part of the institution. Hence, the development of the LSDDA solution for the LSDDA sector might significantly differ from the TPP solution.

As we will see in detail in Section V, many organizational issues that were considered during the TPP still apply during the LSDDA Phase: maintaining favorable conditions, involvement of champions and stakeholders, updating and sharing the project vision, careful planning and monitoring of the project, involvement of the EAT and EDT, assessment of the project progress in relation to good governance principles, etc. Other issues increase in criticality such as identifying and training motivated and skillful employees to join the EAT and preparing efficient and appropriate training programs. An LSDDA development plan should be set at the start of this phase, and monitored and revised during the whole duration of the phase.

Progress must be monitored and appropriate decisions and actions should be performed to address the issues and problems that will inevitably arise during the development of the local solution. At the end of the LSDDA Phase, the local solution and the development process should be assessed and a report should be written and submitted to the institution's authorities. This report should present the primary results of the local solution, its impact on the institution's transformation and the lessons learned toward the full deployment of the solution in the whole institution. The report, assessment and recommendations should be presented and discussed with the main stakeholders to prepare the next phase.

In some cases, the development of the LSDDA solution may result in either partial or total failure. This failure should be carefully analyzed and its causes determined so that the institution can learn from it. In other cases, the institution might not been ready to extend the local solution for a variety of reasons (lack of political and institutional will or support to carry out the transformation in the other sectors of the institution, lack of adequate financial and human resources, etc.). This is symbolized by the NO-GO branch of the diamond shape attached to the Ph2 rectangle in Figure 6.1. This initiates a return to the archaic, fossilized situation/ICT-based local situation, but now the local solution is applied and used in a larger part of the institution. Moreover, in most cases the development of the LSDDA solution will be a success and the institution's top management will approve the launch of the next phase (Ph3). This is the GO branch of the diamond shape attached to the Ph2 rectangle in Figure 6.1. Details of this second phase are presented in Section V.

C. The third phase (Ph3)

The third phase of our generic roadmap is the Global Solution Development/ Deployment/Assessment (GSDDA) Phase. It starts from the archaic, fossilized situation/ICT-based local situation, but the local solution now is applied and used in the LSDDA sector (rounded rectangle input to the Ph3 rectangle). The aim of the GSDDA Phase is to scale up the local solution to the whole institution, hence adapting, deploying and assessing the new ICT4D/e-government system and the corresponding new organization in all the institution's sectors.

The ultimate goal is to develop a global solution that sustains the institution's transformation process. At this point, the institution's top management, influential champions and the EAT should carefully consider the specific issues related to the Scaling-Up Process. Again, favorable conditions must be maintained, with special consideration for the selection and involvement of top management champions who may not be the same as the ones who supported the project during the TPP and LSDDA Phases.

During the GSDDA Phase, the project team will encounter similar issues, problems and challenges as during the LSDDA Phase, but their previous experience is an asset when addressing them. A critical factor is the identification, selection and training of motivated and skillful employees and managers who will support the transition process in the various sectors where the solution will be adapted and deployed. Another critical factor is the creation of a project plan and schedule for this phase which will ensure that the local solution will be adapted to the needs and characteristics of each sector and deployed in a timely and coordinated way. The EAT and EDT are still supporting the transformation process and the scaling up. New members may have joined these teams to include people from the various sectors involved in the transformation process. We give more details about this phase in Section VI.

D. The fourth phase (Ph4)

This phase concerns the transition to autonomy (TTA). It is rarely considered a formal phase in ICT4D/e-government projects, especially in developing countries. Although most people understand the importance of the institution becoming autonomous (with respect to the maintenance and improvement of the new system(s) and associated organizational changes), the institution's top managers are usually not aware of the importance of starting such a TTA Phase early enough that it effectively and successfully leads the institution to the targeted autonomy. We must emphasize that when the EAT and EDT are disbanded, the transformation process can still fail even after the successful deployment of the ICT4D/e-government system in the whole institution. This is often observed in developing countries when international support comes to an end. At this point, it is too late to efficiently intervene in order to ensure that the ICT4D/e-government system and the associated organization will become sustainable without external support. This is an important and strategic issue.

To overcome this difficulty, we formally introduce in our roadmap the TTA Phase. An initial and important goal of the TTA Phase is to sensitize the institution's management to the importance of carefully and formally managing the transition to autonomy. Another significant goal of this phase is to develop a plan so that the transition will be effectively carried out, taking into account the necessary resources as well as reasonable deadlines. We also strongly advise launching this TTA Phase as soon as possible in parallel with the GSDDA Phase. Since the GSDDA Phase will last a significant amount of time before the solution is deployed and routinely used in the whole institution, the project managers, in collaboration with the EAT and EDT, should start to select and train the employees and managers who will be in charge of maintaining the new ICT4D/e-government system and supporting the people who will use it as soon as possible. Beginning this transitioning process early will help the EAT and EDT gradually to disengage, empowering the institution's selected personnel to take over their respective tasks and responsibilities.

We also strongly advise managing the TTA Phase as an independent subproject and assigning an appropriate budget to it, as well as skillful human resources. Failing to do so may result in delaying appropriate measures, missing critical milestones or deadlines and failing to train and hire personnel to carry out these measures. This can lead slowly and surely to the failure of the TTA Phase, and the Transformation Project as a whole.

As shown in Figure 6.1, the GSDDA and TTA Phases are run in parallel and, ideally, are completed at the same time (see rectangles Ph3 and Ph4). This means that as soon as the ICT4D/e-government system is deployed and used in the whole institution, the institution should be able to maintain and to expand it autonomously. Quite often in developing countries, the international funding will fade away before the solution is fully deployed in the institution. Hence, the importance of launching the TTA Phase as soon as possible, with deadlines that will take into account the termination of international aid and the disengagement of the EAT and EDT. We discuss these issues in more detail in Section VII.

Failing to successfully carry out the TTA Phase will leave the institution in what is termed in Figure 6.1 a "global chaotic heterogeneous situation with a blend of archaic and fossilized situations (informal governance)." This means that certain sectors of the institution will be able to mobilize and sustain adequate resources to maintain the ICT4D/e-government system in operation, while other sectors will fail to do so and return to the archaic way of carrying out their business. The institution's top-management will need to urgently assess such situations and make appropriate decisions toward the future that it envisions for the institution.

E. The fifth phase (Ph5)

A positive termination of the TTA Phase leads the institution to the fifth phase called the sustainable ICT-based solution monitored by continuous transformation phase. The objective of this phase is to ensure that the institution is able to support, maintain and expand the ICT4D/e-government system, and to adapt the organization to changing needs, taking into account good governance principles. Such a phase is a true challenge for institutions in both developed and developing countries.

Let us suggest here that it is important that the institution's management officially recognizes and announces the successful management and absorption of the planned transformation and that the institution now enters a new era of its development, emphasizing good governance based on ICT and the management of its continuous transformation.

We will not detail this phase in a specific section since it goes beyond the transformation process per se. The continuous transformation of an institution is usually carried out through the use of change management methods. Numerous change management methods are available. Examples are referenced in *The Change Handbook* (Holman et al. 2009) which documents more than 90 methods or techniques for change management. Let us emphasize that a change management method must be customized to the institution's context to fit its culture and management practices, the availability of human resources, and many other factors. Adopting or developing a change management method, adapting it to the institution's context and successfully implementing it is a project in its own right, or even a series of projects that need to be carefully managed (see, for example, Leloup et al. 2008). This goes beyond the scope of this book.

III. A Common Template for the Five Phases of the Generic Roadmap

Our experience of managing a number of ICT4D/e-government projects led us to identify a set of issues and steps that are common to all phases of our generic roadmap. This was the origin of the common template presented in this section (Figure 6.2).

In Figure 6.2, the big rounded rectangle represents the contents of a phase in terms of processes and activities. It surrounds the elements that are included in the template and is comprised of two parts which are divided by the dashed bold line at the top of the rectangle.

During the ICT4D/e-government projects that we managed, we observed that some processes (supervision, training, assessment, communication) should always run in parallel during the full duration of any phase: they are represented in the upper part of the template (over the dashed bold line). Any phase, moreover, contributes to the institution's transformation process. This is represented as a series of coordinated steps represented in the lower part of the template (under the dashed line). The succession of steps is symbolized by arrows in a similar way to the generic roadmap.

Figure 6.2. A common template for the five steps of our generic roadmap

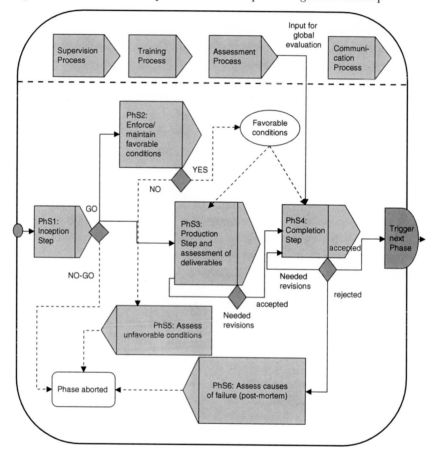

Let's present the four main processes (shown in the upper part of Figure 6.2) that we propose to continually perform during any phase:

1) *The Supervision Process:* It is critical to supervise the transformation process carefully during any phase (using classical management and monitoring techniques, change management techniques, etc.).
2) *The Training Process:* It is important to train, coach and often accompany the institution's employees, managers and the development teams.
3) *The Communication Process:* During any phase, communicating the advancement of the project to all stakeholders is a very important issue. A communication plan must be created and submitted to the institution's management. Reports about communication activities should be regularly

produced and submitted to the top decision makers. Having a good communication plan can help to decrease certain employees' resistance to change and it may motivate others to support the project.

4) *The Assessment Process*: This process is critical throughout the project to measure and assess the progress of the work carried out during each phase, and to identify difficulties and report them to the institution's management so that appropriate decisions can be made in a timely and informed manner toward the completion of the phase and the launch of subsequent phases.

Now, let us consider the steps that are characteristic of a phase (shown in the lower part of Figure 6.2).

The start of a phase is represented by the circle on the left side of the rounded rectangle. It triggers the first step of the phase called the Inception Step (PhS1). This step launches the phase, sets and refines the goals of the phase and ensures that is can be carried out according to available resources and planned deadlines. The successful completion of step PhS1 triggers steps PhS2 and PhS3, but if the Inception Step fails, the phase is aborted (the NO-GO arrow exiting the diamond attached to the rectangle representing the PhS1 step in Figure 6.2).

Let us emphasize that the Inception Step (PhS1) aims at setting clear goals and orientations for the phase and identifying means and resources to fulfill these goals in a set time frame. This naturally leads to the elaboration of a plan for the phase. This plan should be discussed and refined with the main decision makers and stakeholders for their approval and support. This is critical for the success of the phase. If the project team fails to reach an agreement with the decision makers and main stakeholders regarding the phase plan, an assessment of this failure should be readily made and proper action should be carried out since this may imply discontinuing the phase at this point.

PhS2 ensures that favorable conditions hold during the duration of the phase. This issue has already been discussed in Chapter 5. If at any point unfavorable conditions are met, they must be quickly assessed (PhS5) and if appropriate decisions are not made and energetic actions taken, the phase may also be aborted. Preserving favorable conditions is mandatory so that the Production Step (PhS3) can be carried out both timely and effectively. Deliverables of the phase are systematically assessed (diamond attached to PhS3 rectangle) and revisions can be required (return loop). If deliverables are accepted, the Completion Step of the phase (PhS4) can be launched. This step takes advantage of the results of the Assessment Process to assess the work carried out during the phase and to provide recommendations for the next phase. A phase report is presented to the main stakeholders and decision makers. This report can be accepted, possibly after some revisions (back loop of the diamond of the PhS4 rectangle). When accepted, the phase moves to the Trigger Next Phase slot of the template (the gate symbol on the right side of the global round rectangle). If the phase report is rejected by the institution's top managers, then a Post-Mortem Step, "assess causes of failure" (PhS6), should be promptly triggered in order to assess the causes of this failure and rejection. This ends up in the late abortion of the phase and raises a critical issue for the institution's managers to ponder.

In the following sections, we use this template to describe in more detail the different phases of the proposed approach. The goal of these sections is to highlight the main issues that a project manager must bear in mind when launching and managing each phase. These sections will also provide guidelines based on our experience.

Changing our presentation style, we chose to present the contents of these sections in a way that would be easy for a project manager to consult when he/she will have to create and/or adjust the roadmap of a particular project he/she will have to manage. They are essentially presented as check lists of issues, advice and items to be considered in each phase, step and process that are presented in the roadmap.

IV. The TPP Phase

In this section, we discuss the main steps (Inception Step, Production Step, Completion Step), the main processes (Supervision Process, Assessment Process, Training Process) and main elements (favorable conditions, involvement of champions, etc.) to be considered in the TPP. In Chapter 5, we introduced most of the references attached to the description of the TPP: champions, (un)favorable conditions, mission and vision, External Advisory Team (EAT), External Development Team (EDT) and Monitoring and Assessment Process (MAP). Also, it is important to bear in mind that the TPP is managed as an experiment (see Chapter 5 for details and justifications). Please refer to the concepts and notions introduced in Chapter 5.

A. Objectives of the TPP and main stakeholders

The TPP has several objectives which can be associated with the main steps of this phase, hence the following guidelines:

- Obtain a clear mandate with an initial vision (if possible), goals, budget and deadlines from the institution's top managers who are supporting the project.
- Build a dedicated project team supported by enthusiastic champions and arouse and nurture a synergetic and positive spirit about the project and the transformation which will take place in the institution.

- Create a shared vision about how:
  - The institution can adapt its structure/procedures/culture/governance/communications/interactions internally and externally
  - The institution can respond to the forces that motivate the transformation:
    - The vision is about projecting oneself (people as a group) in the future and imagining what/how the institution "will look like and function" in the world when the transformation has been carried out
    - This requires visionary/creative/intuitive capabilities from the Pilot Team and the institution's champions.
- Understand the institution as it is:
  - Understanding clearly the current institution (and its organization) is very important at all levels: political, management, business processes, culture, individual–group relations, communications, relations with external actors, clientele, market drive and forces, regulatory context, etc.
  - Diagnose its problems, identify its strengths and limits, identify the internal and external forces that influence the institution
  - Identify the available resources (people, material, budgets, etc.) and areas where resources are lacking or needed
  - Share this understanding in order to provide stakeholders with "situational awareness"
- Understand the possibilities offered by ICT and change management approaches toward governance and business process reengineering in the context of this institution and its current needs.
- Raise the awareness of top decision makers, champions, stakeholders and the Pilot Team with respect to:
  - The institution's current situation
  - The possibilities of changing it by reengineering, managing change, introducing ICT and inducing organizational or cultural change:
    - At this point, you will achieve a "shared understanding of the situation"
    - You will also raise the enthusiasm of the champions/stakeholders/Pilot Team (increase their "energy"), but be aware that you will also raise expectations.
- Create and refine an actualized project vision and identify expected outcomes:
  - This is a very creative step where "the first orientations to design the solution" are created/refined (co-created and shared with involved stakeholders and champions)
- Propose a solution (i.e., hardware and network, software, management procedures, customer relations, etc.) that will sustain the transformation process and the implementation of an ICT4D/e-government approach, using appropriate technologies (ICT) and taking into account the project vision, as well as the institution's needs and constraints.

- Continually assess the evolving solution and the TPP by using the Monitoring and Assessment Process (MAP) to produce data and progress reports that will readily and effectively support the decision making process (for top decision makers, managers and critical stakeholders).
- Enable top managers to assess and decide if this experiment fulfils their goals and can be used as a basis to carry out the process that will lead to the institution's effective transformation:
  - This goal ensures that the TPP Phase will terminate gracefully and will hopefully launch the next phase

Let us remember that the main stakeholders of this phase are (see Chapter 5):

- Top decision makers and champions
- The TPP champion and the Pilot Team (champions selected from managers and employees):
  - The Pilot Team is composed of selected managers and employees who have the skills, motivation and time to work in the TPP
  - The Pilot Team is supported by the EAT and EDT
- The External Advisory Team (EAT) which provides:
  - Experts with good experience of ICT4D/e-government projects and of transformation management approaches
  - Facilitators/trainers
  - Organizational or social scientist and a communication person (who will play a liaison role with the various stakeholders)
- The External Development Team (EDT) which provides:
  - Project managers, architects and analysts, designers, developers and quality assurance personnel when the initial ICT-based solution will be built during the TPP

Figure 6.3 shows the template of the roadmap associated with the TPP Phase. Let us comment on the steps of the TPP.

B. Inception Step of the TPP

In order to start the TPP and to create favorable conditions, the institution's top decision makers must:

- Officially decide to launch the TPP;
- Identify clear goals for the TPP and create favorable conditions for its operation;

Figure 6.3. The TPP Phase template

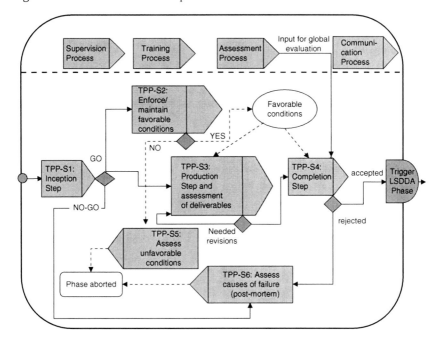

- Appoint a champion with the responsibility of managing the TPP and the Pilot Team;
- Create the pilot cell and assign people to it (officially assign them with responsibilities and adequate means or resources), hence creating the Pilot Team; and,
- Officially announce the launch of the TPP and the creation of the pilot cell/team, their goals and operating conditions.

The TPP champion manages the TPP, reports to the top decision makers and ensures that favorable conditions are preserved all along the phase.

The goal of the TPP is to develop and test a working solution to reach the goals set by the top decision makers, keeping in mind that this is an experiment that may produce only partially satisfying results.

We recommend the official creation of a TPP Management Team, composed of the TPP champion and the managers of the Pilot Team, EAT and EDT. It is important to create such a management team to coordinate the entire project and to make timely decisions in agreement with the institution's top decision makers.

Favorable conditions must be maintained at three different levels: political, managerial and financial resource availability. It is the duty of the TPP Management Team and other involved champions to ensure that conditions stay favorable.

Senior members of the EAT should be involved right at the start of the TPP. In the context of an internationally funded development project, the international agencies will certainly require that the EAT be functional at the project's start. This is a critical issue since the main orientations will be set and the predominant strategic actions will be carried out during the first months of the TPP. EAT's advisors should be involved in the identification and sensitization of champions, the creation and refinement of the project vision, the setting up of the project structure and its management approach, using the assessment of the project's progress (MAP reports should be assessed by EAT's senior advisors).

Bear in mind that the human dimension is most critical in these projects.

Box 6.1. Some favorable conditions for a TPP that we identified in the context of the eFez Project

- Get an (expert/coaching) team to manage/facilitate the transformation (possibly with outside partners)
- Get budget and set a time frame for the experiment
- Set clear goals and formal monitoring and assessment procedures and continuously carry out the Monitoring and Assessment Process
- "Isolate" the pilot cell from the pressure that influences the rest of the institution
- Identify a TPP champion and set up a Pilot Team which drives this phase
- Find people within the organization who are willing to make the transformation happen, and contribute to create/develop/adapt structures/procedures to successfully transform the institution:
  - These people will become the "internal staff champions"
- Set a favorable "atmosphere" for the TPP:
  - Use a partnerships/participatory approach
  - Think of "incentives"/rewards for dedicated employees
  - Establish a "sense of the importance of the TPP for the organization" and communicate it
  - Sensitize top managers about the importance of concretely demonstrating support for the Pilot Team and the project

Main activities for the TPP Inception Step:

- The Pilot Team, EAT and capable champions start to create the project vision. This is a concrete "conceptual view" of the institution's envisioned future situation in terms of a "conceptual picture" that will provide orientations to define the new business processes, internal and external services, governance, culture and modes of interaction (both internally and externally).
- The main deliverables are:
  - A project vision statement
  - A work plan for the Pilot Phase and identification of resources needed
  - A clear list of expected results and outcomes
  - A set of indicators to measure the fulfillment of the project's objectives and the delivery of outcomes
  - A roadmap for the TPP Phase and a schedule
- These deliverables should be presented and discussed with the main stakeholders (essentially top managers and influential institution champions). They will be refined and revised until the main stakeholders reach an agreement.

C. Production Step of the TPP

This process is iterative. The main activities of the TPP Production Step are:

- To plan the iterations of the TPP Production Step and assign responsibilities to the Pilot Team, EAT and EDT
- To carry out the requirement analysis: design new business processes
- To design a conceptual architecture for the management information system
- To develop prototypes of system interfaces to show what the system will look like and validate the interfaces and workflows with involved stakeholders
- To develop the prototype system (application development, database development, integration and tests)
- The prototype system is presented to the various stakeholders who use it, test it and propose refinements
- To iterate the above activities as required until stakeholders are completely satisfied or the TPP production deadline is reached. This refinement step is very important because it helps tailor the solution to the institution's reality and "people"
- To gain the approval, support and enthusiasm of the main champions/ stakeholders
- To "raise the energy" toward the creation of the pilot versions of the solution

The prototype system and associated workflows are documented and tested in a real setting with selected stakeholders and a survey is carried out to get their feedback

- A report is prepared, including a discussion about how the prototype system and the associated workflows (organizational structure, procedures, etc.) meet the goals set for the Pilot Phase, fulfill the overall objectives of the TPP and will help to deliver the outcomes expected by top decision makers
- Problems, shortcomings, limitations and further improvements are exposed
- Recommendations for the continuation of the project are presented

Deliverables: the actualized vision + the global project picture + expected outcomes + indicators/measures + work plan and roadmap + resource list + schedule (milestones)

- All these documents are informally presented to top decision makers/ champions and selected stakeholders by the Pilot Team
- The vision, the global project picture and Pilot Project outcomes should be thoroughly discussed so that all the involved stakeholders have a chance to influence their contents and the proposed solution will reflect the common vision of the targeted solution

D. Completion Step of the TPP

The results of the Pilot Phase and the prototype system are formally presented to all the stakeholders, champions and decision makers who are involved in the TPP.

Feedback is requested, acknowledged and recorded to get all possible information to enhance the proposed solution. At this point, minor adjustments are usually needed since the main refinements and adjustments have been made during the TPP Production Step, with the involvement of selected stakeholders and champions representing the managers, employees and decision makers of the institution.

A GO/NO-GO decision is made at this point and can lead to several situations:

1) The experiment is not considered a complete success and it has to be further refined within a specific time frame (goals might also be refined). We must go back to the TPP Production Step.
2) The experiment is considered a partial failure and a new experiment needs to be launched. The appropriate decision must be made to launch another experiment to capitalize on the lessons learned, and the processes of the TPP start again at the Inception Step.

3) The experiment is considered a complete failure, and the reasons for the failure are assessed so as to consider future courses of action (similar to a post-mortem report of the experiment). The TPP (and the whole project) is stopped at this point.

4) The experiment is considered a complete success, so the GO is given to continue the Transformation Project on a larger scale toward the creation and production of the new system and the setup of new procedures (management, workflows, training, etc.). These will be deployed in a part of the institution under favorable conditions which need to be clearly specified (including sufficient resources and political support). This will continue to the next phase: the LSDDA Phase (see Section V).

This results in the GO/NO-GO decision:

- In the GO case, resources must be identified, and assigned to the next phase of the Transformation Project (the LSDDA Phase).
- The vision and global picture of the project must be communicated widely within and outside the institution, depending on the "image" that top decision makers want to project at this step of the organizational change. This is the final communication action for the TPP Phase, but communication should go on during the next phases of the project.

E. Supervision Process of the TPP

Rigorous management techniques should be applied during this phase by the TPP champion and the involved teams (pilot, EAT, EDT).

It is also advisable to formally create a Transformation Project Board (*"comité directeur" du projet de transformation*) composed of selected key top decision makers and some of their supervisors (politicians), the TPP champion and the managers of the EAT and EDT. The board has the responsibility of making strategic decisions related to the Transformation Project as a whole and to the TPP in particular.

F. Training Process of the TPP

Two main issues should be considered.

Capacity building:

- The EAT and EDT members must become acquainted with the institution's context (political, economic, managerial, cultural, etc.)

- The TPP champion and EAT managers must identify stakeholders (representatives of users, managers, etc.) to be actively involved in the Pilot Phase
- The TPP champion and EAT members must sensitize and train selected stakeholders to enable them to participate actively in the TPP

Empowering people: Actions must be taken by the institution's top managers/ champions to formally give people (employees and managers) the capacities and responsibilities to fulfill the goals that are assigned to them in the project. The TPP champion and the EAT must be aware of this issue that might be critical since top decision makers are not often sensitized to the importance of performing these official actions in a timely way.

G. Assessment Process of the TPP

Let us recall that the Monitoring and Assessment Process (MAP) should be carried out in parallel with the TPP with the aim of observing the TPP from an external point of view (see Chapter 5). The MAP is usually carried out by the EAT. Since the TPP is an experiment toward finding a solution to the transformation that the institution plans to undertake, the outcomes of the TPP must be assessed as well as the transformation process that takes place during the experiment. In an ICT4D/e-government project, it is important to observe, monitor and assess the TPP at all levels (political, organizational, managerial, technical, financial and social), since such observation and monitoring provides a wealth of critical information about the way in which people, groups and institutions react to the changes that are taking place during the TPP. Such a Monitoring and Assessment Process is also very useful to identify and confirm the involvement, commitment and enthusiasm of the individuals (within and outside the institution, such as champions and involved stakeholders) who are key to the success of the TPP as well as the transformation process as a whole.

Consequently, there is a need to launch the MAP as early as possible during the TPP and to use a systematic method of assessing the TPP and how the solution developed may influence the institution. In this book, we recommend using an "outcome assessment analysis approach" (see Chapter 4) that we refined and successfully applied to the eFez Project (see Chapter 7).

H. Communication Process of the TPP

Communicating the advancement of the project to all stakeholders is very important. However, there are usually no human resources in a local government institution both available and trained to devote such communicational activities to the project. In addition, few managers and decision makers in these institutions are aware of the importance of these public relation actions when it comes to an internal project. Consequently, during the TPP, a member of the EAT should be assigned to these communication activities. A communication plan must be created and submitted to the TPP champion who will discuss it with the Pilot Team, EAT and key stakeholders before it may be approved by top decision makers. Once approved, it should be put into action and monitored like any other subproject. The effects of different communication activities should be recorded and assessed to measure the impact on the institution's personnel. Reports about the communication activities should be regularly produced and submitted to the top decision makers. Having a good communication plan can help to decrease certain employees' resistance to change and motivate others to support the project, so this usually proves to be a good investment! Hence, the TPP budget must take into account that resources should be devoted to sustain communication activities.

V. The LSDDA Phase

In this section, we describe the main steps (Inception Step, Production Step, Completion Step), the main processes (Supervision Process, Assessment Process, Training Process) and main elements (favorable conditions, involvement of champions, etc.) to be considered in the LSDDA Phase.

A. Objectives of the LSDDA Phase and main stakeholders

Here are the main objectives of the LSDDA Phase:

- Taking advantage of the results of the TPP, the aim of the LSDDA Phase is to create, deploy and assess the new ICT4D/e-government system and the associated organization (that we call the "local solution") in a significant and well-chosen part of the institution (that we call the "LSDDA sector").
- Assessing the results and outcomes of the deployment of the local solution to prepare the "generalization" of the solution to the entire institution and provide recommendations for the next phase.
- Strengthening the Pilot Team, which then becomes the Transformation Accompaniment Team (TAT), and preparing it to sustain the transformation throughout the whole project.

During the LSDDA Phase, the TPP's main stakeholders usually remain very much involved in the project. Since the TPP has been a success, they are still enthusiastic and hopeful that the expected transformation can occur in their institution. Consequently, we do not usually observe much change in the roles of the top-level champions (top managers). Usually the TPP champion remains in charge of managing the LSDDA Phase, but s/he is now titled the LSDDA champion. This LSDDA champion will still work in close collaboration with the supporting teams (EAT and EDT) that are also extended, if deemed necessary.

The External Assessment Team (EAT) still provides:

• Experts experienced in ICT4D projects and transformation management approaches; they usually play the roles of facilitators and trainers.
• An organizational/social scientist and a communication person (playing a liaison role).

The External Development Team (EDT) still provides:

• Experienced individuals who play the roles of project manager, architect, analyst, designer, developer and quality assurance staff that support the development, deployment and maintenance of the new software solution (the LSDDA solution).

We suggest that the TPP Pilot Team be transformed into (and renamed) the TAT. According to our experience, this seemingly small name change corresponds to an important organizational change, although it is not mentioned in the literature. During the TPP, the Pilot Team was composed of managers and employees who were "pioneers": dedicated and enthusiastic people who believed that the institution was able to move from its fossilized and archaic state to a dynamic and modern mode of operation and governance. In the LSDDA Phase, the Pilot Team will be extended, with new managers and employees joining to participate in the transformation of the operations in their respective sectors. But, in order to start preparing the institution for the significant transformation that it will undergo in the coming years, we recommend to officially change the name of this extended team to the TAT, putting the emphasis on the fact that it becomes the Transformation Accompaniment Team. Changing names is symbolic but significant in ICT4D/e-government projects, not only to recognize the important role played by the dedicated people involved in the project, but also to sensitize top managers about the importance of this TAT that supports and sustains the transformation. As we will see in the next two sections, it is a major challenge to ensure the success of the project in the long term. Through this change of name, all stakeholders will become aware of the change of roles of the Pilot Team members in this crucial phase.

Moreover, beyond the name change, the former Pilot Team needs to "mutate" during the LSDDA Phase by also undergoing a transformation that will prepare it for the upcoming Generalization Phase of the Transformation Project. Following the experiment carried out during the TPP Phase, the project is moving toward the creation of an operational solution implemented, deployed and assessed in a selected part of the organization: the LSDDA sector. After the successful completion of the LSDDA Phase and the top decision makers' GO decision to move to the Generalization Phase (see next section), the extent of the transformation will be considerably enlarged and will ultimately affect all parts of the institution. Hence, there will be an urgent need for additional human resources to carry out the training and coaching of the institution's employees and managers who will have to learn new skills and know-how (new procedures, ICT-based systems, workflows, relationships and responsibilities). Consequently, the capable and dedicated people who have been actively involved in the early stages of the transformation process (TPP and LSDDA Phases) will be solicited to share their experiences and know-how with the other employees. Some of them will need to become coaches and trainers, but such a transformation in roles takes time. We therefore recommend that selected employees and managers are prepared and motivated for these future roles as early as possible in the transformation process. This is why we recommend the creation and training of the TAT during the LSDDA Phase.

In addition, we suggest that the TAT be comprised of two subteams: a Technical Support Team (TST) and a Trainers' Team (TT). These subteams will collaborate with each other and be trained and coached by the EAT and EDT:

- The TST is composed of carefully selected capable and motivated employees who will have to deal with all technical problems related to the operation of the software system (software, hardware, materials like paper, ink, etc.)
- The TT must be set up when there are a large number of employees needing to be trained. This team will have to train all civil servants (managers and employees) who will apply the new administrative procedures and use the software system of the proposed solution.
- As soon as the TST and TT subteams have more than two members, one of the team members in each subteam should take responsibility for coordinating their work, becoming the managers of the TST and TT subteams.

In many cases, the initial people participating in these two subteams have already been members of the Pilot Team. But these subteams need to be readily extended with new capable and motivated people. This is a major

Figure 6.4. The LSSDA Phase template

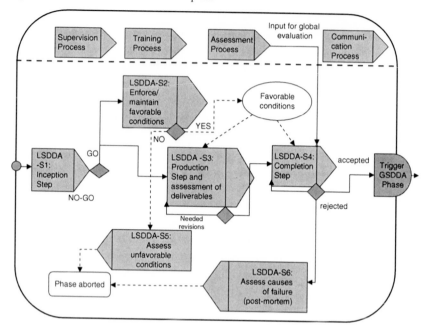

challenge for local governmental institutions in developing countries which lack well-trained people. We also recommend the official creation of the LSDDA Management Team, composed of the LSDDA champion and the managers of the TAT, EAT and EDT. It is important to create such a project management team to coordinate the project as a whole and to make timely decisions in agreement with the institution's top decision makers.

Before moving onto the detailed presentation of the main steps and processes of the LSDDA Phase, let us look at its global template (Figure 6.4). We have classified each step of this phase with the identifiers, starting with LSDDA. Hence, LSDDA-S1 is the Inception Step, the first step of the phase.

B. Inception Step of the LSDDA Phase

Let us recall that for each phase of our roadmap, the Inception Step aims at setting up clear goals and orientations for the phase and identifying means and resources to fulfill these goals in an adequate timeframe. This naturally leads to the elaboration of a plan for the phase. This plan should be discussed and refined with the main decision makers and stakeholders to get their approval and support. This is critical for the success of the phase. If the LSDDA Management Team fails at reaching an agreement with the decision makers and stakeholders about the LSDDA Phase plan, an assessment of this failure should be readily made and proper action must be carried out since that may mean discontinuing the phase at this point. Indeed, many organizational issues that were considered during the TPP still apply during the LSDDA Phase: maintaining favorable conditions, the involvement of champions and

Box 6.2. Some favorable conditions for a LSDDA Phase that we identified in the context of the eFez Project

---

- Sensitize top managers and champions so that they continually support and promote the project
- Officially acknowledge the change of perspective and focus of the LSDDA Phase toward the successful transformation of the LSDDA sector due to the implementation of the ICT4D/e-government solution and good governance principles
- Officially appoint the LSDDA champion and the members of the TAT and officially recognize the role and responsibilities of each individual involved
- Officially recognize the importance of the LSDDA Management Team
- Share and update the project vision with all stakeholders, including new employees and managers who join the transformation process
- Get an appropriate budget and set a reasonable time frame for the LSDDA Phase
- Set clear goals and a formal Monitoring and Assessment Process
- Continuously carry out the Monitoring and Assessment Process
- Provide all the teams (TAT, EAT, EDT) with adequate resources in a timely fashion
- Find people within the organization who are willing/eager to make the transformation happen, and contribute to create/develop/adapt structures/procedures to successfully transform the institution
- The TAT should be given autonomy as soon as possible
- Set up a favorable "atmosphere" for the LSDDA Phase:
  - Use a partnership/participatory approach
  - Think of incentives/rewards for dedicated employees
  - Establish a "sense of the importance of the LSDDA Phase for the organization" and communicate it
  - Sensitize top managers about the importance of concretely demonstrating support for the TAT and the LSSDA Management Team, as well for all involved stakeholders

stakeholders, updating and sharing the project vision, careful planning and monitoring of the project, involvement of the EAT and EDT, assessment of the project progress in relation to good governance principles, etc. Other issues increase in criticality such as identifying and training motivated and skillful employees to join the TAT and preparing efficient and appropriate training programs. Some of these issues can become true challenges to the project success and must be carefully addressed.

Be aware that the project vision may change, at least slightly, as you move from the TPP to the LSDDA Phase. This is normal and should be expected since now the top decision makers, champions and the EAT and TAT have a better and clearer understanding of the institution's situation and its reaction to change. The LSDDA Management Team should be careful to involve all the main stakeholders in updating the project vision so that they will appropriate it and consequently increase their support for the institution's transformation.

The software development plan for the LSDDA Phase should be set at the start of this phase, and be monitored and revised throughout its duration. Progress must be monitored and appropriate decisions should be made and actions performed to address the issues and problems that will inevitably arise during the development of the local solution (software and workflows).

C. Production Step of the LSDDA Phase

Let us emphasize that, even if the LSDDA solution is developed in the same sector in which the TPP was carried out, the LSDDA Management Team should be careful not to try to reproduce the TPP solution as such in the LSDDA sector without assessing its suitability for this part of the institution. Indeed, different strategies might have been explored during the TPP to find a solution to the institution's problems. Since the experiment has been carried out in the pilot cell, which was a small part of the institution, new factors and issues which have not been foreseen yet might arise when considering a larger part of the institution. Hence, the development of the LSDDA solution for the LSDDA sector may significantly differ from the TPP solution.

D. Completion Step of the LSDDA Phase

In the LSDDA Phase, the Closure Step aims at officially recognizing the completion and deployment of the LSDDA solution. It is an assessment of the results/outcomes of the solution for the institution's LSDDA chosen sector. This assessment has to be completed carefully by the EAT alongside selected stakeholders (particularly members of the TAT and the LSDDA champion). The assessment report must clearly present the results of this assessment with proposed recommendations for the next phase, which will generalize the solution to the whole organization (see Section VI). This is a critical step which takes time.

The results of this assessment and the associated recommendations are presented to the institution's top decision makers and discussed with champions and selected stakeholders.

The generalization strategy and plan to be carried out in the next phase (GSDDA Phase) is discussed and adjusted and if all favorable conditions are met, the GO for the generalization can be given by top decision makers.

In some cases, the development of the LSSDA solution may result in a failure (either partial or total). This failure should be carefully analyzed and its reasons explained so that the institution can learn from it. In other cases, the institution might not be ready to extend the local solution for a variety of reasons (lack of political and institutional will to carry out the transformation in the other sectors of the institution, lack of adequate financial and human resources, etc.). Please refer to Section II in this situation.

E. Supervision Process of the LSDDA Phase

As in each phase of the project, rigorous management techniques should be applied during this phase by the LSDDA champion and the involved teams (TAT, EAT, EDT).

The Transformation Project Board (*"comité directeur" du projet de transformation*) may be changed (or extended) to reflect the interests of the different parts of the institution involved in the LSDDA Phase. Let us recall that this board is comprised of selected key top decision makers and some of their supervisors (politicians), the LSDDA champion and the managers of the TAT, EAT and EDT. The board has the responsibility to make strategic decisions related to the Transformation Project as a whole and to the LSDDA Phase in particular.

Carefully monitoring the solution deployment is also critical to this phase. During the deployment of the solution in the LSDDA sector, special attention must be devoted to new issues that might arise when new parts of the institution become involved in the transformation process, especially in the context of ICT4D/e-government projects in developing countries where nothing should be taken for granted. Hence, in each part of the institution where the solution is implemented or deployed:

- The infrastructure must be set and operational;
- The software solution must be installed and tested to ensure that it is operational; and
- The users must be sensitized before the deployment of the system.

When the system is operational, users (civil servants) must be trained by the trainers of the TAT and then coached as they use the system. New procedures and behaviors with clients (citizens, customers) must be explained and effectively implemented in a new spirit (for example, by emphasizing customer satisfaction).

Customers (i.e. citizens) must be introduced to the new way of accessing the institution's services (possibly through the use of software and hardware tools such as a kiosk or online services).

The project must carry out an assessment of the solution and its deployment and record the reactions of users (civil servants), managers and customers (citizens). Surveys must be conducted by independent individuals (usually working under the supervision of the EAT) and results should enable them to measure the degree of satisfaction of the institution's customers and employees while collecting customer input (identified problems, suggested improvements, etc.).

Recommendations about the support to be given to the TAT

The Technical Support Team (TST) and Trainers' Team (TT) must be "empowered" (given official roles, responsibilities and incentives) by top decision makers and their roles and responsibilities must be officially communicated throughout the institution. This is often a challenge in local administrations of developing countries where there is a widespread inertia. Appropriate resources should be allocated to the different teams and parts of the institution to carry out the operations related to the new ICT-based solution. This change in budget and allocation of resources must be acknowledged by the institution's top decision makers and managers.

F. Assessment Process of the LSDDA Phase

Let us recall that the Monitoring and Assessment Process (MAP) should be carried out in parallel with the steps of the LSDDA Phase and aims to observe the progress of the LSDDA Processes from an external point of view. The MAP is usually carried out by the EAT. Following the TPP, the LSDDA Phase is focused on creating and deploying a solution that is adapted to selected parts of the institution. Indeed, the outcomes of the LSDDA must be assessed as well as the transformation process that takes place during the deployment and use of the solution in the LSDDA sector. In an ICT4D/e-government project, it is important to observe, monitor and assess the LSDDA Processes at all levels (political, organizational, managerial, technical, financial and social) since such observation and monitoring provide a wealth of critical information on how the relevant people and groups react to the changes that are occurring. Such a Monitoring and Assessment Process can also identify and confirm the involvement, commitment and enthusiasm of the people within and outside the institution (champions and involved stakeholders) who are key actors on the success of the LSDDA Phase, as well as for the transformation process as a whole.

At the end of the LSDDA Phase, it is also important to evaluate the complete implemented solution with respect to the possibility of deploying it to the whole organization. This is the main objective of the Completion Step in relation to the Assessment Process. The issue of deploying the solution to the whole organization is not trivial.

The capacity of the local solution to support the global operations of the organization must be evaluated and potential new problems identified. Here are some issues to be considered:

- Can the system architecture of the local solution be adapted to support the whole organization?
- Which adaptations must be carried out? Does this require reengineering the software solution? Are there new needs for hardware/connectivity, human resources, additional budgets, etc.?

These issues will be addressed right at the beginning of the GSDDA Phase.

Taking advantage of the analysis of the outcomes of the LSDDA Phase and the lessons learned during this phase, the TAT and EAT should also prepare an actualized vision of the project toward the creation of the generalized solution.

G. Communication Process of the LSDDA Phase

The communication process of the LSDDA Phase is the continuation of the communication process of the TPP Phase, but on a larger scale. Hence, the communication plan should be updated and adequate resources allocated with the support of top decision managers.

H. Training Process of the LSDDA Phase

The members of the Technical Support Team (TST) must be trained and supported by some members of the External Development Team (EDT) to learn their tasks and develop the required skills to deal with all technical problems related to the operation of the new system (software, hardware, materials like paper, ink) that is deployed in the part of the institution involved in the LSDDA Phase.

The members of the Trainers' Team (TT) must be trained by some EAT members (the trainers/facilitators) to become the institution's local trainers. They will be initially trained to use the system perfectly and be involved in the development and use of the new software and the new workflows. A complementary and important part of their training will be to develop the training material to train the future users of the new system/procedures (workflow). This development of the pedagogical material is also carried out under the supervision of the EAT members (the trainers/facilitators) who will provide further support (coaching) to the TT members when they train the institution's employees, at least during the first training sessions.

Box 6.3. Note about the Technical Team EDT

The EDT normally has all the skills to develop the global solution based on the experience gained through their development of the local solution.

The challenge is to make this team grow smoothly (with skilled and trained people) and to ensure that its management team is able to tackle the growing team and the project as a whole. For an established software development team, this is not a challenge. However, this is a challenge for a start-up team in a developing country.

The EDT must also be aware of the importance of staying in close communication with the end users and managers of the institution to develop a new software solution that meets their needs. It is important that end users feel that their needs and requirements are understood to motivate them to adopt the system.

The EDT should also be able to train the institution's capable personnel at a technical level, at least for the basic maintenance/support tasks with the hardware and software. These trained employees will become members of the TST who will maintain and service the new e-government system installed in the different parts of the institution. This is a big challenge in developing countries' governmental institutions (at the municipal level).

VI. The GSDDA Phase

In this section, we describe the main steps (Inception Step, Production Step, Completion Step), the main processes (Supervision Process, Assessment Process, Training Process) and main elements (favorable conditions, involvement of champions, etc.) to be considered in the GSDDA Phase.

A. Objectives of the GSDDA Phase

Here are the main objectives of the GSSDA Phase:

- To spread the local solution to the whole institution
- To help the whole institution undertake its transformation in the best possible conditions

Let us emphasize a practical issue related to champions and stakeholders who have been actively involved in the ICT4D/e-government project during the TPP and LSDDA Phases: some of them might leave the institution or change roles. Such changes may occur when a project lasts several years. This could have a significant impact on the success or failure of this phase which may need several years to be completed. Hence, the institution may need to identify new top management champions who will be eager to support the transformation process in the whole institution. As previously stated, the support given by champions (key top decision makers, managers and employees) at all levels of the institution is one of the most important success factors of ICT4D/ e-government projects.

Hopefully, the LSDDA champion will remain in charge of managing the GSDDA Phase to become the GSDDA champion. He/she will still work in close collaboration with the supporting teams (TAT, EAT and EDT) that are also extended, if deemed necessary. But in certain cases (especially for strategic and/or political reasons), the GSDDA champion role might be assigned to a new person or even to a new group of people. In such a case, the LSDDA champion and the EDT must carefully sensitize and train these individuals so that they will be able to gradually assume the responsibilities and leadership of the Transformation Project. According to our experience, such a situation always induces disturbances in the project and delays the whole transformation process. During this phase, it is still critical to identify, sensitize and train people, such as managers and employees, eager and capable of supporting and promoting the transformation in the rest of the organization. They will become additional champions of the Transformation Project. Another challenge is to keep the motivation of top decision makers as high as possible and make them aware of the importance of their continuous support for the project. They must also communicate their support publically and adopt concrete measures to enforce favorable conditions, so that these conditions become "part of the institution's normal life."

As in previous phases, the project must be carefully managed by the GSDDA management team, composed of the GSDDA champion and the managers of the TAT, EAT and EDT. If new people assume responsibilities

Figure 6.5. The GSSDA Phase template

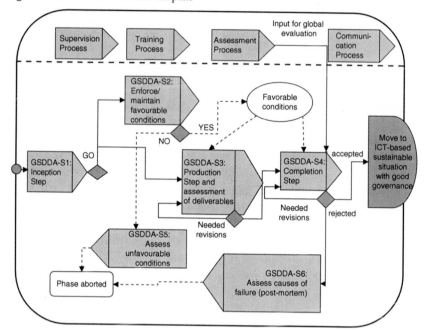

in these different roles, they must have experience in project and team management and be introduced to the specific management culture of this ICT4D/e-government project. Figure 6.5 displays the template of the GSDDA Phase.

It is similar to the LSDDA Phase template. The difference that we need to keep in mind is that the completion of the GSDDA Phase aims to finish the deployment of the new IC4D/e-government solution in the whole institution so that the transformation process takes place toward an "ICT-based sustainable situation with good governance."

Let us recall that this implies that the institution must be able to completely assimilate the transformation and that the GSDDA Phase should be run in parallel with the TTA Phase (see Section II and Section VII).

B. Inception Step of the GSDDA Phase and challenges

The GSDDA Phase starts after the GO decision of the institution's top decision makers. Taking advantage of the analysis of the outcomes of the LSDDA Phase and the lessons learned during this phase, the TAT and EAT should again prepare an actualized vision of the project toward the creation of the generalized solution.

During the Completion Step of the LSDDA Phase, the complete implemented local solution has been assessed with respect to the possibility of deploying it to the whole institution. Hence, during the GSDDA Inception Step the global solution should be planned and designed according to its capacity to support the whole institution's needs and solve problems that have not been encountered during the LSDDA Phase. These new problems may require reengineering the local solution before it can be efficiently deployed in the whole organization. This may also require reengineering of the workflows.

It is also obvious that the generalization of the solution will require additional resources, especially human resources. Hence, the TAT and EAT must convince the institution's top decision makers to allocate these new resources to the project. We mention this issue that might seem obvious to people working in developed countries because it may become a true challenge in developing countries where trained human resources are scarce and politicians are not aware of the real human and budgetary needs when operationally using ICT in their institutions.

Moreover, the GSDDA Management Team needs to provide a list of adequate resources that should be allocated to this important phase of the Transformation Project: time, human resources, training resources, material, budgets, etc.

A work plan should be set up with a schedule for the design and implementation of the global solution, taking advantage of the outcomes of the local solution as well as the feedback from their users and customers.

This plan is presented to the decision makers of the whole organization who are concerned with the project, as well as to champions and key stakeholders, for discussion, refinement and approval.

A communication/sensitization plan must also be discussed with top managers and carried out to sensitize other people in the institution and prepare them for the proposed new ICT-based organization (new hardware, software, workflows, relation with customers, etc.)

Favorable conditions are still crucial during this phase, with:

- Enlarged support for the implementation/deployment of the global solution to other parts of the institution:
  - Support by top managers and decision makers (including champions)
  - Support by additional champions among managers and employees
- Clear commitment to and support for the institution's top management in the deployment of the solution. This commitment must be clearly communicated to all employees.
- Adequate budgets and anything that is needed to carry out the transformation as smoothly as possible.

- Identification and recruitment of human resources (internally and/or externally) that will join the TAT.
- The TAT should be given autonomy as soon as possible.

C. Production Step of the GSDDA Phase

The roadmap of this step is quite similar to the roadmap of the development of the local solution. Special care should be devoted first to the infrastructure (rooms, hardware, etc.) and connectivity issues and to making sure that all parts of the institution are able to install the newly deployed software. Secondly, the development and deployment of the global solution and the training of all categories of personnel that will use this solution should be synchronized, so that they will be ready to use it as soon as it is available.

The GSDDA Management Team must not forget to "revisit" the initial parts of the institution in which the local solution has been deployed and is still currently used. If the global solution is different from the local solution, a plan should be prepared to migrate the local solution toward the global solution when it will be ready for deployment. Consequently, deploying the global solution in the initial part(s) of the institution in which the first local solution(s) were implemented may involve some reorganization (business processes, new training).

The development and deployment schedule of software/hardware must also be carefully orchestrated with the overall implementation of the global solution in the institution. This requires coordinating the schedules for:

- Sensitizing/informing/motivating the various categories of personnel.
- Developing training plans for all categories of personnel (including the training of possibly new trainers/coaches of the TAT who will be needed during the GSDDA Phase).
- The gradual deployment of the solution, incorporating the prioritization of the parts of the institution in which the global solution will be first implemented.
- The creation and implementation of a plan for sensitizing and informing customers (citizens).
- The creation and implementation of a plan to collect data in order to monitor the impact of the global solution in the institution and responses (behavior, satisfaction) of the personnel and customers. Ideally, the technical EDT has already developed functions to automatically collect statistics about system use, embedded in the new system.

D. Completion Step of the GSDDA Phase

At the end of the GSDDA Phase, the Global Solution and Development Process should be assessed and a report should be written and submitted to the institution's authorities. This report should present the main results of the global solution, its impact on the institution's transformation and the lessons learned. The report, assessment and recommendations should be presented and discussed with the main stakeholders in order to prepare the next phase of the project (sustainability of the solution).

E. Supervision Process of the GSDDA Phase

As in each phase of the project, rigorous management techniques should be applied during this phase by the GSDDA champion and the involved teams (TAT, EAT, EDT).

The Transformation Project Board *("comité directeur" du projet de transformation)* may be modified to reflect the interests of all the institution's parts. Let us recall that this board is composed of selected key top decision makers and some of their supervisors (politicians), the GSDDA champion and the managers of the TAT, EAT and EDT. The board has the responsibility to make strategic decisions related to the Transformation Project that now should be completed during the GSDDA Phase.

F. Assessment Process of the GSDDA Phase

The GSDDA Management Team must keep in mind the importance of carrying out an assessment of the global solution, its deployment and the reactions of users (civil servants), managers and customers (citizens). Surveys must be conducted by "independent" individuals (usually working under the supervision of the EAT) and results should measure the degree of satisfaction of the institution's "customers" and employees while collecting comments and suggestions on problems and improvements.

Let us recall that the MAP should be carried out in parallel with the steps of the GSDDA Phase and is aimed at observing these steps from an external point of view. The MAP can still be carried out by the EAT, but some people in the TAT (such as TT managers) can be trained to carry out such an assessment. This will prepare them for the transition to autonomy (see Section VII). In an ICT4D/e-government project, it is important to observe, monitor and assess the GSDDA Process at all levels (political, organizational, managerial, technical, financial and social), since this observation and monitoring will provide a wealth of critical information on the reactions of the relevant people and groups to the changes that are taking place during the GSDDA Phase. Such a Monitoring and Assessment Process is also very useful to strengthen the involvement, commitment and enthusiasm of the individuals (within and outside the institution) who are key actors (champions and involved stakeholders) on the success of the transformation process as a whole.

Regular reports of this assessment must be provided to the TAT and EAT as well as to the GSDDA board and to the institution's top decision makers. Indeed, any problem (political, organizational, managerial, technical, budgetary) which arises during the GSDDA Phase must be promptly reported and assessed and solutions must be found and readily implemented. The GSDDA Management Team should be aware that the magnitude of the problems may increase dramatically when generalizing a local solution to the entire institution. Hence, prompt decision making and actions are essential to the success of this phase.

G. Training Process of the GSDDA Phase

When the system is operational, users (civil servants) must be trained by the TT and then coached during their use of the system. New procedures and behavior with customers (citizens) must be explained and effectively implemented in a new spirit by, for example, emphasizing customer satisfaction.

Customers (citizens) of the whole institution must be introduced to the new way of accessing the institution's services (possibly the use of software and hardware tools such as a kiosk and/or online services). This is in line with what has been carried out during the LSDDA Phase. Now the TT has acquired good experience in carrying out these sensitization campaigns.

Training/coaching of people involved in the project

- During the GSDDA Phase, a large number of people (managers, employees) will need to be trained in the use of the new software and the application of the new workflows. The training demand will increase significantly with respect to the previous phases' needs.
- Hence, the institution faces more big challenges: the strengthening of the TT and helping its members to create training programs (modules) to introduce the global solution to the various categories of employees involved. In addition, the TT managers need to be trained by the EAT to efficiently manage such training programs.
- Moreover, the EAT (coaches, trainers, facilitators) and the trainers of the initial TT play an important role in recruiting and training new trainers. Another challenge is to enable these key persons to enhance their skills

and confidence toward autonomously managing the institution's new training programs. Most of these employees and managers need to develop many skills: team management, meeting management, planning and scheduling, pedagogy and discipline, as well as flexibility, human contact, coaching, etc.

- Considering the different parts of the institution in which the global solution will be implemented, the TT, EAT and the institution's managers should identify the most capable/willing persons to be trained first.
- These persons will become the promoters and champions of the solution in their respective parts of the institution.
- Some of these persons may become future trainers and coaches and join the TT.
- The same issues of empowering/recognition/incentives (see the TPP and LSDDA Phases) must be sensitively handled for these employees to ensure retention of these valuable resources.
- The training plan is usually articulated in three steps:
  1) Train the most capable and willing people first and try to motivate them in order to persuade a few of them to join the TT
  2) Develop a plan with these "first trained personnel" to train other personnel in the institution
  3) Carry out the training program with the different categories of personnel
     - Take the opportunity to train the newly recruited TT members in training and coaching skills
- When considering middle-level and top-level managers, these key persons should be trained with respect to their new roles and activities in relation to the implementation and sustainability of the global solution:
  - This training is carried out through workshops taught by the best trainers/facilitators of the TT and/or the EAT, who have different experiences and the credibility to influence these top-level managers. At this level, the emphasis is not on technical training but on the management aspects of making the global solution sustainable. A facilitation approach is mandatory for this kind of training since conflicts may appear, often as a consequence of scarce resources, past delusions, etc.
  - Two major challenges here are the availabilities of the top decision makers and the challenge of making them aware that an ICT project is not managed like their other projects. It requires their active and continuous involvement and attention to provide adequate resources in a timely manner.

VII. Transition to Autonomy (TTA) Phase

In this section, we describe the main steps (Inception Step, Production Step, Completion Step), the main processes (Supervision Process, Assessment Process,

Training Process) and specific issues (favorable conditions, involvement of champions, etc.) to be considered in the TTA Phase.

A. Objectives of the TTA Phase and main stakeholders

In parallel with the Generalization Process of the ICT4D/e-government solution (during the GSDDA Phase), and in addition to the goal of implementing and deploying the global solution, a critical objective is to help the institution to become autonomous and able to progressively integrate the solution to its mission and operations as a new way of doing business. The aim is to make the solution sustainable after the completion of the Transformation Project. This is the goal of the TTA Phase. Here, autonomy means that personnel (decision makers, managers and employees) will be able to take care of the solution at all levels (politically, technically, in terms of business procedures, budgets, etc.).

This goal may appear obvious, but in ICT4D/e-government projects this is a major challenge. As discussed earlier, the vast majority of apparently successful ICT4D/e-government projects fail shortly after the removal of external financial support and the disengagement of the EAT and EDT. Such failures usually result from the inability of the institution to operate, monitor and adapt the solution without the external support that it benefited from during the ICT4D/e-government project.

The TTA Phase should start before the completion of the Global Solution Deployment Phase (GSDDA Phase). Indeed, if you wait until the completion of the GSDDA Phase, the risk is that budgets provided by external institutions (international development agencies) to your ICT4D/e-government project will run out, and the EAT will not be available anymore (unless another source of funding becomes available).

At first glance, the stakeholders involved in the TTA Phase are the same as those involved in the GSDDA Phase. However, depending on the institution and the workload of the GSDDA Management Team as well as the availability of members of the TAT, EAT and EDT, it might be a good idea to assign a different group of persons to manage the TTA Phase in close coordination with the GSDDA Management Team. As we already mentioned in Section II, it is strongly advised to manage this phase as an independent subproject and assign an appropriate budget to it, as well as skillful and available human resources.

The Transformation Project Board (*"comité directeur" du projet de transformation*) should be actively involved in the GSDDA Phase and the TTA Phase at the same time. The board needs to make informed and strategic decisions which firstly address the issues and possible problems related to the implementation, deployment and appropriation of the global solution by the institution, and secondly aim to make the solution sustainable in the long run.

B. *Inception Step of the TTA Phase*

Here are some major challenges of the TTA Phase's Inception Step:

- The first challenge is to convince the institution's top decision makers and key managers that this phase is crucial and that they need to act as soon as possible to make the transition toward autonomy as smoothly and efficiently as possible.
- Recall that in the vast majority of ICT4D/e-government projects, the sustainability issue is very critical, and a large number of successful projects fail after the external support (funds, expertise, coaching, mentoring) disappears. We suggest that the team:
  - Make the TTA Phase an explicit phase in the overall ICT4D/e-government project (as we propose in this chapter).
  - Manage this phase carefully as another phase with an explicit TTA work plan, schedule, resource allocation, budget, clear milestones and deliverables/milestones toward autonomy.
- The second challenge is to convince the top managers and senior managers to act upon the adoption of the TTA work plan/schedule:
  - All managers will fully agree with the goal of making the solution sustainable and the institution autonomous with respect to the operation of the ICT-based solution.
  - But in practice, in ICT4D/e-government projects and a large number of development projects supported by external organizations, top managers tend to delay decisions, arguing that they do not have the required budget or human resources when very often they do not want to hire new resources or even invest money to train their employees sufficiently so that they become able to sustain the global solution.
  - Here, again, champions play a key role, but be aware that "the early champions" who were very active and enthusiastic about the project at the start may become tired as their enthusiasm fades away, or may have moved away during the project.
    - **Advice:** Keep your critical champions (especially those who are at the top level of the institution) as enthusiastic as possible and try to identify new influential champions who will be able to promote and support the TAT Phase and bring it to a successful completion.

Adoption of the TTA Phase by top decision makers, managers and champions

- The TTA Phase must have high visibility among top decision makers, managers and champions of the solution, and be endorsed as such. All of them must fully understand that the institution will go through a complete transformation.

- A person in senior management at the institution must be officially appointed as the coordinator of the TTA Phase. Ideally, this senior manager is a champion of the project and has lots of authority/recognition and good management skills. We call this person the TTA champion.
- It is important that top decision makers and senior managers of the institution understand that an ICT4D/e-government project differs from the kind of project that they usually manage (in the city infrastructure and construction domains, for example), which consists of contracting some works to private companies and making sure that the work is carried out as planned (e.g., road or street modifications, building renovation, etc.)
- An ICT4D/e-government project requires that managers and employees of the institution adopt new ways of carrying out their activities. New activities take place in relation to ICT and the computerized system, procedures, responsibilities, functions, etc. It is necessary that people act autonomously and responsively.
- One or several meetings (or workshops) must be prepared and enacted by the GSDDA champion and the EAT with the objective of making top decision makers and senior managers aware of the challenges of completing the TTA Phase successfully:
  - The initial meeting will present and discuss the goals of the TTA Phase, as well as the challenges to be met and constraints that may limit or threaten the success of the TTA Phase. The TTA Management Team must then be officially appointed. The TTA Management Team will work in close relation with the TTA champion.
    - **Advice**: Start the Transition to Autonomy Phase as soon as possible in parallel with the GSDDA Phase.
    - **Remark**: During the GSDDA Phase several measures have been taken to prepare the institution to reach the autonomy/sustainability of the solution. Take advantage of close coordination of the TTA and the GSDDA Phase.

C. Production Step of the TTA Phase

- The TTA Management Team should prepare an initial version of a work plan that we call the TTA plan
- When the initial version of the TTA plan is ready, it is presented to top decision makers and senior managers for review and discussion. This meeting is very important and aims to refine the TTA plan in such a way that it is feasible and satisfactory for everyone. This meeting should be

jointly enacted by the TTA champion and the TTA manager, with the latter taking the role of facilitator:
- This enables the TTA champion to fully intervene in the discussions and the TTA manager to appear as the "main architect" of the TTA plan
- The TTA plan can be refined during several meetings
- When the TTA plan gets the agreement of the top managers and support of the senior managers, it must be supported by appropriate resource and budget allocations

TTA Plan: Budget, resources and schedule

- Several important issues should be considered related to the TTA plan:
  - Management/governance of the Transition Phase
  - Allocation/engagement of human resources
  - Redefinition of responsibilities and tasks
  - Progressive assignment of human resources to their new tasks (freeing the persons from previous operational tasks and replacing them with new personnel to carry out these tasks who have been previously trained)
- "Governance" of the Transition Phase (management):
  - This is a critical issue, since clear governance rules should be established and agreed upon in order to formalize and make official the transformation of the institution's organizational structure.
  - This structural transformation should be carefully devised, and one should establish the corresponding business procedures, the descriptions of the new roles and positions, interactions with the other parts of the institution, etc.
  - A transition plan should be proposed to facilitate the transition from the old organizational structure to the new one, taking into account the transformations carried out during the GSDDA Phase (which runs in parallel with the TTA Phase).
  - The plan includes the assignment of resources to the new positions proposed to sustain the new organizational structure.
- Identification and assignment of resources to the new organizational structure:
  - The persons should be selected, motivated and trained for their new roles and tasks. These persons will usually come from the TAT and therefore be already motivated, knowledgeable and experienced.
  - Note that the TTA Phase runs in parallel with the GSDDA Phase and the people that are members of the TAT are already very much involved in helping, coaching and monitoring the deployment of the global solution.

Hence, giving them official duties and responsibilities in the TTA Phase aims at preparing them to become increasingly active (and proactive) to monitor and support the TTA Phase, and decreasingly involved in the GSDDA Phase when the new global solution will become more and more stable.

- Budgets, resources and schedules must be carefully managed during the TTA Phase.

As already mentioned, the TTA Phase should be managed as a project in itself. As in each phase of the project, rigorous management techniques should be applied throughout.

The role of the EAT and EDT is crucial during this phase. They must train, advise and accompany the TAT Management Team the TST and TT, as well as the institution managers and decision makers as they gradually take over the responsibilities and tasks carried out by the EAT and EDT. Hence, these teams should work in close collaboration with the TAT Management Team as well as the GSDDA team and provide them with all required expertise. The EAT and EDT may need to hire additional experts in business transformation processes.

D. Completion Step of the TTA Phase

Ideally, the end of the TTA Phase coincides with the completion of the GSDDA Phase. Hence, the global solution should be operational in all parts of the institution. Most managers and employees should use the new ICT4D/ e-government system. The new workflows as well as the new administrative and managerial procedures should be used routinely. In addition, the completion of the TTA Phase should have brought autonomy to the institution in the sense that the decision makers, managers and employees will no longer need support, especially from the EAT and EDT.

Practically, some transitory measures should be agreed upon so that even after the completion of the GSDDA and TTA Phases, the institution should be able to punctually access the advice of former EAT members when deemed necessary. However, it may be very difficult for local governmental institutions in developing countries to develop autonomy with respect to the technical tasks related to the development, maintenance and upgrading of software systems of the magnitude of ICT4D/e-government systems. This responsibility should be outsourced to a private software company with good expertise.

E. Supervision Process of the TTA Phase

The Transformation Project Board (*"comité directeur" du projet de transformation*) may be modified to reflect the interests of all parts of the institution.

Box 6.4. Outsourcing the development and technical support of the ICT4D/ e-government system

This is an important strategic issue that should be considered very early in the project. Our advice is that this issue should be addressed, at least by an initial investigation, as soon as the end of the LSDDA Phase, when there are good signs that the project will be carried out toward its generalization to the whole institution.

Two main avenues can be considered: either contracting the software development, deployment and support to an existing software company, or creating a start-up company with the EDT members who have been involved in the project during the TPP and LSDDA Phases. This is a challenge that a young team of well-educated people trained in computer science and business administration might be eager to tackle. Taking the perspective that favors developing the local technical resources of developing countries to narrow down the knowledge divide, such a possibility is appealing and seems preferable to contracting out to big foreign software companies. But this is a strategic issue that needs to be considered carefully for each ICT4D/e-government project.

Let us recall that this board is composed of selected key top decision makers and some of their supervisors (politicians), the GSDDA champion and the managers of the TAT, EAT and EDT. The TTA champion and manager join the board who has the responsibility to make strategic decisions related to the Transformation Project during the GSDDA and TTA Phases.

F. Assessment Process of the TTA Phase

The TTA Management Team and the institution's top decision makers must keep in mind the importance of carrying out an assessment of the outcomes of all the actions and decisions made during the TTA Phase. Such an assessment will be best made by experts who are not involved in the TTA Phase and who are able to step back and analyze that institution's situation and its evolution in a much-needed objective way.

These experts should be able to monitor the progress of the GSDDA and TTA Phases to detect potentially difficult situations as soon as possible and advise the GSDDA and TTA Management Teams as well as the institution's top decision makers.

Hence, a MAP should be carried out in parallel with the GSDDA and TTA that aims to observe the outcomes and outputs of these phases from an external and independent point of view. The monitoring must take place at all levels (political, organizational, managerial, technical, financial and social), since such observation and monitoring provide a wealth of critical information on the way in which relevant people and groups react to the changes which are taking place during the GSDDA Phase and which are reinforced during the TTA Phase.

Regular reports of this assessment must be provided to the TAT and EAT as well as the Transformation Project Board and the institution's top decision makers. Indeed, any problem (political, organizational, managerial, technical, budgetary) which arises during the GSDDA and the TTA Phases must be promptly reported and assessed so solutions may be found and readily implemented. The GSDDA and TTA Management Teams should be aware of the importance of the problems that may arise when generalizing an ICT4D/e-government solution to the whole institution when working toward its technical, managerial and financial autonomy. Hence, prompt actions and decision making are essential to the success of these phases.

G. *Training Process of the TTA Phase*

Training is also a key issue during the TTA Phase. The same advice that we gave for the GSDDA Phase still holds in the TTA Phase. However, we should mention that the emphasis of training programs and actions will plausibly move from the technical and administrative content conveyed to the institution personnel shown during the GSDDA Phase toward a more managerial content that aims at helping the institutions' key decision makers and managers assume the responsibilities and tasks of the EAT and EDT.

VIII. Conclusion

In this chapter, we presented the generic roadmap that we developed, refined and applied over several years in different ICT4D/e-government projects. We hope that the reader will have found interesting information, advice and lessons that can be applied to his or her own project. It is clear that a roadmap, like any analysis and design method, needs to be adapted to the particular context of a given institution and a particular project. This is the duty of a competent project manager or project management team.

In the next chapter, we present the story of the eFez Project and illustrate how the generic roadmap has been applied and customized to this particular context.

Chapter 7

THE EFEZ PROJECT ROADMAP

I. Introduction

In Chapter 6, we proposed a generic project roadmap based on our experience in managing a number of ICT4D projects in different situations and countries. The eFez Project has been an important source of inspiration for us in the creation of this generic roadmap. In this chapter, we describe the instantiation of this roadmap specific to the case of the eFez Project and other related projects in Morocco. This specific roadmap that we call the "eFez Approach" was created and refined during the eFez Project. Our goal is to share the experience that we gained while using this roadmap to develop and successfully deploy e-government systems at a municipal level.

The creation of the generic roadmap (presented in Chapter 6) is chronologically subsequent to the eFez Project, since the conceptualization effort that it required was built on the course of events, knowledge, successes and set-backs of the eFez Project along with a number of other similar projects including the LOGIN Africa Project (Waema & Adera 2011). While the global roadmap was inspired by the eFez Approach, it is very different, with an enhanced structure, content and dynamics. In this chapter, we chose to present the eFez Approach in a narrative manner to enable the reader to feel as close as possible to the way in which things actually occurred in the eFez Project.

In the subsequent sections of this chapter, we present and discuss noteworthy events, decisions and actions that occurred during the eFez Project which have been selected to illustrate the important issues and advice that featured in Chapters V and VI in relation to the four main phases of the generic roadmap: the TPP, LSDDA, GSDDA and TTA Phases. In this way, we also intend to raise the reader's awareness of practical problems and important issues that may arise in the course of e-government projects in developing countries. We also hope that the reader will understand that the generic roadmap can be used as a set of guidelines that should be customized to the particular context of any new e-government project.

It is also relevant to mention that the characteristics of the International Development Research Center's (IDRC) international funding program which financially supported the eFez Project and influenced its "project timing." The project was financed in two stages. The first stage, named "eFez Project Phase 1," aimed to prove the feasibility of developing an e-government system: practically deploying it, assessing its impacts and outcomes in a scientifically sound way and engaging Fez's main stakeholders. This first stage was carried out between mid-2004 and mid-2006 and corresponds to the TPP Phase of the generic roadmap (Chapter 6). eFez Project Phase 1 was successfully completed and the IDRC agreed to support the project in its scaling-up stage, named eFez Project Phase 2, which was carried out between mid-2006 and 2009 and corresponds to the LSDDA, GSDDA and TTA Phases of the generic roadmap.

II. The eFez Approach

From the very beginning of the eFez Project, we (the eFez Team leader and external advisor) were convinced that the project's success was dependent on the disciplined application of a structured approach for the creation, development and deployment of the envisioned ICT4D/e-government system. We were also very conscious that we would need to advise and accompany Fez's decision makers, managers and employees throughout the project duration to help them smoothly navigate the transformation that the creation and deployment of the future eFez System implied. We were certain that we required a method that not only provided practical guidelines during the different phases of the project, but which would also provide the means to raise the awareness of the various stakeholders involved in the project with respect to the impact of their decisions on the governance changes. Such a method would be of paramount importance to guiding the eFez Team as well as Fez's involved stakeholders throughout the entire lifecycle of the eFez Project.

This issue of raising the main stakeholders' awareness about the various facets of the project (including good governance, the importance of managing the institution's transformation, the human factors, etc.) through this method was an important aspect of the eFez Project which was not discussed in Chapter 6.

With this in mind, before the end of the first year of the eFez Project, we established the following set of fundamental principles that guided the elaboration of the eFez Approach:

• Introducing e-government systems usually results in major changes in citizens' habits and administrative services (especially in developing countries), and these systems should aim to improve citizens' interactions with administrative services and ensure cost efficiency.

- Numerous decisions have to be made at different levels of the institution's hierarchy with constant concern for improving good governance.
- The primary issues are not technological, but, rather, are related to individuals' openness and willingness to change their habits and assume responsibility for successfully carrying out these changes. This leads to the need for the development and deployment of e-government systems that emphasize good governance.
- A vision should be developed during the earliest stages of the project and upgraded and sustained throughout. This vision should be developed with the aim of improving governance as much as possible.
- It is of the utmost importance to involve all stakeholders in the project as soon as possible, and explain the project's vision and orientation to them with a primary focus on the improvement of governance while supporting their deliberations. All stakeholders need to share, adopt and possibly contribute to the project vision.
- It is necessary to assess and monitor the indicators measuring the project outcomes continually to ensure and highlight governance improvements and to enable a prompt reaction to any difficulties that inevitably arise.

The eFez Approach is quality driven and inherits from the principles of software quality engineering (Tian 2005). It encompasses all the phases of software system development, deployment and assessment with a special emphasis on the harmonization of the different views of all stakeholders in relation to governance improvement. Here are some important principles and assumptions:

- All stakeholders should be involved as early as possible in the project and their motivation should be kept as high as possible throughout the entire project
- Special care should be given to sustain favorable conditions for the project from its onset to its completion
- Special care should be devoted to the creation and updating of a project vision to which all stakeholders must adhere
- Outcomes and outputs of the project should be identified as early as possible and refined throughout the project with special concern for governance improvement
- The method should cover all the traditional steps of information system development, delivery and deployment with an emphasis on quality software development related to improved governance

Figure 7.1 presents a graphical overview of the eFez Approach which includes four main phases:

1) Sustaining favorable conditions during the whole project
2) Inception
3) Development and deployment of ICT/e-government system
4) Systematic assessment of project outcomes.

In this figure, graphical conventions were applied:

- The method's *phases or steps* are represented by *plain rectangles*.
- The main *actors* such as stakeholders and champions are represented by little *"human" icons*.
- The main *data or knowledge stores*, which are inputs or outputs, are represented by *rounded rectangles*.
- An *arrow* drawn from a rounded rectangle (data or knowledge store) to a rectangle (phase or step) shows that the associated store is an input to the associated phase or step. If the arrow is drawn from the rectangle to the rounded rectangle, it means that the associated store is an output of the associated phase or step.
- Sometimes the same set of rounded rectangles may be related to different rectangles, as, for example, the *expected deliverables*, the *updated vision and expected outcomes* and the *system quality attributes* in Figure 7.1. In such cases, we may embed all these rounded rectangles in a *surrounding rounded rectangle*: the arrows coming from and going to this surrounding rounded rectangle are equivalent to arrows reaching each of the rounded rectangles individually.
- A double arrow shows a bi-directional exchange between a rectangle (phase or step) and the associated rounded rectangle(s) (stores). The same representation rules apply to the links between rectangles and actors.
- A *cloud-like shape* represents the relevant elements of the milieu in which the method is carried out. In our case, these elements essentially correspond to the conditions that influence the project (what we call the situation). The *situation* encompasses all the elements of the institution (ministry, municipality, company, etc.) that influence the *institution's functioning* in relation to its *clients* (mainly citizens in public settings, or the whole society if we consider a global governmental point of view) as well as to the organizational, social, political and economic circumstances. Let us first emphasize that we distinguish three situations that characterize the institution: before, during and after the system development and deployment. They are represented by the cloud-like shapes in Figure 7.1. It is important to distinguish these situations to make all stakeholders aware that the institution's characteristics change

Figure 7.1. Overview of the eFez Approach

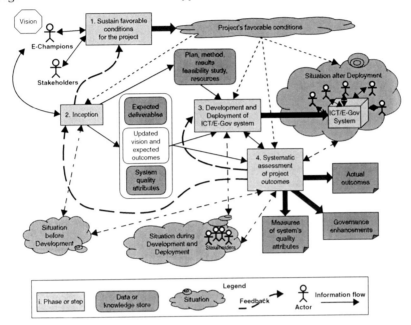

during the project and that these changes should be carefully considered and monitored in order to make appropriate and timely decisions.

For reasons already mentioned in the introduction to this chapter, we chose to present the original version of the roadmap here that we developed for the eFez Approach. Let us look at its similarities and differences from the generic roadmap presented in Chapter 6. Historically, the eFez Approach was developed and practically applied during the eFez Project Phase 1 (corresponding to the TPP Phase of the generic roadmap in Chapter 6). During the scaling-up stage that took place over the three years of the eFez Project Phase 2, we found out that the eFez Approach still applied with minor variations. Thus, the general template that we propose in the generic roadmap (Section III of Chapter 6) reuses the steps of the eFez Approach and adds the supervision, training and communication processes that were not formally pictured in the presentation of the eFez Approach.

Conversely, let us also observe that Figure 7.1 presents much more details than the general template of Section III in Chapter 6. We think that showing these details will help the reader understand how such a general template can be customized in the context of a particular phase (in our case, the TPP Phase) of a particular project (in our case, the eFez Project).

Let us now detail the different steps of the eFez Approach.

A. Creating and maintaining favorable conditions step

This step is active throughout the whole project. It consists of creating and maintaining all the conditions that will stimulate the project's progress. This step involves the different concerned stakeholders, among whom we distinguish the project's champions (called e-champions) that promote and support the project at all the critical levels of the institution's hierarchy. The project's management team must be aware that certain stakeholders and e-champions may change over time and that it must act accordingly in order to maintain favorable conditions for the project even with the changes taking place in the institution. The thin dashed arrows in Figure 7.1 show that these favorable conditions influence every step of the project.

B. The Inception Step

This step is critical for an e-government project which can only start when a minimal set of favorable conditions are met, among which the strong will and influence of high-ranked e-champions who support the project are of paramount importance. These favorable conditions should build up as early as possible. The e-champions and the project management team must develop a clear and structured vision of the future e-government system and the outcomes it must provide to the institution and its clients. The Inception Step is paramount to helping e-champions shape their vision and refine their expectations with respect to the project's outputs (main deliverables) and its outcomes. During this step, most critical stakeholders are led to share this vision and reach a consensus on the project's main targets (outputs and outcomes).

The Inception Step (see Figure 7.2) is composed of several substeps that help one understand the relevant elements of the "before development situation," mainly by carrying out a feasibility study (incorporating models of organizational procedures, identification and the characterization of existing relevant systems) and establishing a diagnosis related to the possibility of achieving the goals set for the project. During the Inception Step, the development team must help the e-champions and stakeholders clarify how the vision and project's outputs and outcomes will enhance the governance. This is a critical issue that aims to assign the right goals to the project for the right reasons.

From a technical point of view, the development team (which corresponds to the EDT of Chapter 6) and certain technical stakeholders should also set technical norms and goals based on quality criteria which foster improved

Figure 7.2. Inception Step of the eFez Approach

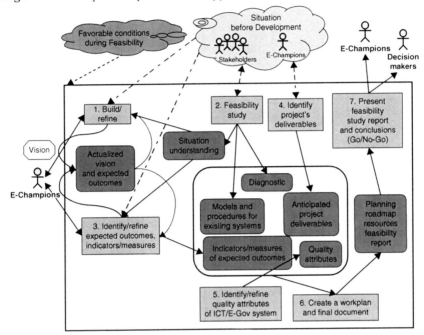

governance to orient technical decisions related to the system development and deployment (to be used in the next step). The Inception Step ends with a general presentation of the main findings to the e-champions and decision makers who will have to decide to continue or end the project (GO/NO-GO decision), taking into account the available resources, anticipated risks and presence or absence of favorable conditions.

As shown in Figure 7.2, the main outputs of this step are the "expected deliverables," the "updated vision and expected outcomes" and the "system quality attributes" as well as the plan, method, resources and results of the feasibility study which are all inputs to the Development and Deployment Step.

C. The Development and Deployment Step

This step starts whenever the GO decision has been made after the completion of the Inception Step. A critical success factor is to maintain favorable conditions throughout this step. All the Inception Step's outputs are available during the development of the e-government system. The Development and Deployment Step (see Figure 7.3) mainly consists of substeps similar to those

Figure 7.3. Development and Deployment Phase of the eFez roadmap

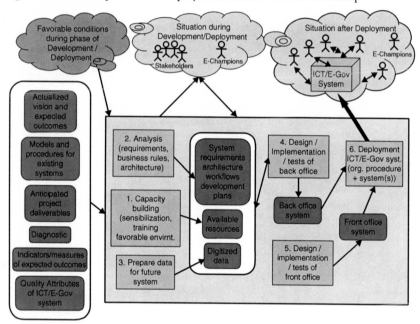

found in traditional analysis and design methods applied to the creation of information systems such as:

1) Requirement analysis
2) Creation of a "solid" system architecture
3) Business analysis refinements and development of new workflows, taking into account the introduction of the e-government system in the institution
4) Usability analysis, creation of interfaces
5) Analysis and design of the software
6) Implementation, integration and tests of the software
7) Deployment of the software, implementation of new workflows and required adjustments

Again, during this step both organizational issues (procedures, workflows, business rules, etc.) and software development issues are addressed. The technical norms and goals, based on quality criteria fostering improved governance and set during the Inception Step, are refined during the Development Step and give strong directions to the development and deployment of the ICT4D/ e-government system. As in all the method's steps, a special emphasis is put on respecting the project's vision which strongly influences the system's architecture and the different technical decisions that are made with the aim

Figure 7.4. The "systematic assessment of project outcomes"

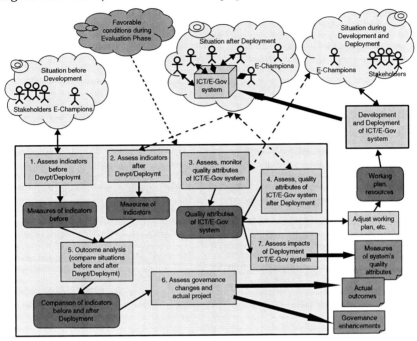

of achieving the outcomes set in the previous step. Hence, there is a guarantee that the project will provide the best outputs and outcomes possible given the situations that prevailed before and during the development and deployment of the system. This emphasis on working toward a significant improvement of governance should be adopted by all the development team members as well as the majority of stakeholders.

D. The "systematic assessment of project outcomes"

The "systematic assessment of project outcomes", or the Assessment Step (rectangle 4 in Figure 7.1), is also a very important step of the eFez Approach that is carried out in parallel with the other steps. Its goal is to systematically assess and monitor the evolving situation during the course of the project with respect to the achievement of the expected project outcomes and system quality attributes with the aim of improved governance. During this step, favorable conditions should be maintained. They may be different and/or complementary to those that must prevail in the other steps, since the right environment must be established in order to conduct the various investigations needed to carry out the assessments.

Figure 7.4 presents the main substeps of this Assessment Step.

A scientific analysis of the results must be done to assess, explain and justify the outputs delivered by the project against the expected results and the project's impact compared to both the anticipated outcomes and the project vision of improved governance. Hence, a first assessment of the situation is carried out in parallel with the Inception Step to obtain the data which will be used to measure the indicators associated with the expected outputs of the system.

We developed a specific approach to identify such indicators and measures and applied it to the eFez Project (Kettani et al. 2006). The first steps of this approach (mainly the selection, definition and refinement of suitable indicators and measures) significantly contribute to the refinement of the anticipated outcomes established during the Inception Step (represented as a feedback loop by a dashed curled arrow linking rectangles 4 and 2 in Figure 7.1). In the same way, the assessment of the system's quality factors, in parallel with the Development and Deployment Step, can raise some warnings that will enable the project managers to adjust the course of this step. This is also shown in Figure 7.1 by the dashed curled arrow between rectangles 4 and 3. More details are provided in Chapter 4 of this book.

As already mentioned, the eFez Approach has been successfully applied with minor variations to all phases of the eFez Project (corresponding to the TPP, LSDDA and GSDDA).

In the following sections, we discuss some prominent facts that illustrate the effective application of the eFez Approach with reference to the phases of the generic roadmap. We will use the terms used during the eFez Project, such as the eFez Team, as well as terms introduced in Chapter 6 such as the Pilot Team, EAT and EDT.

III. The TPP Phase of the eFez Project

The main objectives of the TPP Phase, as stated in the generic roadmap, are to:

- Elaborate a clear mission, vision and goals to be presented and agreed upon by the institution's top managers;
- Build a dedicated project team supported by enthusiastic e-champions;
- Understand the current situation and status of the institution and arouse and nurture a synergetic and positive spirit among all stakeholders about the positive impacts/changes the ICT introduction will have on the institution as a whole and on individuals who are a part of it;
- Create and maintain favorable conditions;
- Create, refine and update the project vision and identify expected outcomes;
- Propose a solution (i.e., hardware and communication network, software, management procedures, customer relations, etc.) that will sustain the

transformation process and the implementation of an ICT4D/e-government approach, using appropriate technologies (ICT) and taking into account the project vision as well as the institution's needs and constraints;

- Continually assess the evolving solution to produce data and progress reports that will readily and effectively support the top managers' and stakeholders' decision making process; and
- Enable top managers to assess and decide if this experiment fulfills their goals and can be used as a basis to carry out the process that will lead to the institution's effective transformation.

Retrospectively, we can say that most of these objectives have been addressed and met by the eFez Phase 1, through activities and actions that took place in the four steps of the eFez Approach. Let's visit some salient details with respect to these in the following sections.

A. Vision, mission and objectives of eFez Phase 1

Our research vision was, and still is, to promote ICT as an important vector to support and induce socio-economic changes in Morocco through its dissemination in different sectors of activities.

Our research mission was, and still is, to develop different pilots in different sectors and elaborate a roadmap to speed up their dissemination process along with an impact/outcomes assessment to convince decision makers to support their adoption decisions.

Our research mission was to develop a pilot e-government system to enable online delivery of citizen-oriented services to the local community of the city of Fez. The project aimed to: (1) propose a method (or roadmap) that can be used to replicate the experience in other Moroccan cities; and (2) assess the influence of such systems on the everyday life of Moroccans and on enhancing governance in general.

B. Champions, stakeholders and team building

A special emphasis was put on mobilizing and motivating all relevant stakeholders to share our mission, vision and goals and on the careful elaboration of indicators and measurement techniques to assess the project outputs with respect to enhancing governance quality. The team adopted a participatory approach from the very beginning of this phase and started by communicating and explaining the eFez Project's main idea and its related objectives to Fez's decision makers. This was important to sensitize and mobilize Fez's local decision makers to embrace and support the eFez Project vision.

In the eFez Approach, the term 'stakeholders' refers to the institutions and individuals concerned with succeeding and benefiting from the eFez experience. These stakeholders include Fez parliamentarians, politicians at the Fez local government, administrative executives at Fez's local administration and citizens' representatives. Let us look now at the main actors who actively participated in the TPP Phase.

As the city of Fez had no employees with the knowledge and expertise to develop computerized systems, the eFez Team was created at the project's startup and was responsible for managing the project and delivering the TPP outputs. The eFez Team was composed of the project leader and two collaborators from Al Akhawayn University (AUI) in Ifrane, and was counseled by an external advisor from Laval University in Canada. Some developers were also hired by the eFez Team and worked in the ICT4D Lab at AUI to support the various technical activities during the TPP including the development of the required software pieces. During the TPP, it was not possible to include employees and officers of any *bureau d'état civil* (BEC) in the eFez Team because nobody was trained and ready to participate in the project management activities. Fortunately, some BEC officers and employees who were actively involved in the design, testing and use of the first prototype of the eFez System during the TPP showed their interest and capacity to engage more actively in the project as trainers and coaches of their peers. They will later become part of the Transformation Accompaniment Team (TAT) in the LSDDA and GSDDA Phases.

After building the foundations of a shared vision, the eFez Team engaged all stakeholders throughout the different phases of the project to ensure that the project met local needs and aspirations. Since they were local actors, these stakeholders were eFez agents of change, assisting project efforts and activities by effecting concrete change on the ground. Therefore, the eFez Team identified stakeholders explicitly showing interest in actively participating in the eFez Project and called them "e-champions." In this respect, the eFez Project had various e-champions at the political, organizational and civil society levels to facilitate a smooth transition to the new e-government approach.

The Agdal Arrondissement's president was one of the main champions of the eFez Project.[1] He strongly supported the project and proactively took the responsibility of supervising the legal aspects and the administrative validity of certificates delivered via the eFez System. When the project started, Agdal Arrondissement officers were somewhat reluctant to support us because of past bad experiences with similar initiatives. Nevertheless, with the instructions

---

1   The Commune of Fez is divided into five arrondissements (counties), each of which have an average of five BECs (*bureau d'état civil*) under the authority of the arrondissement's chairman (president).

and engagement of the arrondissement president, we received all the support that we needed.

C. Refining the project objectives

eFez Phase 1 started with the official launch of the eFez Project in June 2004 during the Kick-off Workshop which assembled distinguished participants from the city of Fez, representatives of AUI in charge of the project, representatives of the Moroccan Ministry of Interior, Canadian advisors and representatives of IDRC. This workshop helped participants present and discuss the project's goals and main challenges, potential solutions, anticipated impact on the local and national governance and similar e-government projects carried out in other countries.

At an organizational level, the eFez Team worked closely with BEC executives and employees throughout the project. Accordingly, the eFez Team assessed the service delivery system existing prior to the eFez System implementation to gain insight into BEC regulatory and legislative framework, organizational structure and functionalities and their related defaults, and employees' expectations. One of our findings is the fact that Morocco's legal and regulatory policies are lagging far behind ICT progress. To enable the project implementation, the eFez Team invested in the groundwork necessary to understand the legal framework regulating the service area in which the project was introducing ICT. Such an understanding was a prerequisite for developing ICT applications that comply with the existing legal policies, and thus maintaining the trust of BEC executives.

To modernize the BEC service delivery, it was decided not only to automate the back office (i.e., offer software support to the employees and managers of the BEC), but also to create an electronic front office that would enable citizens to access the BEC services autonomously, using either a digital kiosk in the BEC office or the Internet. As a first service, the eFez Team chose to develop a system computerizing the BEC citizens' life records.[2]

---

2   The eFez Team is the name that was chosen by the group of people who were very much involved in the eFez Project since its beginning. This group was mainly composed of the project leader and his collaborators at AUI, the external advisor from Laval University, Canada and key employees and managers of the city of Fez. The eFez Team evolved over the years, but the core of initial participants remained stable during the whole duration of the project. In this chapter we will often refer to the eFez Team, although sometimes we will use the terms that we introduced in Chapter 6, namely the TAT, EAT, EDT and TT to emphasize the specific roles of team members.

D. Proposing / developing an ICT platform

The eFez Team realized at the outset of the project that the involvement and active participation of ordinary citizens was crucial for the project's success. Accordingly, at a social level, the eFez Project used many research methods to gain insight into citizens' needs and aspirations and gather their input and feedback with regard to the project progress and its ICT-deployed outputs. The eFez Team proceeded to find out about citizens' expectations on the BEC automation.

For instance, in October 2004, the eFez Team launched a survey on Fez citizens' readiness to use an e-government system deployed on their behalf. Specifically, the survey aimed to identify the demographic profile and ICT habits of the main citizen groups requesting BEC services, as well as their attitudes toward the Fez e-government portal that was underway. The main outcome was to discover citizens' positive attitudes toward the initiative of building the Fez e-government portal and to highlight the desire for three public services to be made available on the Fez portal: online local government information on administrative procedures, the online possibility to request/ receive public services and interactive areas for posting comments and complaints. A large proportion of respondents preferred the portal content to be in Classical Arabic (63.1 percent) and to access it without interacting with BEC employees.

Based on these encouraging findings, the eFez Team proceeded to design the ICT-related outputs of the eFez Project. The eFez Team made several site visits to assess the need for building and deploying a functional e-government system. The team realized the need to build everything from the ground up because of the overall lack of electronic infrastructure in the Fez municipal administration. The existing networking infrastructure was obsolete and not functioning. The eFez Team decided to work with only one pilot BEC during the TPP Phase: the Agdal BEC located in the Fez–Agdal Arrondissement. The team also had to choose which services to automate. The advice of the officers and especially the senior officer of the *État Civil Division* at Fez–Agdal Arrondissement were very useful. With his intimate knowledge of BEC services, the senior BEC officer suggested that the team start by electronically enabling the service delivery of birth certificates because they are widely requested throughout the year and the regulations determining the workflow are simpler and less bureaucratic than other BEC services. Thus, the TPP experience was limited to the development and deployment of a system for the electronic delivery of citizens' birth certificates.

One of the first activities of the TPP Phase was to conduct a complete study to identify and compare technology enablers (benchmarking), including considering open source solutions. This identification was very important since it allowed the eFez Team to gain insights about available technology and software suitable for Moroccan municipal institutions. Then, the eFez Team selected the technology enablers suitable for the project's needs.

Early in the TPP Phase, the EDT proceeded to install the necessary IT infrastructure (e.g., cabling, wiring) with the involvement and active participation of Fez IT personnel (only comprising of one person at that time!) The installation activities were conducted in such a way as to enable and assist the IT personnel to acquire technical skills needed for the maintenance work. Therefore, involvement in this activity was something of a training opportunity for Fez IT personnel.

In order to design, implement and deploy the system for birth certificate online delivery, electronic access to citizens' life event records was needed. The eFez Team expected such electronic access (citizens' database) would be available in other institutions such as the police administration, the Ministry of Interior or any other institution in Morocco. However, the team discovered that this data had never been digitized in any city or BEC in Morocco. For example, Agdal BEC keeps life event records of around 17,000 citizens on paper. The EDT attempted to scan these paper-based records, but with this method the margin of error exceeded 60 percent due to the inconsistent handwritten Arabic script. This meant that the EDT had to build the system from scratch, not only deploying an online delivery platform but also computerizing and digitizing the data that the platform would need to process for the delivery. In other words, the eFez Team realized they would need to work on both the BEC front and back offices, as well as developing the digitizing software and associated workflows. Citizens' records are critical data that need to be accurately and securely digitized and validated.

To automate the BEC's back office, the eFez Team and the EDT were required to design, implement and deploy a citizens' database and system that digitizes and electronically manages citizens' recorded life events. Building this part of the back office system demanded precise system requirements and the teams had to complete this task without assistance, as the city employees were unqualified to help in this regard. Furthermore, BEC service delivery was not documented, partially because BEC law was not issued until 2003. In fact, lack of documentation is a serious ongoing problem plaguing Morocco's public administration (Ourzik 2006). In addition, the eFez Team discovered that employees working in BEC offices had not received any formal training in BEC service delivery. Most of the employees had informal on-the-job training by simply observing how their experienced colleagues carried out BEC-related tasks in a mechanical way, without understanding the legislations and regulations governing their functions. Only one senior BEC official was knowledgeable with regard to BEC legislation and regulations, having earned a Bachelors degree in law in 1975 and through 30 years of experience working in BECs. Therefore, the team worked with this expert daily for at least the first two months of the system design and implementation. Such intensive work was important because information about the BEC service delivery was only available through his knowledge. He also helped the team understand the regulations governing the BEC service delivery so that it was able to identify and collect the requirements that would determine the system's characteristics.

After the identification and selection of technology enablers, the eFez Team and the EDT proceeded to conceptualize and design an initial version of the platform architecture in which the main components of the software system were organized in a functioning and secured way:

- The software for digitization and validation of citizens' records in the database (back office)
- The system software to exploit the citizen records database and provide them with birth certificates (front office)

Then, a number of design and development activities took place:

- Creation of the client server architecture for the software application
- Identification of public services that could be delivered online
- Database design to record citizens' life events (citizen records)
- Software design and development, security and authentication protocols
- The design of an initial version of the graphic user interface (GUI) for the system

The EDT proceeded to design and implement the software to digitize the citizens' records and the system for online delivery of birth certificates (the early version of the eFez System back office).

The eFez Team worked with the Agdal BEC personnel in designing, implementing and deploying the system to digitize the data and to automate the local service delivery method (workflows). BEC officers (i.e., BEC experts) actively participated throughout the creation steps of the system and validated the new system. The development and implementation of the application was very iterative: the application went through cycles of testing and adjustments. The input garnered from Agdal BEC's personnel upheld the integrity of the digitizing system as it pertained to actual BEC business processes and internal operations. The eFez Team invited and encouraged the BEC personnel to lead in directing and guiding the design and implementation of the application's graphic user interface (GUI). Agdal BEC personnel insisted on having a

GUI that was predominantly similar to a BEC record book, reasoning that the simplicity and practicality of this representation would reduce familiarity problems and streamline the learning process.

Building the BEC back office application proved to be a very sensitive task since the BEC officers were not satisfied until the platform perfectly respected and complied with BEC regulations. For instance, mistakes that were originally made in the handwritten version of the record needed to remain in the computerized record as well because they could only be disproved through a formal court intervention. In the absence of this, corrections were not considered legally valid and regarded as punishable fraud. The eFez Team and EDT met weekly with two or three BEC officers who provided advice on the building of the database and the data entry interface. With the great number of inconsistencies in the BEC manual system, it was very difficult to find a systematic approach to building the application, but, through the full involvement of dedicated BEC officers, the eFez Team and EDT succeeded in completing the BEC database design and implementation.

Shortly after the deployment of this digitizing tool, BEC employees used the new system to computerize records of citizens' life events that were then validated by BEC officers. Finally, the personnel of the Agdal BEC shifted operations to the deployed automated system, granting them the ability to now instantly serve citizens with a few simple mouse clicks.

E. Continuing adjustments

By the end of the TPP Phase, citizens of the Agdal BEC were able to use three different modes for the submission and processing of their requests for certificates (i.e., birth, marriage, death, etc.):

- Maintaining the former practice by going directly to a BEC employee's desk
- Using a bilingual interactive kiosk (in Arabic and French) with an easy-to-use touchscreen interface
- Using an interactive bilingual Internet portal (in Arabic and French) from which document requests could be sent. In all cases, citizens were still required to pick up printed documents and pay fees in person at the BEC office

Since the deployment of the initial eFez System and the installation of the kiosk in the Agdal BEC, the eFez Team tracked the usage patterns via qualitative and quantitative data gathering research methods. From November 2005 to February 2006, the eFez Team observed periodically and conducted in-depth interviews with employees and ordinary citizens on their use of the deployed electronic delivery channels. The main finding was that almost all citizens requested their services by approaching the BEC employees in charge and that the online/kiosk delivery channels were severely underused.

In response to the kiosk underuse over the first four months of deployment, the eFez Team investigated possible means of promoting the use of the new kiosk. The kiosk channel was deployed as a mechanism to mitigate the digital divide evident in Moroccan's low access to ICT, PC and Internet. It was also a mechanism to address the high illiteracy rate which is a challenging social obstacle for Morocco. Accordingly, the eFez Team developed the kiosk to be universally accessible, usable and acceptable among local community members, regardless of the degree of literacy and familiarity with ICT. The underlying rationale was to avoid socially excluding illiterate people from BEC automated service delivery as one form of resolution of the digital divide. To solve the problem of kiosk underuse, the eFez Team started an iterative process with ordinary citizens, including the illiterate, and as such, the team was able to adjust and readjust the kiosk system to conform to citizens' feedback over the period February 2005 to March 2006. As suggested by citizens who participated in these iterative processes, the kiosk includes clear voice instructions guiding the user through the process of making his/her request step by step: the instructions were created in Morocco's dialect based on the input of the participating citizens group. The kiosk also includes culturally sensitive illustrative images to represent the different BEC services. The kiosk is built on Morocco's existing cultural conventions, allowing citizens to enter their digit information in a GUI that resembles a cellphone shape and keypad with a clearly distinguishable red button for corrections and green button to validate. Once these adjustments were incorporated into the kiosk, the eFez Team proceeded to test its use with a test group of about 70 illiterate men and women of different ages. The testing revealed that all the participating illiterates without sight and hearing problems who were able to differentiate between figures could successfully complete a kiosk request by themselves after the first initiation. The testing proved the ease of use in making requests by using the kiosk.

Nonetheless, the kiosk usage rate remained unsatisfactorily low. The eFez Team proceeded to investigate reasons behind the low usage rate regardless of the newly proposed GUI that had been validated by a large number of citizens. Observation and in-depth interviews were again conducted. The investigation revealed that the local Fez community was unaware of the existence of the touchscreen kiosk. The community recognizes bank ATMs but had no knowledge that a kiosk facilitating instant requests for BEC services was also available. The eFez Team realized that the reason behind the kiosk low usage rate was not technological but rather human and social. Citizens were not informed about the availability of such a kiosk as it was the first to be deployed in Morocco. The eFez Team proceeded to launch a communication campaign targeting visitors to Agdal BEC requesting BEC services. Specifically, the eFez Team assigned an assistant to the kiosk responsible for informing citizens about its availability, inviting them to use it, assisting them if needed and administering questionnaires so that they could participate in assessing the BEC changes from their perspective.

As a result of this iterative method, the eFez Team not only produced a kiosk to be introduced into Morocco's culture but also an adapted process with a high daily usage rate. Since March 2006, more than 90 percent of citizens' daily requests are conducted via the kiosk. There are some citizens who perceive the kiosk as a way of "making a phone call" to their BEC records to get their needed certificates! This shows that despite its unique introduction to the culture, the kiosk is the preferred local mode of conducting business with the BEC compared to the other two delivery channels. In this respect, citizens no longer approach employees to get the needed services. The kiosk is perceived as a liberator from dependency on the employees!

F. Training, communication and ownership

The project team offered employees tailored training on the new system provided at Al Akhawayn University in Ifrane (AUI). Such a training location proved to be a very good choice as most of the employees had never been to the beautiful city of Ifrane. They perceived it as a resort area and also appreciated the prime opportunity to benefit from the research facilities of AUI. In this sense, the training became very appealing to these employees. In addition to their arranged stays at AUI, the project team also rewarded the employees with monetary incentives to complete their BEC computerization training quickly and precisely. What seemed to further boost employees' motivation to achieve the eFez goals was the highly visible political leadership, as evident in influential formal delegations to Agdal BEC for site visits. These included the Canadian Governors' visit in November 2005 and the visits of Morocco's mayors and walis. With such visits, the BEC personnel realized a sense of importance. They realized they were actively contributing to a development project of high national and international significance.

Fez's stakeholders also became more interested in the successful implementation of the eFez Project due to the project's growing visibility via extensive coverage in Morocco's print and television media. Furthermore, BEC personnel were very grateful to one specific gesture from the project team subsequent to the successful eFez implementation. After the opening session of the eFez closure workshop held on July 2006 at AUI, all the participants (including national and regional decision makers) were invited for a site visit at the Fez BEC. The project team then presented them with personalized symbolic prizes and accompanying certificates commemorating their participation and signed by the project director, Dr Kettani, the IDRC officer, Dr Adel Zaim, and the Fez Mayor, Mr Chabat. Each prize and signed certificate personally stipulated the name of the person receiving them and acknowledged his/her contribution. Photos were also taken with the workshop participants. BEC personnel were very grateful for these gestures of recognition and they appreciated being acknowledged publicly with such a high-ranking audience for their part in the project's success. They indicated that one main problem of working in public administration is the fact that active employees are not widely recognized for their efforts and actions.

G. Outcomes assessment

The use of automated records, the immediate printing of birth certificates and their delivery to citizens at the employee desktop proved a success as soon as the system was deployed and put into operation in the Agdal BEC. This Pilot Project has been truly successful, receiving excellent feedback and with great satisfaction expressed by all stakeholders ranging from the city authorities to the BEC's officers and employees, as well as citizens. A survey conducted during May and June 2006 with more than 500 citizens (7.9 percent illiterate, 6.4 percent with only primary education, 32.9 percent with secondary education, 6.4 percent with junior high school and 45 percent with university education) showed that 95 percent of them used the kiosk located in the BEC office. The satisfaction was exceptionally high: 91.2 percent of respondents were very satisfied (7 percent were satisfied) and 93 percent of respondents considered the service delivery to be excellent (3 percent rated it as good).

At an organizational level, the eFez Project has revolutionized the functionality of BECs by introducing ICT and modernizing their internal operations. These unprecedented concrete improvements confirmed the great significance and value of the project to the city of Fez's employees and management and, as such, have facilitated the project's appropriation at an organizational level. In the automated BECs, employees rapidly abandoned the manual way of work and their main wish was to see the extension of the project to include other services not yet automated.

At a social level, the eFez Project improved BEC governance tools and practices, and hence enabled an unprecedentedly citizen-friendly service delivery through diversified electronic delivery channels. These new electronic modes of BEC service delivery have allowed citizens to: 1) use a simplified request/receipt process for the desired certificates; 2) decrease their dependency on employees; 3) gain instant and convenient access to the needed certificates through the kiosk or Internet to receive printed, high quality certificates, as opposed to the former handwritten ones. The instant access to the certificate delivery has eliminated queuing and the need to make repeated personal visits to the BEC. Consequently, the ills of queue jumping by "tipping" employees or using social connections were also eliminated, due in part to the timely and instant receipt of the requested certificates as well as to the reduced person-to-person interaction. In this respect, the electronic/automated service delivery allowed citizens to have access to BEC services on an equal basis.

At a political level, one major outcome of the TPP was the strong project appropriation. As previously mentioned, the president of the Fez–Agdal Arrondissement offered absolute support to the eFez Project and facilitated the provision of all needed logistics to enable the smooth implementation of the project. His strong political leadership augmented the visibility of the project at the local level as well as at the regional and national levels through the engagement of his network of influential actors, including Fez's mayor (elected position) and Fez's wali (appointed representative of His Majesty, the King of Morocco).

The TPP succeeded in demonstrating the possibility of transforming local governance structures by introducing an e-government system which enabled online delivery of citizen-oriented services. The project's research component emphasized the importance of the assessment of results, changes, outcomes and the effects of an e-government deployment on local governance quality. All initial objectives were fulfilled, including:

- The deployment of an e-government portal providing the Fez–Agdal local community with easy, speedy and convenient access to government information. This portal also includes a platform enabling the online request/receipt of one of the most actively used citizen-oriented services using a variety of devices including cellphones, PCs and touchscreen kiosks, which are located at the municipality building and available for public use free of charge.
- The elaboration of a roadmap to serve as a reference for e-government systems in other cities of the kingdom. This roadmap aims to guide and inform local and national government practitioners about good practices toward the successful implementation of e-government systems.
- The proposition of a framework of assessment and analysis of changes and outcomes generated by the deployment of electronically enabled services at the political, organizational, social and governance levels.

eFez Phase 1 was considered a true success and the arrondissement's top decision makers decided to continue the project upon the completion of the TPP. As an official recognition of its outstanding achievements, the project team was awarded the prestigious national prize, eMtiaz 2006, as the best e-government project in Morocco.

IV. The LSDDA Phase of the eFez Project

The main objectives of the LSDDA, as stated in the generic roadmap, are to take advantage of the results of the TPP in order to create, deploy and assess the new system and associated organization in a significant and well-chosen part of the institution. Usually, the LSDDA Phase is carried out in the same institution sector in which the TPP has been performed to capitalize on the momentum gained and because there are already active and supportive champions in this sector. Many (but not all) organizational issues that were considered during the TPP generally still apply during the LSDDA Phase, including:

- Maintaining favorable conditions
- Involvement of e-champions and stakeholders
- Updating and sharing the project vision
- Careful planning and monitoring of the project
- Training and coaching
- Assessment of the project progress in relation to good governance principles

Within the global vision and mission of the eFez Project, the specific objectives of Phase 2 were to improve stakeholders' readiness and awareness and to make sure that the proposed solution could be easily scaled up to the whole city. eFez Phase 2 corresponds to the two steps that follow the TPP in the generic roadmap, namely the LSDDA and GSDDA Phases. In particular, in eFez Phase 2 the LSDDA Step corresponds to the adjustment/redesign of the pilot system and its deployment in all seven BECs of Agdal Arrondissement, while the GSDDA concerns itself with the generalization of the platform to the 33 BECs of the five arrondissements of Fez Municipality.

In this section, we concentrate on salient details associated with different steps of the LSDDA Phases, as presented in the generic roadmap.

A. Maintaining favorable conditions

The Agdal Arrondissement was chosen as the LSDDA domain because the TPP had been carried out in this arrondissement where favorable conditions still held, especially the enthusiastic support of several champions including the arrondissement's president, general secretary and several employees and officers who heartily backed the project. Hence, it was decided to adjust, refine and expand the initial pilot system to a larger number of BECs of the same arrondissement.

B. Involvement of e-champions and stakeholders

The eFez Team continued to apply a "participatory action research methodology" which allows (and encourages) those involved in a project, including citizens, politicians, employees and researchers, to be active contributors to the research activities at all stages. The project led and managed the transformative changes produced by the project deployment in close collaboration with eFez partners/stakeholders. Since many of the project partners are local actors, these stakeholders are the agents of change ("e-champions"). They were integral in assisting the eFez Team to carry out change on the ground. They were encouraged to actively participate in monitoring the project implementation toward accomplishing the expected results. The project e-champions were fully engaged and encouraged to participate in further improving the eFez initial roadmap to facilitate its evolution into an applicable, reliable, and practical guiding tool toward the generalization of e-government projects in Morocco.

C. Training and dissemination

The eFez Team developed two types of training packages targeting two different audiences. The first training package targeted eFez stakeholders, who include BEC employees/officers, IT personnel and elected politicians. Such a training package aimed to enable these partners to acquire the knowledge, understanding and skills needed to use the eFez System and to become autonomous in maintaining and keeping the system functioning. The second type of training package targeted regional/central government actors: specifically, actors at the Ministry of Interior and officials operating in Moroccan cities interested and concerned with the eFez experiment. Such training aimed to raise their awareness about ICT importance, the growing dangers of the digital divide and the urgent need to advance and facilitate ICT projects' diffusion in Morocco's governmental institutions. The ultimate goal of this training was to sensitize stakeholders about the feasibility, utility and significance of generalizing and diffusing ICT within Morocco's local government structures through the replication of tools like the eFez platform to other cities in Morocco.

D. Careful planning and monitoring of the project

The project leader began to devote one full day a week to meetings with key Fez stakeholders and periodic visits to automated BECs. The weekly meetings proved to be very useful and influential for the day-to-day progress of the project. They provided a conducive environment to think collectively about project difficulties and challenges and to elaborate action plans for problem solving.

E. Updating and sharing the project vision

After conducting an "eFez stakeholder analysis," the eFez Team organized a series of workshops with selected actors to explain the eFez Project's objectives in the context of the LSDDA Phase, the proposed gradual approach of transformation and expected/desired results. In these vision sharing meetings, stakeholders agreed on the urgent need to address a common challenge: successfully conducting BEC records digitization to benefit from BEC automation.

F. A more suitable ICT platform

The LSDDA Phase aimed to generalize the automation operations so that they could be applied to any BEC. The eFez Team decided to:

1) Rebuild the eFez software by migrating to open source technologies;
2) Transform the system architecture so that it became a web application (as opposed to an application that runs locally in BECs); and
3) Add new functionalities for BEC management to deliver new categories of certificates and collect statistical data, and issue automated reports about the system usage.

The new eFez System included the following improvements:

- An enhanced module for digitizing BEC birth paper records: quality, breadth, and depth of digitization accuracy further improved. Hence, the conformity and consistency between BEC data on paper and its digitized version are more greatly developed.
- A new module to deliver life events certificates that are not generated from BEC record books and are known as *attestations administratives*. There are eleven different types of them including betrothal (i.e., engagement to be married), marriage and divorce. To enable the electronic issue of these certificates, an additional database was built, tested, validated and deployed in automated BEC offices.

- A module to digitize BEC death paper records was built, tested and validated. It was deployed for on-site testing at Adarissa BEC office. Then, after readjustments, it was deployed in other automated offices of the Agdal Arrondissement.
- An application module to generate periodic statistics associated with citizens' life events was developed and implemented. BEC offices need to send these statistics to the National Planning Department at the Ministry of Interior. Using these statistics, the Central Government carries out analyses to plan citizen-oriented services in health, education and the utilities. This module enables instant generation of the necessary statistics to further streamline employees' work and, equally as important, to improve the accuracy and timeliness of this data vital to central planning. In this regard, the module was intended to enhance BEC office external relations (i.e., reporting requirements) with the Ministry of Interior.
- A new module that enables automated counting/tracking/monitoring of two major operations: digitization operations (data entry/validation) and electronic certificate issuance.

The EDT also designed and developed a new e-government portal and its related touchscreen kiosk with a selection of the most suitable technology platforms and software to be used. This software also included content creation tools, content management tools and content delivery tools. The selected tools needed to meet and comply with the new n-tier architecture that had been chosen for the eFez system.

G. Training and coaching

During the LSDDA Phase, a few skilled and devoted BEC officers and employees were trained by the eFez and the EAT Teams to become peer trainers. They rapidly appropriated the project and became its new critical champions. They naturally led the design and development of the training pedagogic material and delivered this training to their peers under the eFez Team's supervision. Once training sessions were complete, the BEC trainers, as they were now called, shifted focus toward coaching their peers (their former trainees) to, in turn, provide support, attention, guidance/advice and on-site re-training to others as required. They conducted their coaching activities during their daily BEC visits, a valuable opportunity for them to gather statistics on weekly automation progress for each pilot BEC office. Retrospectively, and from a management point of view, this smooth creation of the "BEC Trainers' Team" was a critical success factor for the project.

H. Assessment and adjustments toward GSDDA

The new platform was successfully deployed in several BECs of the Agdal Arrondissement. The increased responsiveness of the new platform to BECs' needs helped to convince their officers of the benefits of automation. As a result, at least 30 BEC officers shifted from skepticism and disbelief to full acceptance and adoption of the system over a two year period (2007–2009).

One year's experience (March 2007 to March 2008) with generalizing automation operations provided a learning opportunity for the eFez Team and its assessment emphasized the urgency essential to rethinking the scaling-up model and making some adjustments. Several worrisome facts were revealed during the assessment of the LSDDA Phase, including that the BEC-oriented approach (digitization of citizen records in the BECs) was labor intensive and too geographically dispersed, required high coordination, monitoring and maintenance costs and, most importantly, the required trained human resources were not available in sufficient numbers. It became increasingly obvious that a model shift was strategically needed.

After a careful analysis of the situation, the EAT reached the conclusion that more centralization and control were needed to curb the inefficiencies observed and to preserve and foster favorable conditions for the efficient deployment and use of the system.

Considering the possibility of generalizing BEC automation not only at a city level but also a national level, and that the Ministry of Interior was contemplating the possible creation of national data centers to centralize the citizen records data and related services, the EAT proposed to adopt a data-center-oriented approach at the city level. The completion of the LSDDA Phase coincided with new financing from IDRC for the scaling up of the eFez System to the entire city of Fez. The objective of this new phase was to build a "sustainable" e-government system for the whole of Fez. Retrospectively, this decision and the associated new funding marked the completion of the LSDDA Phase and the start of the GSDDA Phase of the eFez Project.

V. The GSDDA Phase of the eFez Project

The main goal of the GSDDA Phase is to develop a global solution that sustains the institution's transformation process. At this point, the institution's top management, influential champions and the EAT need to carefully consider the specific issues related to the Scaling-Up Process. Again, favorable conditions need to be maintained, with special consideration given to the selection and involvement of top management champions who may or may not be the same as the ones who supported the project during the TPP and LSDDA Phases.

Another critical success factor for this phase is the identification, selection and training of motivated and skillful employees and managers who will support the transition process in the various sectors in which the solution will be adapted and deployed. Still another critical factor is the creation of a project plan and schedule for this phase that will ensure that the local solution will be adapted to the needs and characteristics of each sector and deployed in a timely and coordinated way.

In the following sections, we describe the important actions/decisions that have been made during the different steps of the GSDDA Phase of the eFez Project, according to our generic roadmap (Chapter 6).

A. *Revisiting the strategy with an extended team*

During the first three months of 2008, the eFez Team devoted much effort to sensitizing Fez's main stakeholders to the new project challenges, including motivating the other arrondissements in Fez to join Agdal Arrondissement in the eFez Project and actively participating in the scaling-up of the automation and transformation processes. Another main action of the eFez Team was to share the new project vision with all these major stakeholders to reach a consensus toward the implementation of a data center approach for the digitization and management of citizen records and service delivery through the use of the eFez System. Such a consensus was mandatory since the new vision would lead to important transformations at different levels (legal, organizational, budgetary and cultural) in the way citizens' records were managed and related services were delivered to the public. The agreement and support of the city authorities (the City Mayor, the Wali and the arrondissements' presidents) were obtained around March 2008 and the new project vision had to be readily implemented.

The next challenge faced by the eFez Team was to find an efficient strategy to create and put into operation the data center approach, taking into account the realities on the ground. The main limitation was the lack of qualified human resources, although the eFez Team had started its training efforts and devoted Fez BEC officers were beginning to train their peers. For instance, out of at least 50 BEC officers and employees who benefited from training sessions in 2007, only one officer and two employees were capable and motivated enough to lead and coach their peers in automation scaling-up activities. This reflected unaddressed problems related to the management of behavioral difficulties and control issues within the BEC.

B. Requirements for the scaling-up

The data center approach needed to provide solutions at different levels: hardware and software infrastructure, workflows and organizational settings, recruitment, training and the supervision of human resources. The initial idea was to create a fully equipped data center at the city level. The City Data Center would host the data servers connected to thin, cost-effective client computers supporting the eFez software used to digitize the citizens' records. The idea was to centralize the digitization of citizens' records from all BECs in the City Data Center which would host the teams of PN people in charge of the digitization process under the supervision of trained BEC officers and employees.[3]

The data center solution also required the development of a complete strategy for the recruitment, training and supervision of adequate human resources at several levels:

• Teams of PN people trained to digitize citizens' records
• BEC officers and employees trained to validate the digitized citizens' records
• BEC officers and employees trained to use the eFez system to provide services requested by citizens
• Trainers to teach PN people as well as BEC officers and employees how to use the digitization software, the validation system and the eFez software

In addition, the data center approach needed to provide a solution to the problem of scarce IT human resources for the ongoing maintenance of the hardware used in the Data Center and in the automated BECs. As odd as it may sound, one important practical problem that arose on a daily basis was to keep the printers operational in all the automated BECs: paper jams, lack of ink and paper alignment faults were major hurdles for BEC employees. Since technical people with minimal training in computers were not available in the BECs, it was proposed to create a Technical Team at the City Data Center level to service the BECs on a daily basis.

C. Appropriation and ownership

In April 2008, a two week session of intense work took place in Ifrane under the supervision of the external advisor and with the participation of key

---

3   PN is a French abbreviation. It stands for "promotion nationale," which is a government national program that allows municipalities to hire short-term personnel to conduct specific tasks during a defined period that ranges from couple of months to couple of years. The city of Fez allocated most of its PN labor to the citizens' records digitization activities of the eFez Project.

members of the eFez Team and a select group of BEC officers and employees (including the BEC trainers) to develop the most important parts of the data center approach, mainly:

- Appropriation of the data center vision by selected BEC officers and employees
- Development of an organizational strategy and workflow plans for the Data Center and the automated BECs
- Revision of training material for PN personnel as well as for BEC officers and employees
- Training of the selected BEC officers and employees to enable some of them to become trainers and coaches to their peers
- Creating a "team spirit" for the group of future trainers who would become responsible for the management of the Data Center and all related operations
- Creation of training plans for the Data Center group of technicians
- Organizational procedures to enable all these groups to efficiently operate when the Data Center is launched

With the close involvement of the eFez Team, the external advisor and the involved BEC officers and employees, this ambitious agenda was completely fulfilled. Most importantly, the team spirit grew during these intense days of work and a new team was created (equivalent to the Transformation Accompaniment Team, or TAT, in Chapter 6) for the training, mobilization and coaching of BEC human resources. Team members chose to call it the CERCL (Centre de renforcement des capacités locales).

During the intense working sessions in Ifrane, senior BEC officers raised a fundamental legal issue that might prevent the successful implementation of the data center solution. According to Moroccan law, only BEC officers can validate citizen records, and paper registers cannot be physically moved out of the BEC. Having the Data Center at the municipal level not only involved moving citizens' paper records out of the BEC, but also moving the records out of the arrondissement to which they belong. Such movement of data legally required the explicit approval of the arrondissement's president who is ultimately responsible for the BEC offices of his arrondissement. After few weeks of discussions with a large number of stakeholders, the eFez Team and the CERCL came up with a compromise that mitigated this legal difficulty: to locate the Data Center at the arrondissement level. This would require the creation of a data center in each of the city's arrondissements. It was also suggested to keep the CERCL at the city level. This solution was presented by the eFez Team and the CERCL supervisors to the city's top decision makers (the mayor and arrondissement presidents) and it was approved.

D. Maintaining favorable conditions

During the whole project, the eFez Team had to be constantly alert and monitor favorable conditions because unfavorable conditions would often arise without notice and create undesirable, negative outcomes. Such an unexpected situation did occur during this initial period of the GSDDA Phase, when timing was critical and preserving the enthusiasm of key stakeholders paramount. For BEC officers and employees to become members of the city CERCL, they need to be officially assigned to their new positions and be relieved of their responsibilities in their BECs. As strange as it may appear, this was a difficult issue in the context of municipal bureaucracy and lack of resources. It took several months and numerous interventions of different stakeholders before the few BEC officers and employees could be officially assigned to their new positions in the CERCL of the Data Center. Again, the eFez Team had to devote much effort to sensitively convincing the city's main stakeholders of the importance of the creation of the CERCL and the need to execute mandatory actions to operationalize it. The dedicated BEC officers and employees optimistically worked extra time to start organizing the Data Center operations, mainly creating training material, organizing training sessions for BEC officers and employees of the newly digitized BECs, coaching them in the daily operations of the eFez System and participating in the validation of the new version of the eFez2 System with the EDT.

E. A new organization

Figure 7.5 illustrates the principle dynamics of the data center solution, mainly showing the interactions and movements of different categories of personnel in the Data Center (technical people, PN people, trained officers and employees supervising the digitizing process, the coordination team and Trainers' Team) and in the computerized BECs (officers and employees needing to get training from the CERCL to use the eFez System when back in their BECs). BEC personnel would convene in groups at the city CERCL for training, then go to the data center in their arrondissement for hands-on experience by supervising the PN digitizing process, and finally return to their respective BEC offices to conduct correction and validation operations remotely via the eFez web application.

The CERCL members proposed practical organizational solutions to operationalize this new solution with regard to the movements of registers and BEC personnel:

- *Paper records' physical movement*: It was proposed to designate a person responsible for facilitating this operation, and that a records book should

Figure 7.5. The conceptualization of the data-center-oriented model with CERCL at the city level

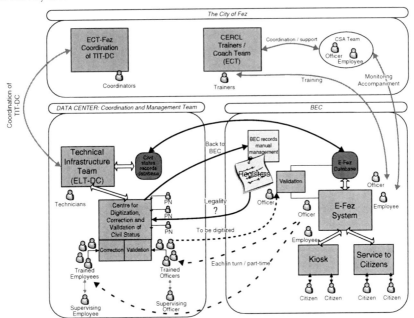

stay at the Data Center for a maximum of two weeks. During this period, an employee of the BEC should be located at the arrondissement data center to process citizens' request transmitted by the BEC and to issue the corresponding records.

- *BEC officers'/employees' movements for training*: It was proposed to maintain an up-to-date and clear planning calendar for the movements of BEC personnel.
- *Official signatures*: It was proposed to expand the signing authority for official documents so that employees and officers remaining in the BEC could continue serving citizens regardless of personnel movement. Such signature expansion needed the approval and written decision of the arrondissement's president.

F. System design and reinforcement of the ICT platform

So far, we have essentially discussed strategic and organizational issues, but the reader will easily guess that this new data center solution required important adjustments to the eFez System and the associated software modules. Fortunately, the eFez2 platform had been designed as a web application during the LSDDA Phase. This critical design decision helped the smooth evolution of the platform during the GSDDA Phase.

Once the participatory conceptualization of the data-center-oriented model was completed, the EDT moved to developing and implementing the related technological capabilities. Design and experiments were first carried out in the ICT4D Lab at AUI to build the new software platform before deploying it in the first pilot site, the Agdal Arrondissement. The data center solution was intended to enable an unprecedented opportunity in Morocco: web-based BEC processes and services. This experiment was made possible because the eFez2 software, as a web-based application, could be installed in BEC offices and run locally while remaining remotely accessible from a data center.

The eFez System's architecture has been designed to offer the possibility of interconnecting all of Morocco's 4,200 BEC offices to a national data center once Morocco's legislators officially approve this interconnection idea. The implication of enabling such interconnection was to allow citizens to request and receive their BEC certificates from any BEC convenient to them as opposed to the current situation in which an individual can only access his certificates at the BEC office where they were registered at birth, which involves high traveling costs for citizens.

Figures 7.6 and 7.7 illustrate the interconnection solution of the eFez2 Platform.

Figure 7.6. The networking architecture of the Data Center

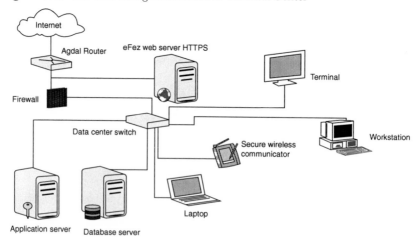

Figure 7.7. The architecture of Data Center interconnection capability

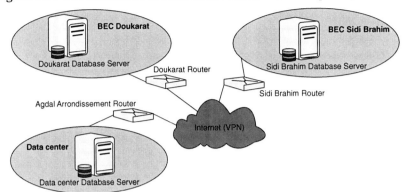

In December 2008, the Data Center platform moved from the ICT4D laboratory to the Agdal Arrondissement where the first data center was created. The EDT's engineers deployed and tested different configurations of the system. Some technical difficulties arose, such as the inability to visualize certain computerized and digitized records. Once configuration testing was completed and the infrastructure of the Data Center was operational, the new organizational solution was enforced and PN personnel moved to Agdal's Data Center to resume records digitization operations. Simultaneously, officers of Agdal's automated BECs were able to connect to the Data Center via the eFez2 web application to visualize the digitized records and correct and validate them remotely from their respective BEC offices.

G. Training and coaching

While the Data Center provided a way of accelerating the digitization of BEC citizens' records, it also offered an environment where BEC officers and employees could convene in groups. They received their initial tailored training from the CERCL trainers and then received more advanced training from the supervising officer of the arrondissement data center, who involved the trainees in the correction and validation of records digitized by PN personnel (often records from their own BECs). So, overall, they gained a wide range of concrete exposure to real life aspects, issues and cases of automation. Once approved by the supervising officer/employee, the groups of trainees could go back to their respective BECs and start remote correction and validation of the records at their BECs that were digitized in the arrondissement's data center.

H. Starting the scaling-up

The data center implementation and operation at Agdal Arrondissement provided a convincing demonstration to the other Fez arrondissements, which helped to strengthen their engagement in the city's e-government transformation process. In the meantime, each of the other Fez arrondissements (apart from Agdal) had one "pilot BEC" fully automated. The BEC personnel were trained, digitization operations were completed by PN personnel in the BECs and the eFez2 system was subsequently used by BEC employees and officers on a daily basis to provide services to citizens and to validate digitized records.

The presidents of all the arrondissements of Fez were now enthusiastically supporting the project. Some arrondissements were less advanced than others in the transformation process and were not ready to implement the data center solution, essentially due to the lack of trained human resources (BEC employees and officers) to operate the Data Center. Consequently, a scheduling plan was developed by the eFez Team, the EDT and the CERCL for the creation of the remaining data centers.

Table 7.1 illustrates the timings of the main steps toward the creation of the various data centers. The reader will appreciate the importance of adequately planning such major operations and mobilizing all the needed resources.

As it can be observed, the last data centers were put into operation in September 2009. Retrospectively, December 2009 can be considered as the end of the GSDDA Phase and the beginning of the TTA Phase of the eFez Project.

VI. The TTA Phase of the eFez Project

As stated in Chapter 6, this step aims to prepare and deploy the necessary structures and elements to enable a sustainable autonomy in the institution that is using an e-government system. Autonomy means that the institution (decision makers, managers and employees) is able to use, manage and sustain the automation at all levels (politically, technically, in terms of business procedures, budgets, etc.). Autonomy is a clear indicator of a successful institution transformation using ICT4D, and its maturity toward the usage of ICT to enhance good governance.

Unfortunately, due to a significant lack of awareness about the importance of the TTA Phase, most successful e-government initiatives in developing countries fail shortly after the removal of external financial support and the disengagement of the Pilot Project team members and the EAT. Such failures are usually the result of the institution's inability to operate, monitor and sustain the solution autonomously. In the eFez Project, given the importance

Table 7.1. Data center replication status within Fez

Fez's Six Counties	When was the data center idea accepted?	Data Center Implementation Steps					When was the data center operational?
		County's venue allocation	Venue repairs (doors, paint, electricity)	Cabling installation (entrusted to AUI)	IT material delivered (by AUI)	Office supplies (tables, chairs, etc.)	
Agdal	Fall 2007	December 2007	January 2008	February 2008	March 2008	February 2008	Since March 2008
Zouagha	November 2008	December 2008	December 2008	December 2008	April 2009	December 2008	Since January 2009
Fez-Medina	February 2009	February 2009	March 2009	March 2009	April 2009	June 2009	Since February 2009
Maryneen	February 2009	March 2009	March 2009	April 2009	April 2009	September 2009	Since September 2009
Jnan Ward	January 2009	January 2009	January 2009	February 2009	April 2009	September 2009	Since September 2009
Saiss	March 2009	March 2009	April 2009	September 2009	April 2009	September 2009	Since September 2009

Figure 7.8. Model of change emerging with eFez2 implementation

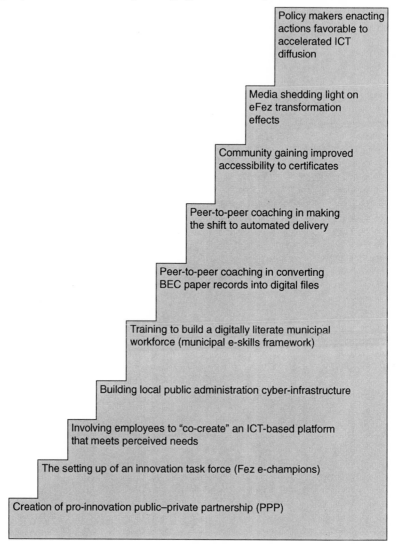

of the early preparation of this stage, the eFez Team started working on it long before December 2009, the date of the official end of the financial support of the project by the IDRC. Most notably, several data centers were not yet fully operating and a significant number of BECs were not yet automated. The lack of resources (financial and human) and the inertia of the institution as a whole were important constraints to the steady advancement of the e-government transformation. Our research team started first with the "e-champions' profiling analysis" and followed a formal "outcomes mapping framework" to track partners' behavioral changes and predict the long term viability of the project stakeholders. This facilitated the gradual implementation of eFez action research that shaped and endorsed the following model of change:

Clearly, the eFez Project generated several outcomes in behavioral changes at the community level, public administration level and policy level. Such influence on stakeholders' attitudes, behavior and decisions rest on the eFez Approach: creating an environment where research results are systematically converted into practice fully materialized on the ground. In this sense, it built a collaborative atmosphere where research is not conducted and perceived as a "luxury," but used as a facilitating tool to transform and mobilize aspired changes.

During the year 2009, concrete interventions were carried out in order to prepare the city of Fez to move to the TTA Phase. The eFez Team leadership and the Agdal Arrondissement's president and general secretary devoted important energies and time to sensitize the other presidents and general secretaries on the importance of becoming autonomous as soon as possible.

In April 2009, a critical step was reached with the organization by the EAT of a special training session on change management. Two Canadian experts of the EAT prepared and supervised parallel workshops in Ifrane (see Table 7.2). The general secretaries of the six Fez arrondissements participated in the first workshop with the aim of preparing the TTA Phase. Several important issues were discussed including the BECs' reorganization assessment approach, lessons learned, the creation of city-level coordination structures and methods to implement the project in a coordinated way. Members of the CERCL, officers of the pilot BECs and four Fez IT technicians participated in a second workshop as an introduction to change management techniques and related communication plans and to elaborate drafts of change management plans for the BECs and for the data centers. The six general secretaries, the pilot BEC officers and the four Fez technicians also held several separate meetings in May 2009 which facilitated city-level coordination of automation issues.

These two workshops had a positive impact by raising the awareness of all attendees and providing them with tools to manage change in their institutions and prepare for the transition to autonomy. The eFez Team focused on not only producing technology solutions but also developing the needed capacities to prepare the institution's autonomy. Capacity development actions intended to address capacity gaps in comprehensive ways, including (put on a gradual scale):

• Training on describing what the eFez System is;
• Training on reasons to use the eFez System;
• Training on how to use the eFez System;

Table 7.2. Local capacity building planning

Capacity Development Activities	Number of Training Beneficiaries	Training Objectives	Training Results Expected	Emerging Outcomes

Training of BEC trainers
• **March 16–25 2009**
• **Led by: Rabia Mekkaoui, Alami Mostafa, Asmae El Mahdi**
	At least 50:
	• 14 BEC officers (Fez)
	• 30 employees (in charge of birth certificates and administrative documents in Fez)
	• Six networking technicians (Fez)
	• Teams from Larache, Ksar Kebir, Boumalne, Dades, Ifrane and El Hajeb
		1) Learning how to use eFez2 (features and functionalities)
		2) Preparing potential new BEC trainers
		3) Becoming our contact reference (arrondissement coordinators / champions)
		4) Be fully available to Data Center / CERCL
			BEC personnel applying what they learned at their respective BEC offices:
			• Using *all* eFez functionalities
			• eFez work model is respected:
			  a. eFez database regularly updated
			  b. delivery of electronic *attestations administrative*
			• Being available and ready to coach BEC peers at the Data Center
				• Sense of "community of interest" was formally rebuilt (very positive group dynamics / energy). City-level team rebuilding
				• Back in their BEC offices, they've occasionally restated the eFez vision and gains
				• Explicitly claimed equipment support for their leadership to comply with e-BEC model
				• Welcomed the idea to coach / train their peers. Many peer-training cases have emerged, namely Atlas BEC

Training of IT trainers • **March 25 2009** • **Led by: Alami Mostafa, and Aboubacar Diarra**	• Six networking technicians (Fez) • Three technicians from Larache, Ksar Kebir; Boumalne and Dades	1) Learning how to maintain / troubleshoot eFez2 to reduce BEC technostress 2) Preparing potential new BEC trainers	Learning the theory application aspects of eFez2 maintenance	• Technicians of three counties (arrondissements) became autonomous in troubleshooting eFez2 to reduce BEC technostress: 1) Saiss 2) Fez Medina 3) Merinides

		3) Becoming our contact reference (arrondissement coordinators / champions) 4) Be fully available to Data Center / CERCL IT help desk 5) Ensuring smooth functioning of software	• Jnanae Ward and Zouagha counties still need Agdal interventions because of lack of technicians • Technicians started replicating Alami's role (with varying degrees of success)
Change Management Strategy • **April 16 2009** • **Led by:** **Two Canadian experts**	• Six general secretaries (SG) (Fez) • Pilot BEC officers • Four technicians (Fez)	To prepare for eFez2 autonomy post-IDRC funding. Two parallel training workshops: 1) SG workshop (led by Mr Moulin) to disseminate BEC reorganization steps / lessons and discuss creating city-level coordination structures 2) BEC officers / technicians workshop (led by Mrs Greene) to elaborate change management in eight steps and a related communication plan	SG workshop led to: • Raising awareness about BEC reorganization matters • Validating the design of city-level coordination structures BEC officers / technicians workshop led to: • Exploring change management in eight steps • Elaborating related communication plan • Fez's six SGs held meetings in May 2009 • Pilot BEC officers held meetings in May 2009 • Four technicians held meetings in May 2009 • Many of these meetings facilitated a city-level coordination of automation issues, with the major result that the Fez municipality SG (Mr Dahbi Mohammed) became more involved in organizing these meetings and following them up

Figure 7.9. Growth in BEC certificate issuance

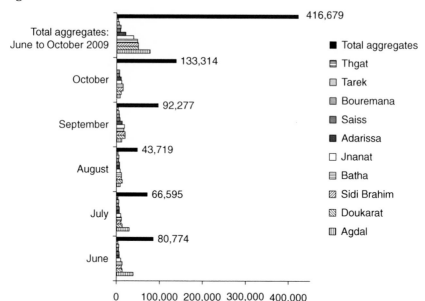

- Training on how to transfer eFez knowledge and skills to peers; and
- Training on the preparation, management and reinforcement of the eFez changes.

These intensive training sessions underpinning the participants' motivation were intended to prepare the local government of the city of Fez to appropriate and to autonomously use the developed system As an illustration, the following table shows a summary of the capacity development activities that were carried out in March and April 2009, along with their training objectives, expected results and outcomes.

Up to the time of writing (February 2012), we had not heard about any problems encountered by the city of Fez in the actual use of the deployed e-government system. Sporadic checks, information from media and feedback from citizens indicate that the system is still being used efficiently with a significant increase in good governance. The team of employees and officers of the city of Fez that were trained and prepared during the TTA Phase totally appropriated the system and is managing it smoothly. The number of certificates/documents delivered with the automated system is showing tremendous growth:

In 2010, the city of Fez became completely autonomous vis-à-vis the eFez Team. The six data centers were operational, 28 out of 33 BECs were automated and more than one million citizen records were digitized. This is Morocco's first large scale record digitization experience conducted in a metropolitan area. In addition, all employees of the automated offices have already abandoned delivering handwritten certificates and adopted the platform to generate and print requested certificates.

As a matter of fact, when the eFez terminals are out of service and need troubleshooting, BEC employees refuse to go back to the old way and handwrite certificates. Rather, they call the IT department for technical intervention and do their best to fix the situation as soon as possible. For example, once a BEC office ran out of printing ink. The employees phoned the arrondissement seat responsible for supplies and discovered that the delivery of office supplies had been delayed. Later, the secretary general was surprised when he discovered that employees had collected their pocket money and collectively purchased printing ink for immediate use. He was surprised because purchasing something for the public administration is unexpected of low-ranking civil servants with modest salaries. They justified the purchase by stating their unwillingness to return to the old practice of handwriting certificates and the reluctance of citizens to accept handwritten certificates.

At present, citizens not only expect to receive printed certificates but also have greater expectations in regard to protocol at BEC offices. An increasing number of citizens abandoned the conventional way of requesting certificates (approaching the employee in charge). Instead, they have grown accustomed to using eFez self-service technology, such as the touchscreen kiosk deployed at the BEC office, available to the public free of charge and, more importantly, adapted to the illiterate user profile.

Since its deployment in November 2005, the eFez platform has had a far-reaching, organizational-capacity-building impact on Fez's local government. The ICT-based system not only revolutionized and transformed the BEC functioning and the workflow associated with it but also enabled an unprecedented citizen-friendly instant service delivery and eliminated conditions leading to the pitfalls of bad governance (queue jumping, tipping, abusive and unfriendly treatment, etc.).

The Fez community is now prepared to extend the ICT-based experience to include the 33 BECs of Fez. The eFez2 platform is currently serving over a million people of Fez and several other cities in Morocco including Ifrane, El Hajeb, Guelmime, Settat, Boumalne and Dades. Essentially, the eFez platform has been steadily changing the face of local administrations not only in Fez but also in an increasing number of cities in both northern and southern parts of the country.

VII. Conclusion

In this chapter, we presented the instantiation of the roadmap we proposed in this book (Chapter 6) to the specific case of eFez Project. This roadmap has been created and refined over the course of the project. It is the result of conceptualization and abstraction efforts we exercised along the lifecycle (and associated events, knowledge, progress, setbacks, etc.) of the eFez Project and a number of similar projects we conducted including the LOGIN Africa Project (Waema and Adera 2011). The aim is obviously to document and share the experience we gained from the use of this roadmap for the development of e-government systems at a municipal level.

Throughout the different sections of this chapter, we presented and discussed remarkable events, decisions and actions that took place during the eFez Project. These events have been reported to illustrate important issues and advice in relation to the four main phases of our generic roadmap: the TPP, LSDDA, GSDDA and TTA Phases. We used a narrative style to sensitize and raise the reader's awareness of important decisions, problems and practical issues that may arise when running ICT4D/e-government projects in developing countries.

At the end of this chapter, we wish to recall that our roadmap should be considered as a set of instructions and guidelines that *must* be adapted to the specific context of any new e-government project.

Chapter 8

TECHNOLOGY ENABLERS FOR E-GOVERNMENT SYSTEMS

I. Introduction

In this chapter, we present some important issues related to the design and implementation of e-government systems from the viewpoints of both nontechnological decision makers and the public administration at once. Key technology enablers for e-government systems such as hardware, base software, databases, application servers, heterogeneous network interconnections and security enablers will be discussed in such a way as to help nontechnologists to understand the role of each component in the e-government system. Whenever possible, the advantages and risks pertaining to a particular technology or choice are highlighted.

The topics covered hereafter extend beyond technology enablers to encompass key issues that arise before, during and after the rollout of e-government systems, such as project management and IT service operations, in order to provide a complete view of the "ecosystem" that surrounds the successful deployment of e-government systems. We want to show that the use of e-government technology enablers introduces specific constraints and risks that must be managed in an e-government project.

Not only does the use of these technologies require proper integration and administration to ensure efficient processing, availability, scalability and performance, but it also requires stringent security measures such as personal data protection, strong access control (including citizen identification, authentication and authorization), identity management, confidentiality, integrity, compliance with legal aspects and compliance with government technology standards, guidelines and procedures.

II. Key Issues in the Design and Implementation of E-Government Systems

When efficiently and purposefully implemented, e-government systems are not only major instruments for transparency, good governance, improved and efficient provision of public goods and services, etc., but also important sources of productivity and economic growth (Wimmer 2004). Indeed, the large contracts for the procurement of hardware, software and the services necessary for the implementation, operation, maintenance and security assurance of e-government systems stimulate the private sector and, in particular, the IT sector, especially in developing countries where government ICT procurements represent most of the ICT spending.

When an e-government system makes its way into the lives of citizens and becomes the preferred process to adopt, it is critical to allow for the continued provisioning of government services. Business continuity and disaster recovery measures must be produced to prevent service interruption that can be caused by the suboptimal configuration of technology failures and/or natural disasters such as flooding and power outage and/or malicious cyber-attacks, to name a few.

To ensure the efficient use and widespread adoption of e-government systems by the citizens who are their ultimate consumers and users, careful user interface engineering is required to provide a user experience that is intuitive and delivers the right information at the right time. This calls for a great deal of user-centeredness, flexibility, modularity, information management and context awareness, supported by technologies that lend themselves to delivering a successful user web experience over multiple channels (mobile access, home access and enterprise network access) for a variety of user devices (smartphones, regular desktops and PDAs).

Often, e-government systems need to integrate and interoperate seamlessly at both front-end (that is, "user experience") and back-end levels with existing e-government systems that are associated with their own technological environments and operational constraints. Moreover, the challenges raised by technology occupy an important place in the seamless implementation and operation of these e-government systems. These challenges include service integration through service-oriented architectures, federated identity management, cross-domain security authentication and access control, as well as system interoperability.

Inevitably, the provisioning of public services through the use of ICT requires many complex back office and front office transformations of the internal processes of government and public administration. The public administration may require some reorganization to accommodate both the constraints and facilities introduced by the use of e-government-enabling technologies. Not only will these transformations impact the IT services department, but also core departments of the public administration that will then have to rely on technology to look up records, make decisions and carry out daily tasks. The offering of user support through an IT helpdesk becomes a necessity to mitigate problems related to the use of technology by public administration staff. Users need to be efficiently trained and supported to use the computer systems in carrying out their daily tasks. In addition, a second helpdesk is also needed to support e-government service consumers over the web, perhaps through a call center, which is similar to the helpdesk services provided by telecom operators for their customers. In addition, the various technology enablers need to be supported by maintenance contracts with access to a software editor and/or hardware provider for technical support to be used by the IT department.

As technology and its related complications make their way into the heart of government services delivery and general public administration, IT departments in particular need to adopt practices and standards proven to be the best in IT management, governance and service delivery, which are key success factors.

It is, therefore, clear that the successful delivery of e-government services requires the setup of a complete "ecosystem" to maximize the use of ICT and mitigate its shortcomings during operations. Yet there are many other challenges that the public administration will face, even prior to the system rollout, during the project definition and specifications phases. Unlike the private sector in which enterprise resource planning (ERP) systems emerged as off-the-shelf customizable products for the dematerialization of HR, financials, logistics and other enterprise processes, in the realm of government and public administration, there is not a unique way of doing government business. Since public administrations delivering the same service in different countries, or even different regions, have different process flows and requirements, each of them must have its own separate system built from scratch. Because of the size of the market for such systems, it is rarely feasible for companies to venture into the implementation of off-the-shelf solutions for such things as passport delivery. There are only as many customers as the number of countries recognized by the UN, which is close to 200!

When developing e-government systems from scratch, many projects fail to attain their objectives as they are too large or ambitious. As a matter of fact, there are a number of reasons for an e-government project to fail. Some of these risk areas are:

- The e-government project's scope is too large, or it has a vague perimeter
- The failure to use proven methodology for project management
- The projects are technology-driven, rather than business-objectives-driven
- There is a weak involvement of all stakeholders and underestimation of internal resistance
- There is a weak political will and commitment to the information age and knowledge economy

An e-government project with a large scope or vague perimeter is a recipe for failure. Often these projects can be broken up into smaller, less complex projects. The typical project that many public administrations start with is the conversion of all historical records and forms to an electronic format, with the ability to submit these forms electronically via web-based self-services. This conversion can be complex, very risky and time consuming. A series of smaller projects allow for more manageable endeavors. For example, a first project could start by digitizing existing records. Then a second project would use the digital database internally while service provisioning continues to operate under the conventional (manual) way. A third project would then bring the database and public self-service features to the web. These smaller projects can be completed sequentially with managed risk and more flexibility than the initial large, risky and time consuming project. One such successful experience is the eFez project that aimed to put the birth registration offices in Fez online with the goal of delivering a number of local government services such as accessing birth and death certificates (IDRC 2009). This overall objective has been carefully de-composed into three smaller projects that consisted of:

- Digitizing existing records related to the Civil State Register (citizens' records);
- Provisioning IT services for the introduction of new birth data into the digital registry database; and
- Provisioning online self-services to citizens.

This de-composition helped greatly in managing the independent risks and social engineering aspects, as well as technology challenges and project management aspects associated with each of the three independent yet integrated subprojects.

Furthermore, as information systems (IS), e-government systems require the adoption of proven IS project management and operations management methodologies to reap the expected benefits. The former helps frame all aspects related to people, cost, scope, time and technology throughout the phases of the lifecycle of the implementation of the e-government system including social engineering aspects, while the latter frames and streamlines all aspects related to the operations and support services associated with the e-government system during the production/operation phase. At the heart of these management methodologies is the tetrahedron (Figure 8.1): technology, people, process and data. Indeed, these four elements are put together to

Figure 8.1. Technology, people, process and data tetrahedron: dimensions of the IS (e-government) system

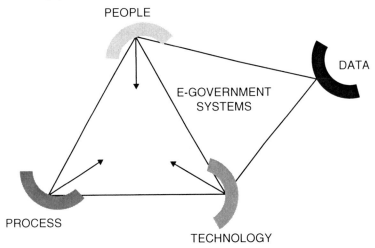

collect, manipulate, store and process data into information and provide an electronic e-government service, as follows:

- *Process*: Series of steps necessary to complete the delivery of the service. It also incorporates activities for administering the system
- *People*: The needs of those involved with the e-government system (end users, managers, etc.) are critical
- *Technology*: Hardware, software, database and network components of the e-government system
- *Data*: The information elements processed by the e-government systems such as citizens' records

Recognizing that the success of the e-government system in meeting its objectives depends on the proper interaction between these four independent dimensions, practitioners have explicitly factored them into their methodologies in terms of planning, architecture, risk assessment and management.

Since information is computerized and stored in digital records, and since this information needs to be exchanged with other government systems in standard computerized formats for public administration (for instance, birth data from the birth registration office must be passed onto passport delivery services or national ID delivery systems), the issue of the standardization of data exchanges has become critical. The eXtensible Markup Language (XML) has emerged as a technology that supports such needs. Standardization includes the data formats, definitions, values and attributes (also called metadata) necessary to interpret received information. If and when these standards exist, the e-government system must adopt them. Usually, standardization efforts are the works of specialized agencies and industry forums whose concerns go beyond the standardization of data exchange to data governance in general.

Notwithstanding the sheer size and importance of the issues involved in the successful delivery of e-government systems, its associated costs and the daunting task of successful delivery, the cost/benefit analysis is largely in favor of a massive shift to electronic governance. During the last decade, some business models have been proposed for the successful operation of e-government systems, and standards exist to support such initiatives.

III. Global Orientations

A. Feasibility and opportunity study for e-government systems

The main objective of the feasibility and opportunity study is to expand the idea, or project definition, of putting in place an e-government system with the aim of framing its scope and perimeter, estimating its timeframe, roughly defining its budget and risk areas, explicitly laying out its expected benefits, building the business case for the e-government system (including nontangible benefits), reviewing the legal aspects and exploring any international commitments that may apply to the system. It is the GO/NO-GO phase. If and when the go-ahead is given, the project is put in the pipeline for budget and then for execution, which usually starts with the elaboration of the detailed project requirements and technical specifications. Many of the conclusions and estimations elaborated during this stage need to be revised as the project progresses through its subsequent stages, namely the detailed requirements and system specification, the development, rollout and operations.

B. In-house development versus contracted development

While the development of an e-government system can be undertaken in-house, especially in small systems, generally, contracting the execution of such a system to external companies is preferred. Using the services of a contractor offers numerous advantages such as controlled costs, limited hiring of new technical personnel for the software development and a focus on processes rather than on technology. However, this option requires the existence of a clear requirements and system specifications document. The elaboration of this document can be a challenging project in its own right, and thus contracting its production can be a better solution for many public administrations.

Even if subcontracting the development of an e-government system reduces the need to hire dedicated software development engineers, it does not completely eliminate the need for a dedicated project management team to oversee the execution of the project. Often, too, independent consultants are needed to help make technical decisions for executions by the contractor Another important issue in relation to subcontracting is whether to contract out the whole system (i.e., software, hardware and development) to a single subcontractor as a turnkey solution, or to spilt the development and deployment of the system into several separate contracts for software development and implementation and hardware procurement and configuration. The disadvantages of the latter option outweigh its theoretical advantages linked to risk management. Fine tuning for performance, incompatibility and overheads in managing the separate contracts are often strong risk areas. Turnkey solutions should be preferred as much as possible. This being said, other innovative models that extend beyond the delivery of turnkey solutions are available. These issues are addressed later in the section which deals with the delivery models for e-government.

C. E-Government project management and quality assurance

The public administration wishing to roll out an e-government system should adopt or impose on the subcontractor a standard approach toward IS project management. Indeed, a standard approach toward IS project management defines the responsibilities and expectations of all parties involved in the project. Project managers, functional managers and the project steering committee use a common referential for project management that eases communication and identifies necessary success conditions such as prerequisites, the level of staffing, etc. All project management approaches require establishing a project management office, designating the key stakeholders, nominating the project management team, setting up a mixed project steering committee and specifying the roles and responsibilities of each actor.[1]

In the production/development of software, effective engineering methodologies follow a formal set of activities/steps and target a set of attributes to be fulfilled in the final product (the software itself). This way ensures that the client gets a product that meets its expectations, while keeping

---

1   http://www.cio.com/article/40342/Project_Management_Definition_and_ Solutions?page=3.

a vigilant eye on quality assurance during all the intermediary steps of the methodology.

Successfully developing an e-government system is only part of the challenge. In order to attain the objectives of e-government systems (G2C e-services, for example), many other aspects need to be carefully considered during the operations (service delivery) phase. ICT system and security management, administration, maintenance and bug fixing management, helpdesk, user and technical support, asset management, compliance with personal data protection laws, etc., are all aspects that need to be handled in a structured way and which need the adoption of a standard proven methodology for managing IT operations.

D. The impact of regulations, laws and standards on e-government projects

In many countries, no specific provision is made by law for the use of electronic and telecommunication services other than the traditional mechanisms and procedures for the delivery of services to citizens. Therefore, when delivering services electronically, e-government systems must comply with traditional law application texts often grounded in the physical world, frequently resulting in a greater overhead in service specifications and upfront planning. The regulations and laws must be addressed as project constraints and factored into the implementation of an e-government project, expanding both its scope and cost.

Some governments also have an agency for setting up a framework for the delivery of e-government systems (Hanna 2010a). These agencies adopt various standards which become constraints for the implementation of e-government systems. When it is necessary to use standards other than those specified in the recommendations of the agency overseeing the implementation of e-government systems nationwide, the public administration is often required to submit a report explaining the reason(s) for using such standards in lieu of unique government standards.

E. E-Government technology risks

In principle, risk assessment, analysis and management must be conducted for each of the four dimensions of the tetrahedron model (people, technology, process and data: see Table 8.1). Risks associated with the technology dimension are defined as any potential adverse effect arising from the use of, or reliance on, technology which leads to hardware damage, data loss, security and privacy violation and/or service disruption. These adverse effects can happen because of computer hardware, software, devices, systems, applications or network failures and disruption. The risks can result from systems flaws, processing errors, software defects, operating mistakes, hardware breakdowns, systems failures, capacity inadequacies, network vulnerabilities, control weaknesses, security shortcomings, malicious attacks, hacking incidents, fraudulent actions and inadequate recovery capabilities. Technology risks can also relate to the obsoleteness of tools, use of and dependency on proprietary technology, as well as the use of open source technology/software without the necessary support assurance.

A risk analysis approach is often used to develop a risk management plan and to adopt a model that protects administration information assets as well as mitigates the potential damages that may arise from unexpected adverse events or incidents (Alberts and Dorofee 2002). A rapid recovery capability under these circumstances is crucial. The ability to keep service and support operations running is mandatory to enable the administration to overcome disruption and adversity. It is senior management's responsibility to ensure due diligence and due care to give the administration the capacity and preparedness to deal with technology risks. A comprehensive risk management plan should also include risks associated with people, processes and data.

IV. E-Government Design and Architecture

System, process and application architectures are key domain architectures in the design of any e-government system. They provide blueprints that show how the structure and components of each of the four dimensions of the people/process/technology/data tetrahedron interact to achieve the desired functions.

The following table shows the various architectures that are usually derived for each dimension of the tetrahedron.

Table 8.1. Various architectures related to each dimension of the tetrahedron

Tetrahedron Dimension	Architectural Domain
People	Organization, planning
Process	Process/business architecture **Service architecture**
Technology	**Systems architecture** **Application architecture**
Data	Data modeling Information architecture

There are many architectural models for each conceptual level or domain. Hereafter we will present some of the common model architectures for service, application and system domains in use in e-government systems today.

A. Application architecture

The application architecture is used to represent the internal structure and modules of the software application (Sommerville 2006). One such architecture is the three-tier architecture. The three-tier architecture is essentially an extension to the client/server architecture in which the processes for the *presentation*, the *business processing logic and rules* and *access to/manipulation of persistent data* are logically separated, with the ability to run on independent processors/machines as in Figure 8.2 (Bass et al. 2003).

The three-tier architecture provides a model for developers to create loosely coupled, modular and reusable applications. It allows for the maintenance of any of the tiers independently as application requirements or technologies change. Delivering the same application over a new device only affects the

Figure 8.2. Three-tier application architecture

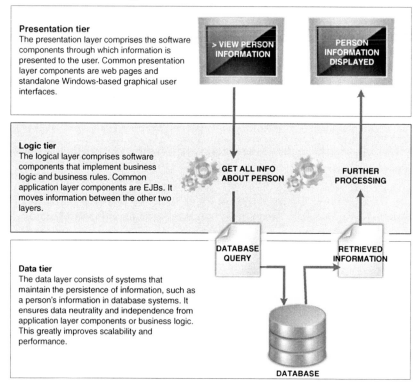

code of the presentation tier. Each of the tiers can be executed on a separate platform/processor. Similarly, the data access tier can be modified without an impact on the other tiers. The tiers usually communicate using standard protocols, such as JRMP/IIOP, HTTP or WAP between the presentation tier and the business tier and JDBC or ODBC between the business tier and the data management tier.

The presentation/interface layer in the three-tier architecture is used through a web browser (or any virtual desktop application) to request services over HTTP (WAP protocol on mobile PDAs). The requests are captured by a web container which then invokes the appropriate component/bean running within an application container such as J2EE or .NET. The service components make use of other specialized data access components to retrieve needed data from a persistent storage through the interfaces provided by the database management system (Ullman 2007).

The business logic tier (also called the middle tier) may be multi-tiered itself, in which case the overall architecture is called an "n-tiers or multi-tiers architecture." Figure 8.3 shows a typical multi-tiered Java Web application where the application server runs two tiers, namely a web container and an EJB container.

Together with a multi-tiered architecture, a design pattern is usually used at lower level to define relationships and interactions between classes or objects within the middle/business tier that reflect the separation between the tiers. One such design pattern is the model-view-controller (see Figure 8.4).

Figure 8.3. eFez four-tier web application architecture

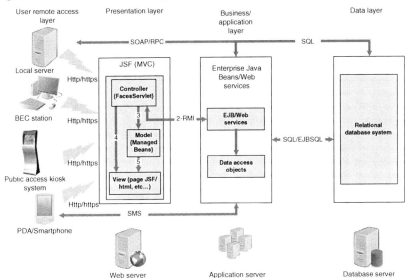

Figure 8.4. MVC design pattern for web applications

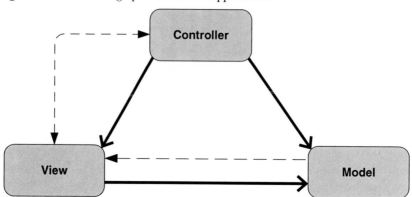

MVC pattern is based on the principle of subscription/notification, whereby interested observers are notified when information changes. The model, embodied in an EJB, encapsulates the business logic and persistent data upon which the application operates (for example, records in a persistent storage medium such as a database).[2] When a model changes its state, it notifies its subscribed "views," embodied in JSPs, so they can be refreshed (Figure 8.3).

The view renders the model into a form suitable for interaction, typically with a user interface element such as a desktop browser or a mobile browser. Multiple views can exist for a single model for different purposes.

The controller, embodied in a Servlet, accepts input (e.g., HTTP, GET and POST requests) from the user and instructs the model and view to perform actions based on that input. All necessary information (such as client socket) about the request is passed with the call to the view and the model to allow the view to respond directly to the user (web browser).

B. System architecture

System architecture defines the structure and/or behavior of a system. It is a plan from which products can be procured and systems developed in such a way that they work together to implement the overall system. It is also a representation in which there is a mapping of functionality onto hardware and software components, a mapping of the software architecture onto the hardware architecture and human interaction with these components.

---

2   Although we use terminology derived from the development of Java Web applications, the MVC model applies equally to Microsoft using .NET Framework and ASP.net environment.

Figure 8.5. eFez local e-government system architecture

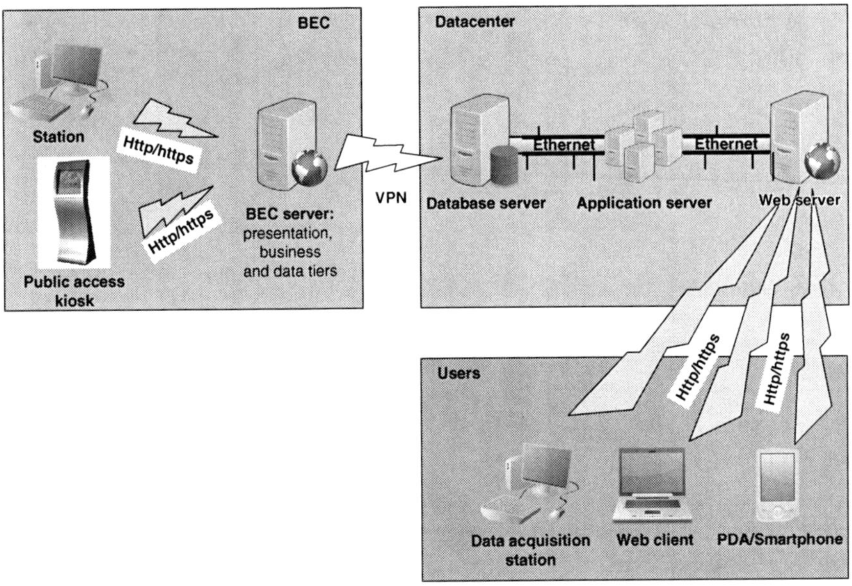

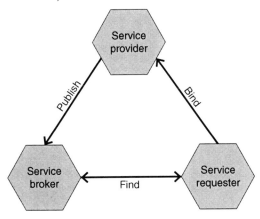

Figure 8.5 depicts the system architecture for the eFez local e-government system.

C. Service architecture

Web services are self-contained, modular applications that can be described, published, located and invoked over the web using XML/SOAP over HTTP Protocols (Ullman 2007). A service broker is used to intermediate between the service provider and the service consumer (Figure 8.6).

Figure 8.6. Web service cycle

Figure 8.7. Web services architecture

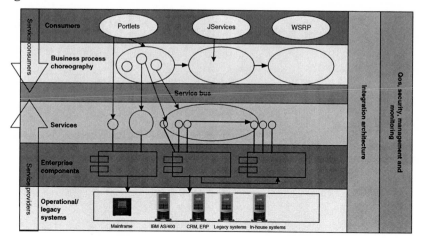

The fundamental concepts in web services include the encapsulation of details, message passing, dynamic binding and service description and querying. Web services are composed and choreographed to map business processes. The composed business process is then delivered through "portlet" technology (see Figure 8.7).

Web services are bound dynamically at runtime. A service requester describes the capabilities of the service needed and then uses the service broker infrastructure to locate it. Once a service with the required capabilities is located, the information from the service's description is used to bind to it. Dynamic service discovery and invocation are enabled through publish, find and bind yield applications with looser coupling, allowing the integration of new applications and services just in time. This, in turn, yields systems that are self-configuring, adaptive and robust with fewer single points of failure (Dodani 2005; Barry 2013). Security, middleware and communications technologies are also wrapped as environmental prerequisites.

As evidenced from Figure 8.6, Web services are a very powerful e-government enabler, for they allow legacy applications and cross-administration applications to be wrapped, exposed as web services, and consumed as part of an e-government system.

V. Security, Authentication and Access Control

In general, security management consists of a set of processes and techniques used to establish, maintain and evaluate security programs at all levels to ensure the confidentiality, integrity and availability of all e-government computing assets (Tipton 2009). Managing security programs (technical, administrative, physical) is an increasingly difficult and challenging task. With the advances in computing and communications technology, it is mandatory to monitor security on a number of levels. Security management efforts deal with the following concerns:

- Policy
- Business impact analysis
- Defining roles and responsibilities
- Identifying owners
- Classifying information and applications
- Ongoing monitoring

In the specific case of e-government service delivery platforms (servers, computers and software), a stringent and meticulous configuration to authenticate users, restrict access to resources and/or to block hacking intrusions and malware infiltration are all orchestrated under a general security policy.

Information security controls aim to preserve the confidentiality, integrity and availability triad of the e-government system assets, namely hardware, software, data and people. This is done through numerous controls including physical security, administrative controls and logical/technical controls. An organization-wide framework is also fundamental to the management of risk both in particular and to security in general. Technical controls are comprised of logical/technical access control, technical defense mechanisms and secure channel establishment through security services.

A. Logical/technical access control

Logical/technical access control focuses on user identification, authentication, authorization, and auditing (IAAA). Identification consists of asking for user credentials that will distinguish them from other users. Authorization, on the other hand, deals with granting the identified remote user access to a particular resource or a service. This is typically done by finding out if the user is a part of a particular group. Access can be granted or denied based on a wide variety of criteria, such as the network address (the IP address) of the client, the geographical zone in which the user is, the time of day or the application being used.

Authentication is the process of verifying that a user is truly who they claim they are. This usually involves the creation of a username and a password, but can include any other method of demonstrating identity such as the use of

PKI credentials (encryption keys, digital certificates) loaded on a smart card or biometric data like retina scans, voice recognition and fingerprints. More and more, a combination of these is being used, commonly referred to as two-factor (or strong) authentication. In general, two-factor authentication refers to any combination of "something the user has," "something the user knows" or "something the user is."

Authentication and identification are closely related and often used together in applications. Flawless authentication is both so critical and so difficult to build from scratch that, in practice, authentication is usually delegated to a specialized third party component and not embedded in the e-government service application per se. Third party authentication systems for web users such as Kerberos, Windows AD, X509 LDAP directory or CAS2 are often used for authentication in e-government system security architecture.

Two types of access control exist: access control to data and access control to services. Typically, if the latter is parameterized at the level of the web container that will be used to invoke the service (see application architecture), the former is usually enforced at the level of the operating system and/or the data management system.

i. Technical/logical defense mechanisms

Securing an e-government system (i.e., preserving the availability, integrity and confidentiality of system assets) is not an easy task. It is a large process comprising of securing both persistent and on-transit data across the internet and within the network of the delivering platform, securing the infrastructures (servers, network switches, administration consoles, etc.) against attacks, authenticating and controlling user access, and delivering services over secure (confidential and trusted) channels. Security architecture with defense mechanisms usually cater for all these aspects.

Defense mechanisms are comprised of firewalls, intrusion detection/prevention systems (IDS), enterprise antivirus solutions (AV) and anti-spam solutions, network access control (NAC) systems and honeypots. Automatic updates on all software are also part of the defense mechanisms.

ii. Secure channel establishment

These are virtual private networks (VPN), TLS (for securing Web access) and IPsec sessions. Cryptography and public key infrastructure (PKI) are at the heart of creating channels between the e-government service and the end user that are confidential, with mutual authentication ensured.

The increasing demand for e-commerce, online banking and e-government services has increased the demand for PKI solutions. PKI is the set of standards and protocols that enable the establishment of secure channels over unsecure networks, such as the internet, for the purpose of transferring sensitive information and money by means of public key cryptography.

In PKI, digital certificates are defined as authenticated bindings of identities with cryptographic public keys. The use of these certificates (i.e., the recipient's authenticated keys) allows the secure and trusted exchange of cryptographic material such as session encryption keys by security protocols including IPsec, TLS and IPv6.

Certificates can identify an individual or an organization such as "minA. gov.ma." The generation of a certificate is a standardized process whereby an organization or an individual presents its public key to a central trusted third party authority, which then returns the signed certificate to them effectively attesting that "this public key belongs to this individual or organization." The signing is unique and its authenticity is verifiable.

Of course, the necessary ID checks are made before the certificate is delivered. When there is reason to believe that the private key corresponding to the public key in the certificate is compromised, the certificate can be revoked and placed in a list of revoked certificates (CRL) so that it is known that the binding "public key, entity" is no longer valid.

PKI certificates follow the X.509v3 standard, and various classes of certificates exist depending on the degree of their background and ID checks, allowing for different types of use such as securing email and web sessions or, eventually, signing other public keys.

The public key infrastructure consists of:

1) A certificate authority (CA) which issues and verifies the digital certificate;
2) A registration authority (RA) which receives and verifies certificate requests for the CA before a digital certificate is issued to the requestor; and
3) An LDAP directory where the certificates (with their public keys) are stored.

Requests are packed in standard file (PKCS#10) and sent by email which delivers to the RA through the web. There are various software solutions for the generation of public/private key pairs for forming a PKCS#10 certificate request.

One typical use of certificates is to exchange them between communicating parties wishing to establish a secure channel, and the parties then verify each other's certificate. The verification process obtains the revocation status of the certificate from the CA who delivered the certificate through downloading the

CRL or using the Online Certificate Status Protocol (OCSP). Key exchange takes place following the standard format PKCS#12.

A number of PKI solutions exist, some of which are:

- RSA
- Verisign
- GTE CyberTrust
- Bull MetaPKI

PKI solutions can be deployed in an organization for the purpose of authenticating internal users, but the organization, CA, has no authority outside of the organization.

B. Technical and administrative controls

Information security controls aim to preserve the confidentiality, integrity and availability triad (also known as the CIA triad) of the e-government system assets. An organization-wide framework is fundamental in the management of risk in particular and security in general. Technical controls comprise logical/ technical access control, technical defense mechanisms and secure channel establishment through security services. Administrative controls represent a set of nontechnical tasks necessary to ensure and strengthen the information security triad. Separation of duties, the need to know who does what and policies are all considered administrative controls.

Generally, there are three types of security policies: organization security, data management security and system security:

- The organization security policy establishes the foundations of data classification as an asset of the organization. This policy usually states that information will be classified based on data value, sensitivity, risk of loss or compromise and legal and retention requirements. This provides the information security officer (ISO) with the necessary authority and framework to develop security programs and obtain funding and other support for the effort, such as executive sponsorship and support.
- The data management policy establishes data classification together with the processes to protect information. It includes:
  - Data and software classification definitions and corresponding security criteria
  - The roles and responsibilities of teams or users entrusted with implementing the policy or using the data

- System security policies are usually explicitly written on a document and configured at both the level of the base software such as the OS and/or the data management system and the level of the PKI (e.g., accepted key exchange methods, authorized encryption algorithms, etc.).

All policies must be enforced and widely communicated within the organization and with the stakeholders, including users of e-government systems.

C. Security management

Managing security programs (technical, administrative, physical) is an increasingly challenging task. With the advances in computing and communications technology, security must be monitored at different levels. Security management is the set of processes and techniques required to establish, maintain and evaluate security programs at all levels to ensure the confidentiality, integrity and availability of all e-government computing assets. Most of the costs associated with this endeavor are front-end start-up costs. Security management efforts deal with the following concerns:

- Policy
- Business impact analysis
- Defining roles and responsibilities
- Identifying owners
- Classifying information and applications
- Ongoing monitoring

When it comes to e-government systems, one cannot ignore the importance of security management. Depending on the size of the system, one might want to consider allocating dedicated certified security management personnel (ISO, CSO, security committee, etc.) to oversee security management and its operations. One such certification that has a sound value in the security industry is CISSP (www.isc2.org).

VI. Hardware Platforms and Cloud Computing for Back-end Systems

A. Processor multi-core technology

The combination of high silicon integration and demand for parallelism are behind the invention of multi-core CPUs. A multi-core microprocessor implements multiple cores in a single physical package and a single integrated circuit. Cores in a multi-core device can share a single coherent L2 cache at the highest on-device cache level or may have independent caches (e.g., current AMD dual-core processors). The processors, however, transparently share the same interconnect as the rest of the system (data and address bus, interrupt lines, etc.). Each core is a CPU in its own right, implementing optimizations such as superscalar execution, pipelining and multi-threading. A multi-core CPU is effective when it is solicited to execute more than one thread concurrently, that is, when the application is multi-threaded or composed of multiple cooperating processes. As separate execution entities, virtual machines (VMs) can also take advantage of multi-core technology (see the virtualization section below). All reputed web servers, application servers and even web browsers leverage multi-threading, and therefore can draw on all the benefits of multi-core processor technology. However, depending on how they were coded, different applications may get different performance benefits from different multi-core brands because of the different ways cores are built.

B. Cloud computing

Cloud computing is a new technology that helps reduce IT complexity by leveraging the efficient pooling of an on-demand, self-managed virtual infrastructure consumed as a service (Rhoton 2009). Cloud computing provides a more efficient, flexible and cost-effective model for computing: one that allows IT to operate much more efficiently and respond faster to business opportunities. The goal of cloud computing is to enable IT as a service.

A cloud operating system holistically, dynamically and seamlessly manages collections of infrastructures (CPUs, storage, networking) to create a dynamic operating environment. Just as a traditional operating system manages the complexity of an individual machine, the cloud operating system manages the complexity of a whole data center. Hardware virtualization is the key underpinning technology that enables cloud computing (see the following section).

C. Virtualization technology

Virtualization is a technology that uses a hypervisor (cloud operating system) to create an entirely simulated computer environment (i.e., a VM), for its guest operating system (OS). Typically one can create five VMs for each available CPU/core. Vendors offer specialized calculators to adjust the number of VMs that can be hosted on a computer system. The guest OS works as if

Figure 8.8. A set of CPUs managed by one hypervisor allowing the creation of many VMs

it were running directly on the physical hardware (see Figure 8.8). Access to physical system resources (such as the network access, display, keyboard and disk storage) is multiplexed for the running VMs. Guests can be restricted from accessing specific peripheral devices or may be limited to a subset of the device's native capabilities, depending on the hardware access policy implemented by the virtualization host (the hypervisor).

A virtual machine can be more easily controlled and its configuration is more flexible than a physical machine. A new virtual machine can be provisioned when needed without the need for an up-front hardware purchase. Moreover, a virtual machine can easily be relocated from one physical machine to another as needed. An error inside a virtual machine does not harm the host system, so there is no risk of breaking down the guest OS. Because of its easy relocation, virtual machines can be used to provide high availability and business continuity in disaster recovery scenarios.

D. Data centers

A key concern for e-government systems is availability. That is, the ability to provide services even in the most disastrous situations, such as terrorist attacks, natural disasters and man-made disasters. Ensuring the availability of critical systems, such as e-government systems, is often part of a business

Figure 8.9.  Inside a data center

continuity plan (BCP) and/or a disaster recovery plan (DRP). The DRP in particular focuses on facilities and IT systems, such as computer rooms, power systems, computer systems, network and telecommunication devices, storage systems, peripherals, etc. It is a common good practice to place these pieces of equipment in specialized rooms called data centers. Data centers are often located in carefully selected, often subterranean, locations for physical security and environmental considerations, such as cooling requirements. They are generally equipped with physical access control systems, redundant or backup power facilities, redundant data communications connections, environmental controls (e.g., HVAC systems, fire detection and suppression systems) and security devices.

Four classifications of data center exist, dependent on their readiness to cope with and recover from disasters and to support business continuity. They span from Tier 1 types to Tier 4 types. Tier 1 data centers are simple computer rooms, while Tier 4 data centers adhere to stringent guidelines set to host mission-critical systems. They are characterized by fully redundant subsystems (power, cooling, HVAC, etc.) and compartmentalized zones that are controlled by biometric access control technologies.

A key concern when operating a data center is energy consumption. Indeed, the various computing systems, together with the environmental control subsystems (cooling in particular), can account for many of the operating costs. Power consumption for large Tier 4 facility can reach the megawatts, accounting for over 10 percent of the total cost of ownership (TCO) of a data center.[3]

VII. Software Platforms for E-Government Systems

Software platforms for e-government systems comprise of base software, application server software and database management software. These are off-the-shelf solutions, available in two varieties: vendor specific and open source (license free) solutions.

A. Base software

Base software refers to the OS and some utility software as general purpose applications. The OS consists of the programs/software that controls the execution of user programs (Stallings 2012). The OS is, in fact, an interface between the hardware and the user/programmer. It is responsible for the management and coordination of activities and the sharing of the resources of a computer (processor, input/output devices, peripheries, memory, etc.) among applications (also called processes) running on the machine. It provides a foundation upon which to run application software such as word processing programs, web browsers, web servers and application servers. Examples of operating systems designed for servers include UNIX, Linux, AIX, Solaris, Redhat and Windows 2008. Examples of user/client operating systems are Vista, Windows 7, Linux, and Mac OS 7 and 8.5.

B. Web and application server software

A web server is a computer program (or a computer running a program) that is responsible for accepting HTTP requests from clients and serving back HTTP responses along with optional data contents, which are usually web pages such as HTML documents and linked objects. Apache, Microsoft IIS and IBM HTTP Server are known web servers. Typically, a web server runs on a separate machine or physical server that is accessible from the outside world through the enterprise network. Although web servers have extensions for returning HTML pages dynamically (i.e., generated by a program based on the parameters passed to the web server with the request), they are best

---

3   http://sakthidww.com (accessed February 2014).

suited for delivering static pages (i.e., static files stored on disk such as images, web objects, etc.).

An application server is a middle tier software engine that hosts and executes the programs (or business logic) of a web application (Figure 8.3). Enterprise Beans, where the logic is implemented/coded, access persistent data (data tier) using specialized database connectors. IBM Websphere, Jboss, Microsoft, .NET Server and Oracle Application Server are all examples of application servers. Beyond the dynamic behavior, an application server brings numerous advantages to the application developer such as transaction handling, connection pooling, development frameworks, security and access control, etc.

C. Data management software

A database management system (DBMS), also called a database manager, is a software that lets one or several users and programs write and retrieve data and records in a database. The database is a collection of persistent and organized records (Ullman 2007). The DBMS receives and serves user and program requests for records, hiding their physical location on storage media and, in a multi-user system, lets other users access the data. In handling user requests for the retrieval, updating, and insertion of new records, the DBMS ensures the *atomicity* and *integrity* of the data (that is, making sure that it continues to be accessible and as consistently organized as intended), and its *security* (that is, making sure only those with access privileges can access the data). Among the variety of DBMSs, the relational database management systems (RDBMS) are the most widely used. RDBMSs use the structured query language (SQL) as a standard interface for receiving requests. Object-oriented database management systems (ODBMS) are also used for storing persistent data in the form of objects, and are used in conjunction with object-oriented programming environments.

On PCs, Microsoft Access is a popular example of a single- or small-group user RDBMS. Microsoft's SQL Server is an example of an RDBMS that serves database requests from multiple users/clients. Other popular RDBMSs are IBM's DB2, Oracle's line of database management products and MySQL, which is open source software. A popular ODBMS is Versant.

D. Software licenses

There exist three categories of software license, namely, proprietary, free and open source software licenses. If the former mode of licensing has been around for a considerable length of time, and its financial and legal implications are understood, the differences between the latter two have a significant legal and financial effect on the entity using the software. A free open source license makes software free for the inspection of its code, modification and distribution. Some open source software, like the GNU General Public License, allows the product and/or derivative to be commercially sold by integrators.

A software component licensed under a proprietary license remains the exclusive property of its editor. The end user merely accepts the terms of use stipulated in the license contract, such as the number of installations allowed or the terms of distribution. Some software editors apply a license pricing model per declared users, while others apply a pricing model per processor or even per CPU core. Examples of proprietary software licenses include Microsoft Windows and Oracle RDBMS licenses.

VIII. Networking and Interconnection

A computer network is the set of physical media (i.e., optical fiber cables, radio frequencies, coax cable, copper twisted pair cables, etc.), together with the active devices (switches and routers) and associated protocols and services (DHCP service, naming service etc.) that allow for the transfer of information and invocation of e-services in the form of messages between the user equipment (PC, mobile device, etc.) and the e-government system platform.

It is worth mentioning here that the medium itself does not make up a network/technology. Rather, it is the combination of the medium and the active devices (which usually implement one of the networking standards such as IEEE, ATM, etc.) that make a technology. Therefore, it is not accurate to speak of optical fiber per se. Rather, it is more accurate to speak in terms of a technology that uses optical fiber. In what follows, we will try as much as possible to alleviate the confusion between the medium used to build the network and the technology that uses that particular medium.

As shown in the figure below, one can, in the context of e-government systems, distinguish between at least three types of network, namely the local area network (LAN) used to interconnect the components of the e-government platform, the access network that connects the platform to the internet backbone and the access network that connects the user to the internet backbone. A fourth type of network called the administrative metropolitan area network is often used to interconnect the e-government platforms between themselves and to the internet backbone (see Figure 8.10). In what follows we will describe the key features of each of these four types of networks.

Figure 8.10. Network hierarchy: enterprise networks can connect directly to MAN or through regional ISP

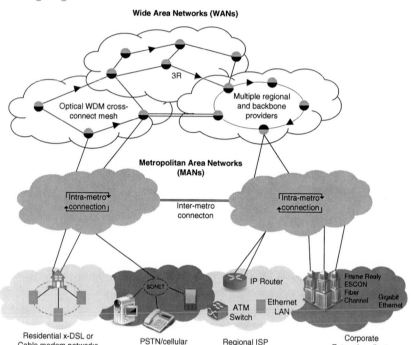

A. Enterprise networks

The networks deployed to connect the various components of the e-government platform fall into the category of enterprise networks. Today, Ethernet and its variants are the dominant technology for this class of networks, and are even making their way into carrier, MAN and WAN networks. Ethernet uses switches to transport frames between computing system components (servers and workstations). There exist standard variants for Ethernet depending on the achievable transmission speed and media/physical layer used.

i. MANs

E-Government platforms are typically interconnected to the internet by means of dedicated point-to-point links with ISPs. For speeds that exceed 2Mbps, these links are usually provisioned over an SDH, a sonnet optical fiber or radio networks. An SLA is often required with the ISP. Although most ISPs would guarantee at least a 99.95 percent uptime, a second link is necessary to ensure high availability. Most firewalls are able to make use of more than one

Figure 8.11. Typical MAN structure

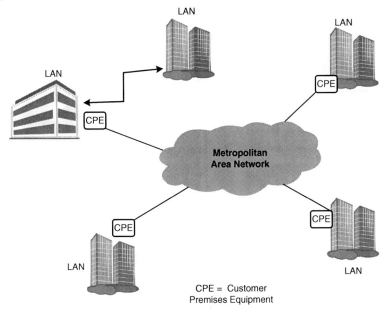

CPE = Customer
Premises Equipment

link in load balancing or resilience modes. Alternatively, enterprise networks are connected to a MAN which regroups a number of LANs using optical-fiber-based high capacity backbone technology (see Figure 8.11) and provides up-link (also called "backhaul" in the context of a wireless network) services to wide area networks and the internet backbone. A MAN might be owned and operated by a single organization, just as it can be owned and operated by a public utility. MANs can be constructed using both wired and wireless network technologies.

ii. WMANS

Two major wireless solutions and technologies are available today for building wireless metropolitan area networks (WMANs). These are WiMax802.16d, a standard-based solution also called fixed WiMax, and long range wireless fidelity (LR Wi-Fi). Although other wireless technologies, such as 60GHz links and microwave links, provide for very large bandwidths, they are not suitable for administrative or urban MANs because of:

1) Their limited range which usually does not exceed 800 meters owing to signal decay; and

2) The type of link that is used (point-to-point rather than point-to-multipoint) does not lend itself to building scalable, cost-effective, medium-size to large wireless networks.

IX. Conclusion

Though we tried to keep the description and technology enablers to a minimum, the sheer number of topics that we explore in this chapter are clear indicators of the challenges that are faced by governments/administrations wishing to deploy e-government services. It is not expected that these technologies be fully mastered as a prerequisite to deploying e-government systems, but a fair understanding of the issues they bring about and the relative advantages and risks they pose is necessary for a successful deployment. Technology is rapidly changing and, regardless of how well staffed the IT department of the public administration is, it is always beneficial to seek advice and technical support from specialized companies operating in the different fields of software engineering, network and telecommunications, network and information system security, project management, etc. Good practice in each of these areas and case studies can provide significant resources for successful e-government system development and operations.

Good practice in software development processes is essential to a successful e-government project. This includes the adoption of a proven methodology for the development process and good requirement engineering supported by use cases, as well as nonfunctional requirements such as performance, well-known industry architecture patterns, adoption of simple design patterns, peer reviewing, testing and performance measurements (Thomas 2009).

Technology and software aspects are only two variables in the whole equation of successfully delivering e-government services. Indeed, the whole technical ecosystem needs to be established, maintained and monitored. Organizational structures for project management and IT operations, as well as security management, proper budgeting and technology watch, are all key to continuously delivering services with the expected success.

Chapter 9

CONCLUSION

A few months before launching this book, we learned with great sorrow about the death of the late Senator Mohamed Titna Alaoui, a man who played an important role in the success of the eFez Project. We believe that without his total support and dedication, this project would never have had the same impact nor the same fate as it has now. In order to express a late thank you to Senator Titna Alaoui and to pay him the tribute he well deserves as a major contributor to the success of the eFez Project, we decided to conclude this book with his own words. In fact, a few months before the death of Titna Alaoui, the journalist Rachid Jankari met him to discuss the secrets or "magic recipe" of the eFez Project.[1] Rachid has always been interested in our project which he has amply covered in many articles in the national and international press. When he learnt that we were writing this book, three years after the deployment of the system and the outcomes and the changes that followed, he proposed to enhance its contents with a testimony of Titna Alaoui. We agreed on his proposal with the intention to include some highlights about Titna Alaoui throughout the book to support our proposals and ideas.

A few months later, Rachid provided us with the results of his work with Senator Titna Alaoui and, indeed, it is very interesting. Unfortunately, the content and structure of this book's chapters were already established and, as such, it was difficult to insert new ideas without the considerable effort of an overall restructure. Accordingly, we decided to overlook this new content and sent the book to the publisher as it was. All that was missing was this conclusion!

As the release date of the book approached, the editor urged us to provide him with the missing conclusion. We searched our archives for available content and documents that could facilitate this task. In this context, when we revisited the material in Rachid Jankari's document, we immediately understood that this was the best possible content for the conclusion of the

---

1 Rachid Jankari is a journalist specializing in new media. His site, www.jankari.org, provides details on his training and skills.

book. These words are full of lessons and information for our target audience (politicians and decision makers).

Thank you, Sidi Mohammed, for the wonderful job you did and for the loyal services you gave to your country!

In the following lines, we provide you with the full document provided by Mr Rachid Jankari divided into four parts:

- eFez mainly as a change management project
- eFez and the challenge of the adhesion of internal human resources and project partners
- eFez as allowing continuous mobilization for sustainability
- eFez as a bet on the future of the modernization of government services

I. Testimony of the Late Senator Titna Alaoui

A. The drive to change

In the beginning, when the eFez Project started in partnership with Al Akhawayn University (AUI), several political and economic actors were wary and felt that it was no more than a lab project and a technology showcase, or a kind of "technological fantasy" for political actors in search of fame and communication in a context marked by the value of the technology theme, especially when considered alongside the government strategy, "e-Morocco 2009." Only the evolution and implementation of the project and its achievements over the years helped to shed that image of experimentation and politico-technological adventure. By capitalizing on its partnership with the International Development Research Center (IDRC) and AUI, the eFez Project successfully managed to drive change in the administration of the city of Fez to a fluid, responsive and immediate service for citizens.

The feedback from the political actors who took part in this "adventure" is that change must first take place in attitudes. eFez is not only a technological project. If the technical expertise in relation to e-government systems is relatively available at both the national and international levels, what is lacking in this context is the willingness and good disposition of politicians who believe in the ability of technology to favorably change the perception of citizens about the public administration and the process of governance in general. Technological expertise is certainly an asset, but alone, without the other remaining elements, remains insufficient. Mostly, there must be a dependence on the political courage and the intelligence of decision makers to manage change. This is a prerequisite for the success of the administration's reform projects through technological innovation.

A politician does not need to be an expert in technology to adopt or promote ICT and e-government. A profound conviction that local administration must be changed to better serve citizens through ICT is the only prerequisite. The familiarization with and understanding of technical components occurs over time and goes along with the development and the deployment of the e-services of the project.

The decision maker should deploy his know-how and experience in order to mobilize, persuade and resolve administrative constraints and fight resistance and reluctance. Such an approach and commitment definitely facilitates the work of the managerial and technical teams, as was the case in the eFez Project.

Remember that in the process of change management in public administration, innovation and change are not only dependent on external factors but also, and more importantly, on the mobilization and membership of the internal human resources. All e-government projects which ignore or underestimate this component are liable to fail.

B. Human resources issues

It is known that the digitization/automation projects aiming to enable document e-delivery in Morocco raised serious problems related to adhesion and ownership in the socio-political ecosystem (district, Wilaya, Ministry of the Interior, etc.). Our first challenge was, therefore, to gain the trust of human resources and to show them that automation is a "win-win" scenario. In fact, an ICT project not only improves the quality of services offered to citizens but is also an opportunity for employees to enhance their capacities and their professional skills. It is not easy to allay the fears of employees immediately. But, gradually, as the implementation of an ICT project progresses, the fear naturally dissipates with the positive outcomes being generated.

Building the trust of human resources inevitably occurs through investments in training and local capacity building, as the feedback of the eFez Project demonstrated. Many training programs and opportunities to strengthen human resources in the field of automation/computerization were organized throughout the project's lifespan. The objective was to ensure an increase in competence and to enable the district's staff to realize the importance of the eFez Project.

The challenge of internal human resources adhesion/ownership is complicated in the absence and/or weakness of motivation mechanisms for staff. With the existing process of promotion and bonus bound by rigid procedures, the administration had to push the project team toward exploring other avenues for motivation and gratification (including a project's financial rewards). Moreover, the project team, which is the base drive, has mainly found motivation in the innovation of the eFez Project. Politicians must be creative to put into practice a clear motivation to override any constraints and rapidly mobilize partners (staff, technical staff, regulators, etc.) throughout the lifespan of the project.

The eFez Project officials succeeded in managing the lack of confidence and financial mechanisms as motivational tools by promising a redeployment of staff, depending on the progress of the project, guaranteeing better job conditions and continuing professional capacity building.

C. Ownership and sustainability

The eFez Project has evolved over the years to become part of everyday life for the citizens of the city of Fez. However, the challenge of this ambitious project is to sustain motivation alongside the deployment of the project's different building blocks. Mobilization is increasingly critical as organizational, technical and financial problems arise along the way. Beyond the technological dimension of an e-government project, adaptation is primarily a long-term process. The political actor must be able to revitalize the project team and fix any situation that threatens the smooth implementation of the project. The politician must constantly be alert and aware of potential issues with the changes and project constraints as they occur, and resolve them quickly. Political and administrative innovation is not easy in developing countries, particularly as local governance is still in the process of growth.

On another note, post-mobilization deployment of the project is especially necessary to avoid demotivation. The optimistic momentum of the technological project results should not overshadow the importance of staying the course to ensure sustainability. The adoption of a computerized service by citizens and human resources must be a primary goal and, as such, gains must be preserved while maintaining a measured pace of innovation.

The challenge is to preserve and ensure the development of e-government service offerings and the growth of the skills of the human resources administration. This paradoxical challenge is undoubtedly the ongoing responsibility of the supporting politician, particularly when technology is the chosen vehicle for change and improvement in the administration services.

D. A challenge for the future

The dematerialization of civil status documents is the first main outcome of the eFez Project. The first challenge is to reform the legal framework for civil status in Morocco. The ultimate goal for the future is to eventually allow any citizen to withdraw their act of civil status in any district of the civil status in Morocco, regardless of their place of birth or residence. The territoriality of the civil status is a major administrative issue that can sometimes be costly in time and money for citizens. This is a legal and technical challenge, but it is within the realm of possibility on the basis of the feedback from the eFez Project. The first steps of scanning the civil status registers and introducing computers and information technology (data center, wireless internet access, etc.) are factors which can accelerate change.

Optimism is important. At the beginning of the eFez Project, it was believed that the civil status area was "reserved" and insensitive to reform and change. However, a few years after the beginning of our project, the prospect of change has become an affordable challenge.

The convergence of political will, scientific research and international cooperation are the ingredients that helped make the ambitious eFez Project feasible. Moreover, the Moroccan Ministry of Interior and the various districts of other cities are following the eFez Project with interest. International recognition of the originality of the experience is an asset that encourages the positive promoters of the efforts to change the legal and regulatory framework governing civil status. This national and international recognition is the true means to advocate expanding both the scope of dematerialization of civil status in Morocco and the commitment of the political administration to a process of innovation supported by the assets and opportunities that e-government technology systems offers. The real challenge is to gradually make the e-government and e-administration an integral part of everyday life in Morocco and to fight against what academics call the "digital divide."

II. Final Recommendations

It is true, as Senator Titna Alaoui said, that academics use more sophisticated terminology and approaches to write papers and books. But, at the end of the day, what we want to convey are specific messages and ideas that politicians and decision makers can "decode" and understand in the easiest way. We believe that most of what we wanted to convey in this book's conclusion has been covered by the testimony of Titna Alaoui but, for the sake of respecting and strengthening the academic standing of this book, we will present in the remaining part of this conclusion some recommendations and tips based on the words of Titna Alaoui, but with an "academic coating."

A. ICT works… the problem is elsewhere!

Yes, ICT does work: millions of dollars are exchanged instantaneously between New York and Japan, Paris and London, Montreal and Rome. If ICT did not work, no one (particularly businessmen) would have risked such money, time and materials. ICT works perfectly for banks, insurance companies, telecoms, aviation, defense, etc., and, better yet, without ICT, all these activities could not have survived a single business day in today's economy, let alone prospered as they have in the last five decades. So, the arguments of many people that don't use ICT because, so they claim, it does not work due to security threats, instability, dysfunctions, unreliability, etc., are absurd and unreasonable. ICT does the job effectively and efficiently. Problems encountered tend to be socio-political rather than technological.

Our experiences with the eFez Project clearly show that ICT diffusion is not a technology problem, but rather a political issue. In fact, very often, politicians and decision makers lack the basic ICT literacy skills and understanding, and this directly impacts on their **awareness** level. Surprisingly, and despite their lack of e-awareness, political actors showed a high involvement in and commitment to the eFez Project shortly after understanding the objectives and expected concrete contributions. This was expressed commonly in Arabic through statements such as: "*chouf rahna maakoum*" ("look, we are with you!") and "*ghir goulounna chnou ndirou*" ("just let us know what we can do to help you"). These statements show the **e-readiness** of policy makers to engage in deploying ICT to support and promote good governance despite their low consciousness of its potential.

With respect to **e-readiness** at the citizen level, we were even more surprised. A large number of citizens clearly voiced their need to interact electronically with government offices, but complained that their political representatives had not been responsive. They expressed themselves with statements like: "*wha chhal hadi bach bghina had chi walakine maddaha fina hadd*" ("we wanted this facility a long time ago, but nobody cares about what we want or need"). Such a reaction showed us that citizens were open and keen to have access to ICT facilities despite their low "digital culture."

B. Decision makers and politicians should make an effort

Without a doubt, the introduction of ICT to an organization does produce deep changes in its structure and dynamics. The reluctance of decision makers to support ICT in our countries is somehow legitimate given the associated risks (organizational, technological, business, etc.) and the necessary adjustment efforts required. The challenge is to find original ways to convince decision makers and politicians that ICT is in their best interests and that there is a possible "win-win" situation for every stakeholder in the ecosystem.

It is not reasonable to think that all decision makers should suddenly become engineers or perfectly master ICT platforms and tools. What is rather required here is to acquire the necessary skills associated with the decision making process as such, so that decision makers are in a position to make informed decisions. They need to manage a new situation in which a significant part of the job depends on technology. It is extremely difficult (but not impossible) to do this without first becoming acquainted with the foundations and evolution of ICT, its conceptual framework and basic operations and techniques. The familiarity of decision makers with ICT impacts a lot on their e-readiness and e-awareness. This is simply because it is difficult to make good decisions about things that substantially change the way work is done and business is run without understanding them. As we stated earlier in this chapter, if Titna Alaoui were not e-aware and e-ready, we could never have succeeded in this project and, similarly, it is unlikely that the generalization of this project all over Morocco will succeed if the minister in charge of this department (Ministry of Interior) is not sufficiently e-aware and e-ready. Indeed, we cannot deny the role and importance of individual initiatives in creating synergies and preparing favorable conditions for ICT projects, but these initiatives will always be limited in their scope and impact if they are not supported by decision makers and politicians. This illustrates the dilemma between the top-down approach and the bottom-up approach. The truth is that there is a need to organize and synchronize the efforts, actions and outcomes of both approaches to succeed at the national level, and inevitably this involves the e-awareness and e-readiness of politicians and decision makers.

C. ICT is an opportunity

The reader may legitimately wonder why one of the main focuses of this book are the benefits of ICT, since this no longer needs to be proven, especially in the business and services sectors (see Section A of this chapter). The opportunity we are stressing in this book is, however, related to the development process of our countries at the macro level, and how ICT can support, accelerate and streamline it. We strongly believe that ICT provides an opportunity for developing countries to catch up. ICT performs operations more effectively, expediently and efficiently for everyone everywhere, regardless of language, gender or social class. We would like to mention here examples of countries that seized the ICT opportunity such as Malaysia, Singapore and Korea and, as a result, became the new dragons of the world's economy. They have made ICT a strategic tool and infrastructure for their social and economic development through clear and explicit political engagement at the highest level, with close monitoring, evaluation and readjustment mechanisms.

ICT is an opportunity because it enables access to, preservation of and processing of data, information and knowledge for everyone and every country (including developing and less developed ones) at an affordable cost. ICT casts off the obstacles of time and space and offers all countries and all individuals the same capabilities. Innovation and creativity are key issues in this sense and every country needs to "invent" an ICT model that fits its context, its constraints and its objectives. ICT offers ways and opportunities to address the developmental challenges at the organizational, national and international levels. Indifference to ICT keeps and sustains the status quo and inevitably fuels all sorts of dangers, including the digital divide.

D. ICT for good governance is the key issue

There is no doubt that ICT alone does not create good governance. What we can confirm, however, is that ICT enables and conditions good governance and it is impossible, nowadays, to achieve good governance without using ICT tools and platforms. Neither is it possible to achieve good governance without applying and using the right organizational and managerial methods and the right supporting environments (legal rules, work conditions, work space, etc.). The high number of requests coming from citizens, their inherent administrative complexity and the anticipated quality of service ineluctably necessitates the use of ICT enablers to not only accelerate the delivery process but also to avoid mistakes, consolidate the rules of law and ease the daily life of citizens.

One original idea that was proposed and implemented in the eFez Project was to embed the attributes of good governance in the specifications of e-government systems and take them into account in the design and implementation phases to enable the monitoring and evaluation of their impacts on the whole governance process. Unlike most existing e-government systems, the eFez platform includes indicators and metrics that indicate how this system contributed to better governance, including time to service, volume of transactions, error rates, gender-related issues, etc. Many organizational institutions, including the UN and the World Bank, are still struggling to find the "right" model to link between government systems and good governance and to enable a fair impact assessment process. In this book, we proposed a whole framework of e-government for good governance which is applicable in all contexts in which the use of ICT is primarily guided and motivated by good governance. This framework gives clear metrics (numbers, facts, diagrams, etc.) on how citizens and employees benefited from the system and illustrates, in a quantitative way, the changes that followed the implementation of the system over a certain period of time. We strongly believe that this framework has tremendous potential to contribute to the important debate related to the evaluation and monitoring of e-government systems and, possibly, revive the dynamism of international organizations in supporting e-government projects by creating a subtle pressure on the politicians and decision makers in developing countries to adopt ICT as an engine to boost good governance.

Appendix

A SYNTHETIC VIEW OF CRITICAL ISSUES FOR A SUCCESSFUL ICT4D/ E-GOVERNMENT PROJECT

One of the goals of this book is to provide the reader with a better understanding of the many diverse and related factors that influence the possible success or failure of an ICT4D/e-government project. Our six years' experience in developing such systems for local government institutions in Morocco enabled us to draw a parallel between the observations and recommendations provided by different authors about the development of e-government programs at a national level and what we observed when we developed and deployed ICT4D/e-government systems at a local governance level. There are strong similarities between the two types of situation that had to be managed and actions that had to be taken (see Chapter 5).

In practice, decision makers, managers of governmental institutions and project managers of ICT4D/e-government projects need to consider numerous related issues and deal with such a large variety of challenges that they may feel overwhelmed. In order to help them grasp "the big picture," we offer in this appendix a detailed view of what we consider to be the main elements that influence the transformation affecting a governmental institution when it adopts and integrates new business policies and practices based on ICT4D/e-government techniques and good governance principles.

Indeed, the institution evolves in a complex context related to its organizational, economic, political, cultural, social, technological, legal and local environments. When this context changes, the institution may no longer be able to deal with it adequately, especially if it does not master ICT or associated business practices. This is often the case in developing countries, particularly at the local governance level. Hence, the institution faces the great challenge of undergoing a multifaceted transformation (at institutional, organizational, business, legal, financial, technological, cultural and human levels) while adopting and integrating ICT and e-government practices as well as good governance principles. We suggest that understanding this transformation process and knowing how to carefully manage it is critical. This knowledge provides an important key for the main stakeholders as they develop the vision that will orient the institution's transformation and proactively deal with all the events that occur during the course of the ICT4D/e-government project. To this end, we propose the following set of tables in which we thematically present the main issues to be considered and the main elements that are involved in the institution's transformation from the initial situation to the target situation when implementing an ICT4D/e-government project. The general themes that we propose are:

1) Managing the context of the ICT4D/e-government project;
2) Good governance (GG) and leadership in ICT4D/e-government projects;
3) Vision and capacity building in relation to the ICT4D/e-government project;
4) Governance and management of an ICT4D/e-government project; and
5) Ensuring the sustainability of the transformation.

Table 5.1-1. Managing the context of the ICT4D/e-government project

Issues	Initial Situation	Transformation Process	Target Situation
Broader context (related to the global environment)	Political, economical, social and cultural contexts	To be monitored for their possible impact on the transformation	Elements that may influence the institution
	Legal context	To be monitored (and adapted?)	ICT-friendly legal context
	Technological context	Technological watch	Select ICT e-government techniques adapted to the institution
Institution's own context (related to its direct environment)	Leadership	E-Champions at all levels Encourage local initiatives	Supportive leadership and participation at all levels of the institution
	Inner politics	Beware of the inner political forces that influence the transformation process	Secure / preserve / encourage a favorable political context for the transformation and its sustainability

(Continued)

Table 5.1-1. Continued

Issues	Initial Situation	Transformation Process	Target Situation
	Institutional context	How institutional policies and rules influence the transformation process (should they be adapted?)	Policies and rules which are favorable to the ICT/ e-government target situation
	Financial context	Obtain sufficient financial support to support the transformation	Sufficient financial support should be secured to sustain the transformation
	Partnerships	Mobilize all necessary partnerships (governmental support, international development aid, academic support, private support)	Create and maintain (and create new) partnerships to sustain the transformation
	Managerial context	Identify managerial practices that need to be customized to adapt the institution to the ongoing transformation and to sustain its targeted new form	Encourage the creation of adaptive managerial structures and practices to support the organization's continuous evolution
	Organizational context	Identify management workflows and practices that need to be adapted	Encourage the creation of adaptive management workflows and practices to support the organization's transformation and continuous evolution
	Cultural context (enterprise culture)	Be aware of the institution's culture and needs for adaptation when adopting ICT/ e-government-based approach	Modern ICT-friendly enterprise culture

Table 5.1-2. Good governance (GG) and leadership in ICT4D/e-government projects

Issues	Initial Situation	Transformation Process	Target Situation
Good governance principles	Awareness of governance and related practices	Assess the top managers' and politicians' governance awareness and practices and help them appropriate GG principles	Consensus about the way to make the institution operate on the basis of GG principles
	Promotion of GG principles	Some top decision makers (politicians, top managers) need to adopt and actively promote GG principles throughout the institution from the very start of the project and until these principles are firmly rooted in the institution	An institution which operates on GG principles at all levels
	Any other issues to be considered?	We let the reader complete these lines	
Leadership	Who will lead the transformation process toward effective GG implementation?	This deep transformation toward GG and the adoption of ICT/e-government approach must be strongly supported by top decision makers and actively passed on to all levels of the organization	Proactive and continuous support of the transformation toward adoption and implementation of GG principles

Table 5.1-3. Vision and capacity building in relation to the ICT4D/e-government project

Issues	Initial Situation	Transformation Process	Target Situation
Vision and willingness to change	Top management's vision of the transformation	Help top managers develop the vision of the target situation to involve key stakeholders and enable this vision to evolve during the transformation	Clear and shared vision of the transformation by top managers and politicians
	Main stakeholders' implication	Identify, sensitize and involve main stakeholders and sustain their interest with respect to the vision and transformation	Main stakeholders' shared vision of the target situation
	Other employees' implication	Develop a plan to sensitize and involve other employees in the transformation process	All stakeholders' willingness to change, adopt and support the transformation process
Sensitization and promotion	All stakeholders (politicians, top managers, middle managers, employees, citizens, other governmental partners, commercial partners)	Assess the awareness of each stakeholder category and develop appropriate sensitization and promotion plans	Awareness of all stakeholder categories of the importance and benefits of the transformation
Education	All stakeholders (politicians, top managers, middle managers, employees, citizens, other governmental partners, commercial partners)	Assess the ICT-related general knowledge of each stakeholder category and develop education plans to help them reach the appropriate levels in order to take advantage of the new technologies and related practices	All stakeholders have sufficient knowledge to adopt and benefit from the transformation
Training	Certain stakeholders (top managers, middle managers, employees)	Assess the ICT-related specific knowledge and skills of each stakeholder category and develop training plans to help them reach the appropriate levels in order to effectively take advantage of the new ICT/e-government systems	These stakeholders have the knowledge and skills to operate the institution using the new ICT/e-government systems and to implement associated practices and workflows

Table 5.1-4. Governance and management of an ICT4D/e-government project

Issues	Initial Situation	Transformation Process	Target Situation
Establish strong leadership	In developing countries, the vast majority of local governmental institutions do not have any resources or knowledge of the governance and management of ICT4D/e-government projects. Hence, they need support from external partners (international partners, universities, companies) to develop the systems and change workflows, business rules and practices to assess progress and risks, to manage the project according to budget and schedule, etc.	Identify key stakeholders (e-champions) at all levels of the institution Identify competent and experienced (external) advisors to manage the project jointly with key institution e-champions	A strong management team well connected to the institution's leadership
Partnerships		Identify the critical and necessary partnerships (both internally and externally)	Efficient and strategic partnerships with international development aid bodies, academic institutions, private companies, etc.
Build the team(s)		Create a team with external advisors and partners involving selected managers and employees of the institution	A core team that will effectively and efficiently move the project toward the institution's goals
Methodologies		Select the required methodologies for all the transformations (business process reengineering, information system design and development, etc.) that will be needed Adapt these methodologies to the institution's context	A set of methodologies to be used in a simple, effective way by the members of the core team, thinking that they will then be integrated in the institution's future operations

Master plan	Build a master plan with the core team and main e-champions to orient and plan the project. Evolve the content of this master plan as needed	A comprehensive and evolving master plan which plans the transformation process toward the achievement of the vision and GG principles taking into account the available resources
Identification of resources	Identify available resources (financial, material, human) and seek all resources needed to support the master plan	Resource mobilization in order to adequately support the institution's transformation
Architectures	Build all needed architectures: business and process, data and information, application and technology. Validate and refine these architectures as needed.	A set of adequate, efficient and evolving architectures to support the development of the new ICT/e-government system and the transformation at all levels
Adopt a progressive approach to the transformation process	Plan for a gradual transformation process based on an initial pilot phase to test the proposed solutions. Then, if successful, propagate the solution more widely (scaling-up)	The institution has a chance to test various solutions to select and adapt the best solution to the local contexts. This evolutionary approach enables the institution to adapt to change at all levels
Top-down versus bottom-up approach	Select the adequate approach at the proper stage of the project. A mixture of top-down and bottom-up approaches might be required	The transformation process is adaptive, oriented by "global directions set by the vision," and encourages local initiatives and adaptations
Business analysis and process reengineering	Based on the master plan, the appropriate business reengineering methodology and the proposed business/process architecture, carry out business analysis and process reengineering to implement the new solution (integrating ICT/e-government techniques and GG principles)	The new business processes integrating ICT/e-government techniques and GG principles. These processes will need to be adaptive to enable the institution to adapt to change.

(Continued)

Table 5.1-4. Continued

Issues	Initial Situation	Transformation Process	Target Situation
Development, adaptation and deployment of ICT-based applications		Based on the master plan, the appropriate design and development methodology and the proposed architectures (data and information, application and technology), this is the global process that orients the deployment of the required hardware infrastructure and the development and deployment of the applications (software)	Functioning and reliable hardware infrastructure and software applications to support the ICT/e-government adapted to the institution's context and implementing the vision of the new solution
Stakeholder management		The core team must take care of the stakeholders of each category to ensure that all key persons are involved and continuously support the transformation process	This is a critical management task that needs time and adequate resources (communication plans, facilitation, training, coaching, etc.)
Stakeholder training		With respect to the transformation process, stakeholders (top managers, middle managers, employees) must be adequately trained	This results in the creation of training programs adapted to each stakeholder category. Do not minimize the need to find "training resources" (trainers) both outside the institution (advisors, facilitators) and inside it (middle managers and employees with adequate skills who may become trainers).
Finance and budget control		Build and maintain a reasonable budget plan which reflects the institution's capacity to finance the transformation. The institution's managers must be sensitized that ICT/e-government solutions need budgets and resources that they are not used to managing. Monitor the expenses (budget control) and proactively adapt the budget to the needs and financial means.	This is a critical task. When an international development aid body provides funds, budget control is mandatory. The institution must go on with such a budget control when the international aid is completed.

Risk management	A Transformation Project is critical for the institution and all sorts of risks must be managed by the core team during the whole duration of the transformation process (and beyond!)	An efficient, multifaceted and evolving risk management plan which is used to monitor the transformation process in relation to the master plan
Communication plan	Communication with all stakeholders is most critical to maintain their interest and involvement during the whole transformation process	A set of communication plans adapted to the various categories of stakeholder and adapted to the changing context of the institution
Scaling-up issues	The Scaling-Up Phase aims to adapt and generalize the solution found during the pilot phase to the whole institution All the elements mentioned above must be revisited in this generalization perspective Getting adequate resources (financial, human, etc.) is of the utmost importance	Revise all plans, architectures, methods, processes, hardware and software solutions. Training, coaching and facilitating activities and related resources must be carefully considered. Schedules must also be revised Beware of keeping and extending adequate support to the transformation process (e-champions)
Situation assessment and progress monitoring	The institution's situation must be assessed before, during and after the transformation process to make sure that the transformation is carried out in a timely and adequate manner to reach the institution's goal (vision, good governance principles, etc.)	A situation assessment plan and a progress monitoring plan. Adequate reporting mechanisms must be created to enable the core team and the institution's managers to intervene during the transformation process when needed.
Change management	The success of the transformation process results from using an adequate change management approach	A change management approach that is adapted to the institution's context and resources

Table 5.1-5. Ensuring the sustainability of the transformation

Issues	Initial Situation	Transformation Process	Target Situation
A vision toward sustainability	The institution has been undergoing a significant transformation with the support of a variety of partners. The danger appears when the support of international development aid bodies fades away and when external advisors cannot help any longer.	The core team (which is often extended during the Scaling-Up Phase) and top managers must develop a vision, a master plan and related plans (especially at the financial, managerial, human resources mobilization and training levels) in order to ensure that the transition toward autonomy will be carried out smoothly	Vision of how to enable the institution to become autonomous in sustaining its new situation resulting from the transformation process. Need to understand that in a modern adaptive institution, the organization undergoes continuous change that must be smoothly and adequately managed.
Sustainability of political support	Strong political support is still needed when the international development aid body leaves the scene	Since the transformation will usually not be completed at the project's planned completion, the steering team will need to secure political support for the continuity of the institution's transformation process	Political support for the continuity of the institution's transformation process
Sustainability of financial support	Adequate financial support is needed	Managers and politicians should be aware that they need to take action so that adequate budgets be secured and sustained when international development funds fade away	Financial plans and budgets taking into account the institution's new financial requirements. Effective actions to secure the required budgets.
New structure to manage the transformation process	The core team that steered the project until completion and that already underwent changes at the scaling-up stage	Actions must be taken in order to enable the core team (usually extended during the scaling-up phase) to be transformed in an autonomous team, considering a diminishing presence of external advisors	The core team becomes a Transformation Steering Team (TST), solely composed of the institution's employees and managers. Institutional members of the core team usually lead the TST, which is augmented with other motivated and capable personnel

Plans for sustainability	Various plans (master, financial, managerial, human resources, training, etc.) to be elaborated for the transformation process	According to the vision for sustainability, the TST and top managers must develop a master plan and related plans (especially at the financial, managerial, human resources mobilization and training levels) in order to ensure that the transition toward autonomy will be carried out smoothly	Set of plans to plan and manage the sustainability of the transformation
Sustainability of e-champions	Current e-champions	The TST must go on keeping e-champions mobilized until the transformation is complete and fully integrated in the institution	Beware that e-champions may change during the course of the whole transformation
Sustainability of ICT infrastructure	Current ICT infrastructure deployed to support the ICT/e-government solution	Plan and take action so that the ICT infrastructure be updated adequately after the project's official completion (sensitize and secure the support of top managers to this end)	Budgets, consumables (paper, ink) and adequate human resources to continuously update and support the ICT infrastructure
Sustainability of new business practices	A large number of managers and employees have adopted new business practices, while other have not	The TST motivates the institution's management to take action so that the new business practices are enforced in the organization after the project's completion	The new business practices should be routinized and sustained throughout the whole organization
Sustainability of ICT/e-government applications	The ICT/e-government applications are now used in a significant part of the institution.	Plan and take action so that the ICT/e-government applications are updated and supported adequately after the project's official completion (sensitize and secure support of top managers to this end)	Budgets and concrete actions from the institution's top managers
Sustainability of human resources for the operation and evolution of technical solutions	Development resources (budget and external expert designers and developers) will fade away at the project's completion	Plan for human and financial resources to continuously support these applications	Needed experienced human resources to maintain, extend and support the ICT/e-government applications (usually through outsourcing to a private company)

(Continued)

Table 5.1-5. Continued

Issues	Initial Situation	Transformation Process	Target Situation
Sustainability of human resources able to use ICT-based solutions and related business practices	A significant part of the institution's managers and employees are trained and use the new workflows, business practices and ICT/e-government solutions. Other managers and employees are not yet trained.	Secure budgets, time and human resources (trainers) to train the personnel to use the new solutions. Plan also for time, budget and human resources to accompany (or coach) managers and employees in their initial experiences with the new solutions.	Adequate budgets, schedules, time allocation and human resources to continue the training and coaching of personnel using the new solutions (business, hardware, software)
Continuity of the situation assessment and progress monitoring	A situation assessment plan and a progress monitoring plan. Adequate reporting mechanisms during the transformation process	Top managers must be sensitized about the importance of these monitoring and reporting mechanisms. Appropriate actions must be carried out to adapt them to the next stage of the transformation.	Plans and associated management and reporting mechanisms must be adapted, taking into account the absence of advisors and the external support of international development aid bodies

These tables are self-explanatory and represent our synthesis of the main issues that should be taken into account when making an ICT4D/e-government project a success. We do not pretend that these issues are exhaustive, but we think that they are a good starting point and a good reference for managers of such projects in developing countries. As a matter of fact, managers in charge of an ICT4D/e-government project may use these tables as check lists during the course of their projects. Indeed they will certainly have to add their own issues, dependent on the project and its context.

REFERENCES

Abowd, G. D. 2004. "Investigating Research Issues in Ubiquitous Computing: The Capture, Integration, and Access Problem." Online: http://www.cc.gatech.edu/fce/c2000/pubs/nsf97/summary.html. Accessed February 2014.

Alberts, Christopher, and Audrey Dorofee. 2002. *Managing Information Security Risks: The OCTAVE (SM) Approach*. Upper Saddle River, NJ: Addison-Wesley Professional.

Aronson, Jonathan D. 2001. "The Communications and Internet Revolution." In *The Globalization of World Politics: An Introduction to International Relations*, edited by J. Baylis and S. Smith. New York: Oxford University Press.

Backus, M. 2001. "E-Governance and Developing Countries: Introduction and Example." Online: http://editor.iicd.org/files/report3.doc. Accessed February 2014.

Barry, Douglas K. 2013. *Web Services, Service-Oriented Architectures and Cloud Computing: The Savvy Manager's Guide*, second edition. London: Morgan Kaufmann.

Bass, Len, Paul Clements and Rick Kazman. 2003. *Software Architecture in Practice*. London: Dorling Kindersley.

Bertucci, G., and A. Alberti. 2003. "Globalization and the Role of the State: Challenges and Perspectives." In *Reinventing Government for the Twenty-first Century: State Capacity in a Globalizing Society*, edited by D. A. Rondinelli and G. S. Cheema, 17–32. Bloomfield, CT: Kumarian Press.

Bhatnagar, S. 2004. *E-Government: From Vision to Implementation. A Practical Guide with Case Studies*. New Delhi: Sage Publications.

Brinkerhoff, D. W. and A. Goldsmith. 2005. "Institutional Dualism and International Development: A Revisionist Interpretation of Good Governance." *Administration and Society* 37(2):199. Online: http://aas.sagepub.com/cgi/content/abstract/37/2/199. Accessed May 2009.

Castells, M. 2000. "The Rise of the Network Society." In *The Information Age: Economy, Society and Culture*, second edition, vol. 1. Oxford: Blackwells.

Cohen, D. S. 2005. *The Heart of Change Field Guide: Tools and Tactics for Leading Change in Your Organization*. London: Harvard Business Review Press.

De Soto, H. 1989. *The Other Path: The Invisible Revolution in the Third World*. New York: Harper & Row.

Denhardt, R., and J. W. Grubbs. 2003. *Public Administration: An Action Orientation*. Canberra, Australia: Thomson Wadsworth.

Dix, A. 1998. *Human Computer Interaction*, second edition. New York: Prentice Hall.

Dodani, Mahesh H. 2005. "Mirror, Mirror on the Wall, Whose SOA Is the Best of Them All?" *Journal of Object Technology* 4(5): 67–74. Online: http://www.jot.fm/issues/issue_2005_07/column6/. Accessed February 2014.

Dybå, T. 2008. *Empirical Studies of Agile Software Development: A Systematic Review of Information and Software Technology*. Amsterdam: Elsevier.

Felts, A. A., and P. H. Jos. 2000. "Time and Space: The Origins and Implications of the New Public Management." *Administrative Theory and Praxis* 22(3):519–33.

Finger, M. 2005. "Conceptualizing E-Governance: European Review of Political Technologies." Online: http://www.politech-institute.org/review/articles/ FINGER_Matthias_volume_1.pdf. Accessed March 2009.

Forman, M. A. H. 2005. "E-Government: Using IT to Transform the Effectiveness and Efficiency of Government." Online: http://go.worldbank.org/XDSYI1P0S0.

Fukuyama, F. 2004. *A New Agenda*. Ithaca, NY: Cornell University Press.

Garridon, M. 2004. "A Comparative Analysis of ICT for Development Evaluation Frameworks." Online: http://www.asiafoundation.org/pdf/ICT_analysis.pdf. Accessed March 2009.

Guida, J., and M. Crow. 2008. "E-Government and E-Governance." In *ICT4D: Information and Communication Technology for Development*, edited by T. Unwin. Cambridge: Cambridge University Press.

Gurstein, M. 2007. *What is Community Informatics (and Why Does it Matter)*. Monza, Italy: Polimetrica.

Hagen, I. R. 2005. "Scaling up Development Initiatives through ICT: Potentials and Challenges." In *Access, Empowerment & Governance: Creating a World of Equal Opportunities with ICT*. Kuala Lumpur: Global Knowledge Partnership.

Haldenwang, C. V. 2004. "Electronic Government (E-Government) and Development." *The European Journal of Development Research* 16(2):417–32.

Hanna, N. 1994. "Exploiting Information Technology for Development: A Case Study of India." *World Bank Discussion Papers* 246.

———. 2008. *Transforming Government and Empowering Communities: The Experience of Sri Lanka*. Washington, DC: World Bank.

———. 2010a. *Transforming Government and Building the Information Society: Challenges and Opportunities for the Developing World*. Springer, NY: Peter T. Knight Editors.

———. 2010b. *e-Transformation: Enabling New Development Strategies*, Springer, NY: Peter T. Knight Editors.

Heeks, R. 1999. "Reinventing Government in the Information Age." In *International Practice in IT-enabled Public Sector Reform*, 9–21. London: Routledge.

———. 2001. "iGovernment: Understanding E-Governance for Development." Institute for Development Policy and Management's Working Paper Series 11. University of Manchester, Manchester. Online: http://www.sed.manchester.ac.uk/idpm/research/publications/wp/igovernment/documents/igov_wp11.pdf. Accessed October 2013

———. 2002. "Information Systems and Developing Countries: Failures, Successes and Local Improvisations." *Information Society* 18(2):101–12.

Heeks, R. 2003. "Most E-Government-for-development Projects Fail: How Can Risks be Reduced?" Working Paper Series 14. University of Manchester, Manchester. Online: http://www.sed.manchester.ac.uk/idpm/research/publications/wp/igovernment/documents/igov_wp14.pdf. Accessed October 2013.

———. 2004. "eGovernment as a Carrier of Context." Working Paper Series 15. Institute for Development Policy and Management, University of Manchester, Manchester Online: http://www.sed.manchester.ac.uk/idpm/research/publications/wp/igovernment/documents/igov_wp15.pdf. Accessed October 2013.

_____. 2006. "iGovernment: Benchmarking E-Government. Improving the National and International Measurement, Evaluation and Comparison of E-Government." Development Informatics Group's Working Paper Series 18. Development Informatics Group, University of Manchester, Manchester. Online: http://www.sed.manchester. ac.uk/idpm/research/publications/wp/igovernment/documents/igov_wp18.pdf. Accessed October 2013.

Holman, P., T. Devane and S. Cady. 2009. *The Change Handbook: The Definitive Resource on Today's Best Methods for Engaging Whole Systems*, second edition. San Francisco, CA: Berrett-Koehler Publishers.

IDRC. 2005. "Stratégie de Programme du Fond pour la Bonne Gouvernance au Moyen-Orient." Centre de Recherches pour le Développement International du Canada. Online: http://www.crdi.ca/FR/AboutUs/Accountability/AnnualReports/ Rapport%20Annuel%202006-2007.pdf. Accessed October 2013.

_____. 2009. "Electronic Government in the City of Fez. Morocco: Scaling up to the National Level." Online: http://www.idrc.ca/en/ev-116196-201-1-DO_TOPIC.html. Accessed June 2009.

InfoDev. 2009a. "E-Government Primer: Information for Development Program." Information and Communication Development, World Bank, Washington, DC. Online: http://www.infodev.org/publications. Accessed June 2009.

_____. 2009b. "Extending Reach and Impact." Information and Communication Development, World Bank, Washington, DC.

ITU. 2006. "Information Society Trends in Africa." International Telecommunication Union's Newslog: *ICT and Development: Applications and Cyber Security Division. Online:* http://www.itu.int/ITU-D/cyb/newslog/Information+Society+Trends+In+Africa. aspx. Accessed February 2014.

_____. 2008a. "Information Society Trends in Africa." International Telecommunication Union's Corporate Strategy Newslog: *Mobile News Related to CSD Research and Analysis. Online:* http://www.itu.int/ITU-D/cyb/newslog/CategoryView,category,World%2BSu mmit%2Bon%2Bthe%2BInformation%2BSociety.aspx. Accessed February 2014.

_____. 2008b. "Report on Electronic Government for Developing Countries." International Telecommunication Union. Online: http://www.itu.int/ITU-D/cyb/ app/docs/e-gov_for_dev_countries-report.pdf. Accessed September 2009.

Jepma, C. J., H. Jager, E. Kamp. 1997. "Business, Government and Lobbying." In *International Economics,* edited by Jepma et al. University of the Netherlands: Longman.

John, J. K., M. S. Nair, P. J. Selvanthan and M. Kuppusamy. 2005. "Using ICT as a Catalyst for Sustainable Development: The Role of National Policy." In *Access, Empowerment and Governance: Creating a World of Equal Opportunities with ICT.* Kuala Lumpur: Global Knowledge Partnership.

Kaufmann, D., A. Kraay and M. Mastruzzi. 2005. "Governance Matters IV: Governance Indicators for 1996–2004." World Bank Policy Research Working Paper 3630. Online: http://www-wds.worldbank.org/external/default/WDSContentServer/IW3P/IB/ 2005/06/15/000016406_20050615140310/Rendered/PDF/wps3630.pdf. Accessed October 2013.

Kaul, Sanjay, Fuaad Ali, Subramaniam Janakiram. 2008. *Business Models for Sustainable Telecoms Growth in Developing Economies.* West Sussex: John Wiley and Sons Ltd.

Kearns, I. 2004. *Public Value and E-Government.* Institute for Public Policy Research, London. Online: http://www.centreforcities.org/assets/files/pdfs/public_value_egovernment. pdf. Accessed February 2014.

Kelly, G., and S. Muers. 2002. *Creating Public Value: An Analytical Framework for Public Service Reform*. London: London Cabinet Office Strategy Unit.

Kendall, J. E., and K. E. Kendall. 2008. "Designing for Positive Outcomes: Using Positive Memes, Distributive Empowerment, Open Source Development and Positive Metaphors." In *Designing Information and Organizations with a Positive Lens: Advances in Appreciative Inquiry*, edited by M. Avital, R. J. Boland and D. L. Cooperrider, vol. 2, 147–65. Amsterdam: Elsevier.

_____. 2010. "Positive Design and Appreciative Construction: From Sustainable Development to Sustainable Value." *Advances in Appreciative Inquiry Series* 3, 137–55. Bingley, UK: Emerald Group Publishing Limited.

Kettani, D., M. Gurstein and A. El Mahdi . 2009. "Good Governance and E-Government: Applying a Formal Outcome Analysis Methodology in a Developing World Context." *International Journal of Electronic Governance* 2(1):22–54.

Kettani, D., M. Gurstein, B. Moulin and A. El Mahdi. 2005. "An Approach to the Assessment of Applied IS with Particular Application to Community-based systems." *Lecture Notes in Computer Science* 4277:301–10.

_____. 2006. "An Approach to the Assessment of Applied Information Systems with Particular Application to Community-based Systems." International Workshop on Community Informatics, OTM Federated Conferences. Montpellier, France.

_____. 2008. "E-Government and Local Good Governance: A Pilot Project in Fez, Morocco." *The Electronic Journal on Information Systems in Developing Countries* 35(1):1–18.

_____. 2010. ""Towards a Roadmap to E-Government for a Better Governance." In *A Handbook of Research on E-Government Readiness for Information and Service Exchange: Utilizing Progressive Information Communication Technologies*, edited by Hakikur Rahman. Hershey, PA: IGI Global.

Kettani, D., B. Moulin and A. El Mahdi. 2005. "Towards a Formal Framework of Impact Assessment of E-Government Systems on Governance." Fourth WSEAS International Conference on e-Activities, 12–20. Miami.

Kotter, J.D. 1996. *Leading Change*. London: Harvard Business Review Press.

Kotter, J.D., and D. S. Cohen. 2002. *The Heart of Change*. London: Harvard Business Review Press.

Kreps, D., and H. Richardson. 2007. "IS Success and Failure: The Problem of Scale." In *Political Quarterly*. New Jersey: Wiley-Blackwell.

Leloup, R., S. Marty and D. Autissier. 2008. "Le Projet Litchi à EDF: Analyse d'une Innovation en Conduite du Changement." In *Editions d'Organisation*.

Lewin, K. 1951. *Field Theory in Social Science*. New York: Harper & Row.

Luhmann, N. 1998. *Observations on Modernity*. Stanford, CA: Stanford University Press.

Macome, E. 2003. "On the Implementation of an Information System in the Mozambican Context: The EDM Case". In *Organizational Information Systems in the Context of Globalization*, edited by M. A. Norwell. Norwell, MA: Kluwer Academic Publishers.

McGuigan, B. 2010. "What is E-Government?" Online: http://www.wisegeek.com/what-is-e-government.htm. Accessed July 2009.

Namba, Y., and Y. Kata. 2007. "City Planning Approach for Enterprise Information Systems." *Bulletin of Advanced Institute of Industrial Technology* 1, 39–48.

Norris, P. 2001. *Digital Divide: Civic Engagement, Information Poverty and the Internet Worldwide*. Cambridge: Cambridge University Press.

Nute, D. 2002. "Net Eases Government Purchasing Process." *American City and County Journal* 117 (1).

Nye, J. S., Jr., and A. W. David. 2000. *Understanding International Conflicts: An Introduction to Theory and History*. New York: Longman.

O'Connell, K. A. 2003. "Computerizing Government: The Next Generation." *American City and County Journal* 118(8).

OECD. 2010. *The Development Dimension: ICTs for Development, Improving Policy Coherence*. Paris: OECD Publishing.

Ourzik, A. 2006. "Gouvernance et Modernisation de l'Administration." Official report of the Moroccan Government. Online: http://www.albacharia.ma/xmlui/bitstream/handle/123456789/31457/1254Gouvernance_et_modernisation_de_l_administration_%282006%294.pdf?sequence=1. Accessed February 2014.

Pertierra, R. 2009. *Technologies of Transformation: The End of the Social or Birth of the Cyber Network*. Singapore: ISEAS Publishing.

Petersen, K., and Wohlin, C. 2009. "A Comparison of Issues and Advantages in Agile and Incremental Development between a State-of-the-art and an Industrial Case." *Journal of Systems and Software* 82 (9).

Picciotto, R. 2003. "International Trends and Development Evaluation: The Need for Ideas." *American Journal of Evaluation* 24(2):227–34.

PRINCE2. 2009. "Managing Successful Projects with PRINCE2." Office of Government Commerce: The Stationery Office. Online: http://en.wikipedia.org/wiki/PRINCE2. Accessed July 2010.

Rhoton, John. 2009. *Cloud Computing Explained: Implementation Handbook for Enterprises*. Recursive Press.

Riley, T. B. 2003. "E-Governance vs. E-Government." *ICT and Governance*. Online: http://www.i4donline.net/issue/nov03/pdfs /egovernance.pdf. Accessed June 2009.

Roy, J. 2006. *E-Government in Canada: Transformation for the Digital Age*. Ottowa: University of Ottawa Press.

Sanjay, K., A. J. Fuaad. and B. Wattenstrom. 2008. *Business Models for Sustainable Telecoms Growth in Developing Economies*. West Sussex: John Wiley and Sons.

Sen, A. 1999. *Development as Freedom*. Oxford: Oxford University Press.

Shah, A., and J. Hurther. 2005. "Public Service Delivery." *Public Sector Governance and Accountability Series*. Online: http:// siteresources.worldbank.org/PSGLP/Resources/PublicServiceDelivery.pdf. Accessed March 2010.

Shally-Jensen, M. 2011. *Encyclopedia of Contemporary American Social Issues*. Santa Barbara, CA: ABC-CLIO.

Shapiro, A. 2010. *Creating Contagious Commitment: Applying the Tipping Point to Organizational Change*, second edition. North Carolina: Strategy Perspectives.

Sisk, J. 2003. "Creating and Applying Knowledge, Innovation, and Technology." In *Reinventing Government for the Twenty-first century: State Capacity in a Globalizing Society*, edited by D. A. Rondinelli and G. S. Cheema, 17–32. Bloomfield, CT: Kumarian Press.

Snellen, I. 2002. "Electronic Governance: Implications for Citizens, Politicians and Public Servants." *International Review of Administrative Sciences* 68 (183).

Sommerville, I. 2006. *Software Engineering*, sixth edition. New York: Addison-Wesley.

Stallings, William. 2013. *Operating Systems, Internals and Design Principles*, fifth edition. Harlow, Essex: Prentice Hall.

Tapscott, D., and A. D. Williams. 2006. *Wikinomics: How Mass Collaboration Changes Everything*. New York: Penguin.

Tian, J. 2005. "Software Quality Engineering: Testing, Quality Assurance and Quantifiable Improvement". Los Alamitos, CA: WILEY-IEEE Computer Society Press.

Tipton, Harold F. 2009. *Information Security Management*, sixth edition. New York: Auerbach Publications.

Traikovik, V., K. Zajazi and Z. Gligorov. 2011. "About ICT for Local Government: Standards, Principles and Best Practices." Skopje: Network of Associations of Local Authorities of South East Europe (NALAS).

Tsui, Frank, Orlando Karam and Barbara Bernal. 2013. *Essentials of Software Engineering*, third edition. Burlington, MA: Jones & Barlett Learning.

Ullman, Jeffrey D. 2007. *First Course in Database Management Systems*, third edition. Harlow, Essex: Prentice Hall.

UN. 2003a. "Global E-Government Survey: E-Government at the Crossroads." UN/DESA. Online: http://unpan1.un.org/intradoc/groups/public/documents/un/unpan016066.pdf. Accessed June 2009.

_____. 2003b. "The Global E-Government Survey 2003." United Nations' Department of Economic and Social Affairs: Division for Public Administration and Development Management. Online: http://unpan1.un.org/intradoc/groups/public/ documents/un/unpan016066.pdf, 2003. Accessed June 2009.

_____. 2008. "The Global E-Government Survey: From E-Government to Connected Governance." UN/DESA. Online: http://unpan1.un.org/intradoc/groups/public/documents/un/unpan028607.pdf. Accessed March 2010.

UNDP. 1997. "Governance for Sustainable Human Development: A UNDP Policy Document." United Nations' Development Programme. Online: http://mirror.undp.org/magnet/policy/default.htm. Accessed July 2009.

_____. 2001. "World Public Sector Report: Globalization and the State, 2001." United Nations' Department of Economic and Social Affairs. Online: http://unpan1.un.org/intradoc/groups/public/documents/UN/UNPAN012761.pdf. Accessed June 2009.

_____. 2002. "Handbook on Monitoring and Evaluating for Results." United Nations' Development Programme. Online: http://www.un.org.pk/ undp/prm/Rules%20&%20Guidelines/handbook-on-monitoring-and-evaluating-for-results-17april-02.pdf. Accessed October 2009.

Unwin, T. 2009. *ICT4D: Information and Communication Technology for Development*. Cambridge: Cambridge University Press.

Waema, T., and E. Adera. 2011. *About Local Governance and ICTs in Africa: Case Studies and Guidelines for Implementation and Evaluation*. Ottawa: Pambazuka/Oxford Press and the International Development for Research Center.

Walsham, G., F. Robey and S. Sahay. 2007. "Foreword: Special Issue on Information Systems in Developing Countries." *MIS Quarterly* 31(2):317–26.

Weiser, M. 1991. "The Computer for the Twenty-first Century." *Scientific American*. Online: http://www.ubiq.com/hypertext/weiser/SciAmDraft3.html. Accessed May 2010.

_____. 1993, "Hot Topics: Ubiquitous Computing." IEEE Computer Society, *Computer* 26(10).

Weiss, T. 2000. "Governance, Good Governance and Global Governance: Conceptual and Actual Challenges." *Third World Quarterly* 21(5):795–814.

Wiley, D. 2006. "On the Sustainability of Open Educational Resource Initiatives in Higher Education." Paper commissioned by the OECD Centre for Educational Research and Innovation for a project on Open Educational Resources. Online: http://www.oecd.org/document/20/0,3746,en_2649_35845581_35023444_1_1_1_1,00.html.

Wimmer, Maria A. 2004. "E-Government: A Catalyst to Good Governance in China." In *Knowledge Management in Electronic Government*, by Ling Lan, edited by Maria A. Wimmer. Heidelberg: Springer Berlin, 317–24.

World Bank. 1991. *Managing Development: The Governance Dimension*. Washington, DC: World University Press.

_____. 2006a. "What is Governance? Arriving at a Common Understanding of Governance." Online: http://go.worldbank.org/G2CHLXX0Q0. Accessed February 2014.

_____. 2006b. "Introduction to E-Government: What Is E-Government?" Online: http://web.worldbank.org/WBSITE/EXTERNAL/TOPICS/EXTINFORMATIONANDCOMMUNICATIONANDTECHNOLOGIES/EXTEGOVERNMENT/0,,contentMDK:20694335~pagePK:210058~piPK:210062~theSitePK:702586~isCURL:Y,00.html. Accessed February 2014.

INDEX

access control 238

accountability (good governance attribute) 60, 75, 77, 81, 84, 86, 93, 130

administrative control 240

advisory/accompaniment role 129, 131, 158; *see also* External Advisory Team, Transformation Accompaniment Team

agile method 110

application server 246

appropriation 14, 17, 33, 67, 174, 200, 208, 209

archaic situation 139, 142

architecture (service, system, application) 40, 75, 103, 106, 110, 153, 165, 188, 196, 205, 227, 231–8, 265

assessment process/framework 19, 48, 69, 71, 84, 111, 147, 156, 164, 171, 179

Assessment Step 189, 129

attestations administratives 204

authentication 238

automatic tracking/monitoring 20,

autonomy 82, 143, 174, 178, 214, 220, 268

back office 84, 188, 193, 195, 197, 224, 235, 242

BEC (*bureau d'état civil* (civil status bureau)) 5, 12, 192, 220, 255

BEC automation 193, 210

biological view of transformation 117

birth certificate 4, 91, 194, 200, 218

bottom-up approach 102, 105, 110, 257, 265

business analysis 109, 188, 265

business continuity plan 244

business process 19, 58, 75, 101, 109, 116, 133, 149, 153, 170, 196, 232, 236, 264

capacity building / reinforcement 16, 37, 44, 55, 58, 71, 108, 155, 217, 221, 253, 254

centralized approach 35, 43, 81, 102, 103, 206

Centre de renforcement des capacités locales (CERCL) 209, 210, 217

change management 103, 109, 111, 116, 145, 217, 219, 252, 267

champions 105, 123, 150, 158, 167, 173, 175, 191, 218

citizen-to-government (C2G) 46, 52

citizen-friendly service delivery 15, 88, 200, 221

client/server architecture 196, 232

closure workshop 209

coaching 132, 152, 159, 166, 172, 202, 205, 213, 216, 266

cloud computing 242

commitment/engagement (top management) 13, 99, 103, 130, 156, 165, 169, 172, 186, 193, 201, 207, 214

communication/sensitization plan 105, 132, 146, 156, 165, 169, 172, 217, 263

communication process 146, 156, 162, 199

Completion Step 147, 154, 162, 171, 178

computer network 247

conceptual architecture 153

consensus-based approach 13, 76, 84, 93, 125, 207, 262

consensus oriented (good governance attribute) 76, 77

continuing adjustments 197

contracted/in-house development 228

critical stakeholders 13, 20, 48, 57, 83, 97, 100, 111, 114, 125, 130, 192
cryptography 238
customer satisfaction 73, 164, 172

database design 49, 196
data center 206, 208, 209, 213, 243; approach 207, 209
data digitizing 125, 195, 204, 208, 214, 226
data management software 246
decentralized approach 43, 81, 102, 105, 110, 131
defense mechanisms 238
Development and Deployment Step 187
development team 124, 133, 146, 166, 186, 189; *see also* External Development Team
digital divide 2, 25, 28, 38, 63, 198, 203
digital (online) kiosk 11, 15, 86, 92, 98, 164, 193, 197, 198, 221, 255, 258
disaster recovery plan 224, 244
dissemination/promotion 4, 21, 36, 78, 95, 109, 113, 190, 203, 262
documentation, lack of 195

e-appropriateness/e-awareness 17, 202, 203, 217, 256
e-champions 84, 186, 192, 203, 260, 264, 269; profiling analysis 217
eFez Approach 24, 182, 217; data center solution 211
eFez Project: awards 20, 202; general description 11; outcomes 71, 85; Phase 1 21, 182, 191, 193, 202; Phase 2 21, 182, 202; roadmap 19, 94, 181, 188; system/platform/ architecture 9, 87, 94, 123, 192, 196, 204, 211, 212, 221
eFez Team 19, 87, 182, 192, 197, 207, 235
effectiveness and efficiency (good governance attribute) 77, 84, 86, 92, 130
e-governance: definition 36, 45, 46, 75; maturity 60
e-government 2, 45, 46; application areas 48; ecosystem 223, 225, 250, 253,

256; evaluation 71, 72; failures 69, 70, 99; sophistication levels 61
empowering (people) 19, 48, 54, 84, 144, 156, 164, 173
enterprise network 248
equity (good governance attribute) 60, 75, 77, 82, 84, 86
e-participation 52
e-readiness divide 64
e-readiness report 4, 13, 17, 48, 61, 97, 104, 194, 202, 256
e-strategy 24
evolutionary approach (progressive) 60, 110, 117, 177, 265
experience-based approach 124, 129, 194, 212
External Advisory Team (EAT) 129, 131, 150, 155, 158, 166, 171, 178, 206
External Development Team (EDT) 133, 150, 158, 166, 178, 186, 195, 197, 205, 212

facilitation approach/actions 173, 177, 266
facilitator (role) 150, 158, 166, 172, 177, 266
failing projects 3, 23, 48, 58, 59, 68, 70, 98, 99, 174, 214, 225
favorable conditions 24, 121, 124, 152, 167, 169, 183, 186, 202, 210
feasibility study 138, 182, 187, 203, 228
front office 11, 15, 46, 55, 60, 80, 188, 193, 195, 224

generalization phase/plan/strategy 13, 157, 159, 163, 169, 174, 179, 202, 257, 267
generic roadmap 19, 24, 137, 139, 140, 145, 181
global solution 142, 169, 170, 173; *see also* Global Solution Development Deployment Assessment
Global Solution Development Deployment Assessment (GSDDA) 138, 142, 166, 202, 206
good governance: definition 2, 11, 20, 41, 47, 54, 65, 71, 75; attributes 76, 131;

measurements 74, 79, 80; and the eFez Project 183
government-to-business (G2B) 26, 47, 60
government-to-citizen (G2C) 3, 47, 53, 60, 230
government-to-government (G2G) 3, 26, 47, 54
graphical user interface (GUI) 196, 198, 232
guidelines for e-government projects 14, 19, 109, 148, 181, 223

help desk 225
human resources, lack of 207

inclusiveness (good governance attribute) 77
Index of Governance Quality (IGQ) 80
illiteracy 198, 221
information communication technology (ICT) 33, 35, 127
information communication technology for development (ICT4D) 28; fundamental issues of 31, 99
information security officer (ISO) 240
information system: analysis and design method 40, 70, 110, 183, 188, 226, 229, 264; urbanization 40, 42
incentives / rewards 103, 108, 112, 152, 164, 108, 112, 152, 161, 173, 199, 200, 253
Inception Step 147, 150, 160, 168, 175, 186
iterative development/process 90, 110, 153, 196, 198
iterative method 110

kick-off workshop 193
knowledge barrier 100

leadership 15, 46, 98, 103, 104, 107, 108, 112, 136, 167, 199, 218, 260, 262, 264
leapfrogging 40, 42
legal issues 50, 77, 99, 108, 192, 209, 223, 228, 230, 247, 254, 260
life records 193, 195
local area network (LAN) 249

local solution 157, 162, 165, 207; see also Local Solution Development Deployment Assessment
Local Solution Development Deployment Assessment (LSDDA) 138, 141, 157, 202; sector/domain 141, 157, 159
LOGIN Africa Project 181, 222

maintain favorable conditions step 147, 202
management team 151, 160, 167, 169, 170, 176, 178, 229
master plan 109, 265, 26–9
media coverage 199
metropolitan area network (MAN) 248
mission statement 127, 191
model shift 206
model-view-controller (MVC design pattern) 234
Monitoring and Assessment Process (MAP) 129, 150, 156, 164, 171, 179

n-tier architecture (multi-tier) 205, 232

official signatures 211
open source solution 31, 195, 204, 247
outcome analysis (eFez Method) 20, 71, 83, 130, 190
outcomes assessment 84, 153, 162, 200
outsourcing 179, 269
ownership 93, 108, 110, 199, 208, 254

participation (good governance attribute) 60, 75, 77, 81, 84, 85, 93, 107, 130
participatory approach 152, 191, 193, 203, 212
participation index 80
personnel movement 211
phase plan 161
pilot BEC 88, 194, 205, 214, 217, 219
Pilot Project 121, 200
Pilot Team 122, 124, 131, 150, 158
portal (e-government) 194, 197, 201, 205
post-mortem step 148, 153
processor multi-core technology 241
Production Step 147, 162, 170, 176
project appropriation 14, 200, 201
project governance 109
project objectives 193

project outcomes (measures) 20, 83, 86,131, 154, 183, 185, 189
project plan 67, 103, 135, 143, 207
promotion nationale people (PN) 208, 213
prototyping 110, 153
public key infrastructure (PKI) solutions/ certificates 239

quality assurance/management 2, 56, 72, 110, 150, 158, 183, 189, 229

recruitment strategy 208
reengineering 101, 109, 169, 111, 116, 149, 169, 264
resources, scarce 169, 175, 208, 210, 214, 216
responsibility management 110
responsiveness (good governance attribute) 47, 77, 81, 84, 86, 93, 130
responsiveness indicator 82
risk management 56, 226, 229, 231, 267
roadmap 19, 137, 191
rule of law (good governance attribute) 76, 77, 79, 85, 95

scaling up 13, 103, 121, 134, 137, 202, 206, 208, 21
schedules (coordination) 130, 133, 170, 175, 177, 207, 214, 267
security architecture 238
security (policy) 30, 47, 55, 73, 97, 107, 196, 223, 241
security enablers 222
security management 230, 236
service provider/broker 235
situational awareness 149, 182
software license 246
software platform 212, 245
software quality engineering 183
spiral method 110
stakeholder engagement/involvement/ sensitization 109, 113, 132, 138, 183, 191, 203, 207
standards, standardization 35, 84, 93, 100, 103, 108, 110, 228, 229, 239
standard protocols 233
statistics generation 205
status quo 25, 118, 120, 140, 258

strategy 24, 86, 98, 104, 107, 127, 207, 209
supervision process 146, 155, 163, 171, 179
sustainability 12, 29, 48, 103, 106, 135, 138, 140, 144, 174, 206, 254
system quality attributes 186, 189
system requirements/design 188, 195, 211, 228

team spirit 209
Technical Support Team (TST) 159, 165,178, 208
technology enablers 194, 223, 258
technology risks 230
top-down approach 48, 100, 102–6, 257, 265
Trainers' Team (TT) 159, 166, 172, 178
training criticality / challenges 70, 109, 112, 162, 172, 195, 205, 211
training plan/program 17, 21, 103, 107, 173, 203, 205, 209, 253, 263
training process 108, 112, 146, 155, 165, 172, 177, 180, 199, 213
Transformation Accompaniment Team (TAT) 157, 158, 171, 177, 192, 209
Transformation Pilot Project (TPP) 121, 129, 139, 148, 190
transformation process/project 113, 117, 130, 167, 174
Transformation Project Board 155, 163, 171, 174, 178
transformation sustainability 137, 174
transition plan 177, 207
Transition to Autonomy (TTA) Phase 139, 143, 173, 214
transparency (good governance attribute) 60, 75, 77, 82, 84, 86, 92; lack of 48, 100
trust 52, 74, 193, 238, 253
turnkey solution 229

United Nations Development Programme good governance attributes 76, 84
unfavorable conditions 125, 146, 151, 160, 210
usability analysis 188
usage patterns 88, 90, 197, 224

values 19, 59, 78, 102, 127, 228
vision 21, 24, 40, 82, 84, 93, 107, 123,
    126, 149, 153, 162, 165, 168, 183,
    186, 204, 207, 209
vision statement 128, 153, 191
virtualization technology 242

waterfall method 110
web application/services 204, 211, 224,
    233, 235, 236

web server 245
web service architecture 236
wide area network (WAN) 248
wireless metropolitan area network
    (WMAN) 249
work plan 153, 169, 170, 175,
    177, 214

XML (eXtensible Markup Language) 227

Lightning Source UK Ltd.
Milton Keynes UK
UKOW03n1515230514

232202UK00001B/29/P